Are \
in a Disa...

Are We Living in a Disaster Movie?

How Genre Conventions Predict the Plot of the Covid-19 Pandemic

BRIAN A. SHAER

McFarland & Company, Inc., Publishers
Jefferson, North Carolina

ISBN (print) 978-1-4766-8729-2
ISBN (ebook) 978-1-4766-4755-5

LIBRARY OF CONGRESS AND BRITISH LIBRARY
CATALOGUING DATA ARE AVAILABLE

Library of Congress Control Number 2022031087

Front cover images © 2022 Shutterstock

Printed in the United States of America

*McFarland & Company, Inc., Publishers
Box 611, Jefferson, North Carolina 28640
www.mcfarlandpub.com*

To all those whose lives were affected, however tangentially, by the Covid-19 pandemic. To the scientists, doctors, first responders, and others who worked tirelessly and selflessly to make sure we arrived at the light at the end of the tunnel.

Additionally, this book is dedicated to those people who, throughout my life, fostered and encouraged my lifelong love of cinema.

Thank you!

Table of Contents

Acknowledgments

Where to begin? I am so grateful to have so many people in my life that, over the course of the past year as I was writing this book, encouraged me with words of support that kept me going when I thought I would never finish. For reasons I am not quite sure of, they believed in me and knew I would make it to the finish line even when I wasn't so sure. I truly thank them for this. But I also must thank everyone who has endured my incessant yammering about my book over the past year since I know I didn't shut up about it.

I do, however, need to offer a special thanks to some special individuals who helped this prospect come to life, whether they are aware or not. There is my good friend Job Guzmán in New York, who at some point in 2020, after I had given a presentation at one of the conferences I attended, suggested I write a book. Well, I've always been the suggestible type.

My editor Layla Milholen of McFarland remembered me (at least she acted convincingly as though she did) when I called her up after the Midwest Popular Culture Association/Midwest American Culture Association conference in October of 2020 and pitched her the idea for this book. She was always there if I had a question and if there is one thing I find so hard to come by these days, it's accessibility and follow-through. Layla left me alone to do my thing, but I knew she was always there if I needed her.

I would also like to acknowledge my professors in the Department of Cinema Studies at NYU's Tisch School of the Arts, a place in which I felt invigorated when breathing the air and honored to walk the hallways, surrounded by the best minds and most passionate people studying cinema. Professors such as William Simon, Richard Porton, Laura Harris, Josslyn Luckett, and Neta Alexander. My time at NYU while I completed my master's degree constitutes some of the best years of my life. Go ahead and use that for marketing purposes if you want, NYU.

My close friends—these lucky people know who they are—deserve thanks for putting up with me over the past year. Now that my time will free up substantially, they will get to know the real me. Come to think of it, I'm not so sure they are going to be my close friends for very much longer. Included in this group is Irv, the newest addition to this rarefied circle, who always gave me the space I needed to write and always had a look of quiet admiration on his face when I would talk about disaster movies (told you I wouldn't shut up!). His belief in me did not go unnoticed and is very much appreciated.

I need to call out my family as well and thank them for never being anything but encouraging and excited about this project. My big brother, Jon, and all the others with whom I share a blood relation. In particular, my mom, Ellie, and dad, Steve, for always congratulating me when I reached milestones in the writing process and for keeping me going with their pride and enthusiasm. Just seeing their faces when I would mention my book was enough to get me back to my laptop.

And to all those people who I was horrible enough to forget to acknowledge, I want to simultaneously apologize and offer a sincere thank you. Whether we know it or not, people occupy a place in our lives, for however short or long a period of time, for a reason. Everyone we meet as we navigate through the days and nights of our lives gets us to the moment in which we now find ourselves, like writing the acknowledgments for a debut book. So, I say to all of them, from the bottom of my heart, thank you.

Author's Note

Warning: Massive Spoilers Throughout!!!

If you have NOT seen any of the following movies, I would highly recommend that you do so before you read this book. Endings will be divulged without reservation.

Airport (1970)
The Andromeda Strain (1971)
Skyjacked (1972)
The Poseidon Adventure (1972)
Airport 1975 (1974)
Earthquake (1974)
The Towering Inferno (1974)
The Hindenburg (1975)
Flood (1976)
The Cassandra Crossing (1977)
Airport '77 (1977)
Fire (1977)
The Swarm (1978)
Avalanche (1978)
The Concorde.... Airport '79 (1979)
City on Fire (1979)
Meteor (1979)
Disaster on the Coastliner (1979)

Cave-In! (1983)
Speed (1994)
Outbreak (1995)
Twister (1996)
Independence Day (1996)
Daylight (1996)
Dante's Peak (1997)
Volcano (1997)
Titanic (1997)
Deep Impact (1998)
Armageddon (1998)
The Core (2003)
The Day After Tomorrow (2004)
Snakes on a Plane (2006)
2012 (2009)
Contagion (2011)
San Andreas (2015)
Geostorm (2017)
Greenland (2020)

The concept for this book came about as an outgrowth of two academic papers the author researched, wrote, and presented. Both papers concern, in varying respects, the cinematic subgenre known as the disaster film, present throughout cinema history but widely popularized in the 1970s in movies such as *The Poseidon Adventure* and *The Towering Inferno*.

The first paper, titled "Canonical Films of the 1970s Disaster Genre vs. the Genre Resurgence of the 1990s," was presented on February 21, 2020, at the Southwest Popular/American Culture Association conference in Albuquerque, New Mexico. The subject matter of this paper concerned the similarities as well as the differences between the popular genre cycle of disaster films made and released in the 1970s (films including but not limited to *The Poseidon Adventure*, *The Towering Inferno*, *The Swarm*, and the *Airport* series) and the subsequent cycle resurgence of the genre in films made and released in the 1990s (films including but not limited to *Speed*, *Twister*, *Independence Day*, and *Deep Impact*). The paper sought to examine both cycles of disaster films and attempted to conclude if all or most of the genre conventions observed in the cycle of 1970s movies were, indeed, still in practice in the cycle of 1990s movies. If not, what had changed in the ensuing years and why?

The second paper, titled "*The Poseidon Protocol*, or the Pedagogy of Survival According to Disaster Film Conventions in the Age of Covid-19," was presented virtually on October 3, 2020, as part of the Midwest Popular Culture Association/Midwest American Culture Association annual conference. With this second paper, I endeavored to explore the similarities between the genre conventions set forth in the mainstream disaster movie and the commonalities in the trajectory thus far of the global battle with the Covid-19 pandemic. I posited, and still believe, that the life cycle of the pandemic paralleled a real-life disaster movie. When and how were certain fictional generic benchmarks hit in reality during the course of the pandemic, and furthermore, what could the conventions of the disaster subgenre inform us as to how the true-life narrative surrounding the pandemic might eventualize? If we were, in fact, living in a disaster movie, then surely a member of the generic canon would be able to offer some insight into this troubling scenario and how it might play out.

It has been during the process of writing this book that I have attempted to make some sense out of all of the sickness and misery that fiendishly surrounded everyone over the past few years. I viewed this pandemic through the one lens that has never let me down: that of the movies. I observed very early on the parallels that could be observed between the Covid-19 pandemic and the standard disaster film and realized, to my astonishment, that I was actually *living* in a disaster movie. I was one of the passengers on the doomed cruise liner. I was in the burning building. I was in the path of the tornado. And realizing this, understanding the pandemic through the language of the cinematic disaster film, would be how I could survive. Not necessarily survive physically—that was up to sheer common sense and diligence—but mentally.

Over the course of my research, I encountered and drew upon various facts and statistics that have, of course, remained unchanged throughout the writing of this book. I imagine that this comes standard with the production of any work of non-fiction. Several of these statistics refer to reported Covid-related deaths and New York City government-related programs that were implemented following the outbreak of Covid-19 in the New York City area. In several instances, many of these statistics are written as verbatim from the corresponding passages in both papers I authored: "Canonical Films of the 1970s Disaster Genre vs. the Genre Resurgence of the 1990s" and "*The Poseidon Protocol,* or the Pedagogy of Survival According to Disaster Film Conventions in the Age of Covid-19." I have used quotations and cited the appropriate paper where necessary.

This book is an examination of the cinematic subgenre known as the "disaster movie" and should not be construed to be a comprehensive accounting of the Covid pandemic. My intention is to undertake a deconstruction of the dominant tropes and general facets of the disaster movie and filter them through the lens of what is arguably the real-life disaster movie that the global population has been unwittingly co-starring in since early 2020. In my desire to articulate and make clear the parallels with the Covid pandemic, I have devised a hypothetical movie within this ongoing real-life scenario titled *The Sibylline Scourge.*

In his review of the 2000 dance movie *Center Stage, Variety* film critic Emanuel Levy began his review with this line: "Based on the assumption that every generation needs to have its own folkloric dance film...." (Levy). Using this train of thought, one might say that every generation needs its own viral plague movie. This was my generation's *The Andromeda Strain.* This was my generation's *Outbreak.* This was my generation's *Contagion.*

This was *The Sibylline Scourge.*

Introduction

The following is a chat exchange that took place on Monday, March 23, 2020, between the managing editor of *Film Threat*, an online magazine with a concentration on independent film news and reviews, and me, an occasional contributor to the publication. We were discussing certain films that were available for me to review at that time.

> MANAGING EDITOR: "OK, we'll move on to another. You want a pandemic movie?"
>
> ME: "No thanks!! I'm LIVING in a pandemic movie!!"

As we slowly fade in on those innocent first few days of January 2020, individuals around the world manage as best as they can to recover from the hangovers of New Year's Eve celebrations. Sporting dark sunglasses to shield their eyes from the harsh glare of the sun reflecting off snow-covered ground and wrapping their coats and parkas tightly around their torsos to keep in the warmth, folks make their way to their cars, subways, and buses, begrudgingly returning to their everyday work lives and routines. Students of all ages prepare to hit the books following a leisurely winter break, office buildings across continents roar back to life as companies welcome back their employees, retail stores reopen to service their customers after the usual madness of the holiday rush, and cities everywhere begin to bubble with the cadence of their normal activity. Nothing is out of the ordinary. It is an inauspicious yet optimistic beginning to what is expected to be a busy year with both the Summer Olympics and a presidential election on the horizon.

In the wintry infancy of the year 2020, the United States was as ensconced in the throes of political fever as ever. Hopeful Democratic presidential candidates, at least those who had not dropped out of the race yet, were galvanizing their campaigns in the run-up to March 3, Super Tuesday, and fighting to outdo each other in their intense, robust hatred for Donald Trump, the controversial incumbent Republican commander-in-chief they were all clamoring to unseat. If anything, 2020 was shaping up to be an historic year, especially when one considered the political future of the American democratic ecosystem.

However, there was a mystifying darkness approaching from far away that would soon entwine itself into the global population and catch everyone off guard. You see, buried beneath the blustery political lead stories in newspapers and across digital media outlets, items concerning a curious occurrence across the Pacific Ocean in China were being published. An alien, never-before-observed flu-like illness was affecting people in the Asian nation's Wuhan region.

The reporting of a suspected outbreak of a mysterious illness was, on its face, seriously troubling but not entirely novel. The early 1980s coverage of what would come to be known as the AIDS epidemic, for example, involved news outlets describing the puzzling deaths among homosexual men in New York City and San Francisco that were apparently caused by a particularly lethal strain of cancer. "Rare Cancer Seen in 41 Homosexuals" read the headline of an article in the July 3, 1981, *New York Times* (Blakemore), the first mainstream news outlet to cover the story.

Yet, the perceived irrelevance of the *New York Times* story is evident in the article's location in the newspaper and in its placement on the page. The article appeared in Section A, page 20 of the July 3, 1981, edition in a narrow, almost insignificant column to the left of a more attention-grabbing, almost full-page advertisement for Independence Savings Bank (Altman). This out-of-the-way situation in the newspaper foreshadows the initial coverage of the novel coronavirus, an early article concerning which, similarly, would be published in *The New York Times* on January 7, 2020, in Section A, page 13 (Wee and Wang). Hardly what one would refer to as front-page news.

Now, it is natural to expect a healthy amount of guarded trepidation when a person is made aware, either through media channels or other means, of a strange sickness that has surfaced overseas. Who wouldn't at least raise an eyebrow? But the sense of foreboding was magnified in mid-January 2020, when John F. Kennedy International Airport in New York City (JFK), San Francisco International Airport (SFO), and Los Angeles International Airport (LAX) all implemented ominously heightened security measures directed at passengers arriving in the U.S. from the afflicted Chinese region ("Public Health Screening"). A troublesome scenario was beginning to take shape: if whatever this illness was could not be contained and eradicated quickly, a disaster of global proportions was not necessarily outside the realm of possibility.

Sometimes it bears reminding that human beings are earthbound creatures, members of the animal kingdom in the same way that dogs, cats, or chimpanzees are. There are illnesses existent in nature that will, like a food we don't much like the taste of, cause our senses to recoil and instruct our immune systems to react in such a way as to eliminate the particular offense from our bodies. Oftentimes, a couple of sneezes, some time in bed, and chicken soup will do the trick. However, there are some pathogens prevailing in the natural world that will prove poisonous to human beings and that cause conditions our highly evolved and advanced immune systems have only minimal tools to combat, such as Ebola or many forms of cancer.

So as the 2019–20 winter season entered its most unforgiving leg in those first few months of the new year, frightening developments in relation to this mysterious illness continued to ensue. On February 5, barely one month after that early article in *The New York Times* appeared, more than three thousand six hundred vacationing passengers aboard the luxury cruise ship Diamond Princess were forced to quarantine onboard following an outbreak of what the world would come to know as Covid-19. Not long afterward, on February 7, Dr. Li Wenliang, a Chinese physician later to be renowned as the retroactive whistleblower who had attempted to warn the world about the conceivability of widespread infections were the outbreak not contained in China, passed away from its effects (Taylor). A snowball effect was strengthening; the sense of looming disaster was now inescapable.

Across the Atlantic Ocean in Europe, Italy issued lockdown orders on February 23 for towns in its northern Lombardy region as positive tests for this novel coronavirus cropped up in the area. As though this progression was now imitating a particularly sick game of global whack-a-mole, reports of infections popped up in nations around the world as the virus spread internationally; both Iran and Brazil were soon identified as hotbeds of virus activity (Taylor).

Then, on February 29, for those of us in the States watching helplessly as this enigmatic sickness engulfed the globe like an errant oil spill, the unthinkable yet inevitable happened: it was announced that the United States had reported what was believed to be its first coronavirus death, a man in Washington State (Taylor). A few days later, on March 3, 2020, a case was confirmed in New Rochelle, New York, a suburb located in the New York City metropolitan area, the most populous metro in the United States (Lombardi). The disaster had landed. If these genuine occurrences were written in the narrative of a mainstream Hollywood disaster movie, the arrival of the virus in New York City would be right on schedule. Ladies and gentlemen, I present to you, *The Sibylline Scourge*.

A genre as evergreen to the cinema as the Lumière Brothers, the disaster film is a thrilling piece of entertainment particularly suited to and comprised of the cross-pollination of more salient dramatic tropes. The formal design of the disaster movie can arguably be construed as a subgeneric form of the standard action-adventure genre, seeing as how within the basic chemistry of disaster stories there exists the race against time to survive a catastrophic event. However, in most disaster films one will find elements of romance or melodrama as in *Airport 1975* (Jack Smight, 1974), which really lays it on thick, or in *Titanic* (James Cameron, 1997), with its Rose/Jack storyline. Perhaps the element of the thriller might be more prominent in film, such as in *Outbreak* (Wolfgang Petersen, 1995), or maybe even comedy, whether intentional or unintentional, like in *Snakes on a Plane* (David R. Ellis, 2006), for example.

Disaster in film can be traced almost as far back as the advent of the motion picture itself, though the term "disaster film" wasn't explicitly used until the 1930s (Keane 13). More than one hundred years ago, for example, Edwin S. Porter's seven-minute short *Life of an American Fireman* (1903) silently documented the titular hero as he responded to a residential blaze. As the film industry matured, so did the disaster film. With D.W. Griffith shepherding the modern-day epic film onto cinema screens with the one-two punch of *The Birth of a Nation* (1915) followed by *Intolerance* (1916), as well as the introduction of sound film technology in the 1920s, the stakes grew ever higher for studios to produce more elaborate and awe-inspiring pictures and spectacles, in order to entice ticket buyers.

In his essay "The Cinema of Attractions: Early Film, Its Spectator and the Avant-Garde," theorist Tom Gunning defines what he refers to as a "cinema of attractions," which "directly solicits spectator attention, inciting visual curiosity, and supplying pleasure through an exciting spectacle—a unique event, whether fictional or documentary, that is of interest in itself" ("Cinema of Attractions" 73). Gunning's definition is as apt and accurate a raison d'être for the disaster film as one is likely to find, and it will be referred to liberally in this book.

On a particularly rudimentary level, as the movie industry entered into what some might define as the Golden Age of Hollywood, studio executives now began to realize the need to include the spectacular element in their pictures for their product to become more elaborate, more dazzling pieces of entertainment. In one regard, large-scale sweeping epics such as *Gone with the Wind* (Victor Fleming, 1939) or superior technical achievements such as *The Wizard of Oz* (Victor Fleming, 1939) delivered the necessary spectacle. But as their filmmaker impresario kin would copycat years down the road, the studio powers that be also looked to disaster, and in particular natural disaster, as a means of procuring the spectacle. In fact, the 1930s saw a mini genre cycle of natural disaster films emerge, including the tsunami extravaganza *Deluge* (Felix E. Feist, 1933), *San Francisco* (W.S. Van Dyke, 1936), which showcased the 1906 California earthquake, and *In Old Chicago* (Henry King, 1938), which reimagined certain events surrounding the Great Chicago Fire of 1871.

As decades passed and movies evolved both in economy, scale, and creativity, cinematic disasters became more involved and the spectacles that were offered to audiences became more vivid and eye-popping. More bang for more buck, if you will. Significantly, however, the noticeable commonalities present in the narratives of disaster films were becoming more identifiable. If genre can be envisaged in an academic sense as more or less a taxonomic system of grouping movies that contain similar tangible traits, one could then ask his or herself, as professor and film scholar Stephen Keane articulates in his book *Disaster Movies: The Cinema of Catastrophe*, not how "such and such a film is a disaster movie, for example, but rather asking what are the properties that might go towards identifying a film as a disaster movie" (3).

In his foundational essay "The Bug in the Rug," Maurice Yacowar identifies eight overarching "types" of disaster film: Natural Attack, The Ship of Fools, The City Fails, The Monster, Survival, War, The Historical, and The Comic (335–41). Recalling Yacowar and depending upon which criteria one uses to define a disaster movie, products as diverse as the *Titanic* dramatization *A Night to Remember* (Roy Ward Baker, 1958), the gooey B-movie *The Blob* (Irvin S. Yeaworth, Jr., 1958), the seminal zombie classic *Night of the Living Dead* (George A. Romero, 1968), or even the mother of all monster movies *Godzilla* (Ishirô Honda, 1954), might qualify as mid-century disaster pics.

Inarguably, the disaster genre, as most people nowadays popularly apprehend it, reached its pinnacle of mainstream visibility in the extraordinarily successful cycle of films released in the 1970s, beginning with George Seaton's *Airport* in 1970. Based upon the popular novel by Arthur Hailey, *Airport* employed a star-studded cast including Dean Martin, Burt Lancaster, Jacqueline Bisset, Jean Seberg, George Kennedy, and Helen Hayes, along with pulpy melodrama and on-the-ground as well as in-the-air disasters. In utilizing this formula of an all-star cast, plus disaster, plus melodrama, disaster movies achieved massive profitability and renown in theaters across the country as America entered the Me Decade.

Airport was produced on a budget of $10 million in 1969 and released the following year to the tune of a worldwide gross of more than $100 million ("Airport–Cast | IMDbPro"). When we translate that picture's haul to 2021 dollars, *Airport*'s budget would amount to roughly $74.4 million, and its worldwide gross would balloon to more than an astounding $707 million ("Inflation Calculator"). With that kind of monetary take, it is crystal clear why and how *Airport* would have incentivized those with green-lighting power behind an entire industry to develop and release their own cinematic output utilizing the template provided by *Airport*, and, in the process, pretty much birthing the disaster genre as we contemporarily reference it.

In the wake of the tremendous success of *Airport*, the disaster genre took flight and proved a popular draw for audiences throughout the 1970s. Two years after the release of *Airport*, *The Poseidon Adventure* (Ronald Neame, 1972) was released, followed soon thereafter by two other founding members of the disaster film canon: *The Towering Inferno* (John Guillermin, 1974) and *Earthquake* (Mark Robson, 1974). All manners of disasters were exploited in the 1970s ranging from natural, such as *Earthquake* and *Avalanche* (Corey Allen, 1978), to the technological, *Westworld* (Michael Crichton, 1973), and even to outer space, as in *Meteor* (Ronald Neame, 1979). Most notably, the massive success of *Airport* spawned a smash series of air-bound disaster movies released throughout the decade, including its immediate sequel *Airport 1975*, as well as the water-bound *Airport '77* (Jerry Jameson, 1977) and the series' inadvertent parody, *The Concorde.... Airport '79* (David Lowell Rich, 1979).

As the 1970s drew to a close, the disaster genre weakened in distinction, both critically and economically. As a matter of example, we have only to look at the clanging death knell of the 1970s disaster movie, the odious *When Time Ran Out...* (James Goldstone, 1980) and the pointless sequel *Beyond the Poseidon Adventure* (Irwin Allen, 1979), which, in my opinion, can't even be justified as a disaster movie. (This is primarily due to the fact that the entire movie is predicated on a disaster that already occurred, in the earlier, and much better, *The Poseidon Adventure*; there is no new disaster to be thwarted. A collapsed ventilator is hardly on a disaster par with the capsized cruise ship.) The decline in cinematic quality of product in the latter years of the 1970s was no doubt due in part to media overexposure of the genre, which had now become a parody of itself. Steve Neale quotes Thomas Schatz's theory of "generic development": "Finally, once 'the genre's straightforward message has "saturated" the audience ... a genre's classic conventions are refined and eventually parodied and subverted...'" (qtd. in Neale 211–12). Indeed, the riotous spoof that mocked the entire *Airport* series, *Airplane!* (Jim Abrahams, David Zucker, Jerry Zucker, 1980), can, more or less, be regarded as the de facto film which terminally punctuated the popularity of the 1970s disaster cycle.

Movies in the disaster vein would sporadically turn up in the 1980s and early 1990s, including the capstone film in mega-producer Irwin Allen's feature arsenal *When Time Ran Out...* and Chuck Russell's 1988 remake of *The Blob*. But the next official disaster movie genre cycle did not occur until the mid to late 1990s, conceivably beginning with Jan de Bont's *Speed* (1994). This end-of-millennium disaster cycle included a close cousin to *The Sibylline Scourge*, 1995's *Outbreak* as well as the alien invasion epic *Independence Day* (Roland Emmerich, 1996), cyclone smash *Twister* (Jan de Bont, 1996), and the twin volcanic eruption movies of 1997, *Dante's Peak* (Roger Donaldson, 1997) and *Volcano* (Mick Jackson, 1997). This cycle also contained the competing asteroid-hurtling-towards-earth extravaganzas *Deep Impact* (Mimi Leder, 1998) and *Armageddon* (Michael Bay, 1998) as well as Emmerich's own reimagining of *Godzilla* (1998).

Throughout the early aughts and continuing right up until the present, the spectacles continued to grow in both size and impression. Since the dawn of the new millennium, filmmakers have treated audiences to gigantic doomsday pieces such as *The Day After Tomorrow* (Roland Emmerich, 2004) and *2012* (Roland Emmerich, 2009) (gee, maybe it was just one guy!), monstrous monster movies including Peter Jackson's interpretation of *King Kong* in 2005 as well as yet another version of *Godzilla* (Gareth Edwards, 2014), historical disaster spectaculars such as *Pompeii* (Paul W.S. Anderson, 2014), apocalyptic zombie scenarios such as *28 Days Later...* (Danny Boyle, 2002) and *World War Z* (Marc Forster, 2013), updated natural disasters including *San Andreas* (Brad Peyton, 2015) and *Geostorm* (Dean Devlin, 2017), biological disasters such as *Contagion* (Steven Soderbergh, 2011), and proving Schatz's genre theory, the disaster send-up *Sharknado* (Anthony C. Ferrante, 2013) and its offspring.

Throughout the decades, the disaster film has persevered and adapted as filmmakers continue to up the apocalyptic ante, whether in the scope of their narratives or in (or sometimes in addition to) the technologies that allow them to realize their spectacles. But amidst the decades of massive hits and disastrous flops, visual spectaculars and lackluster wannabes, the fundamental stories and the generic tropes have largely remained the same. Allowing for reasonable overlap and variation, Yacowar uncovers several generic conventions that appear to be inherent in disaster films, such as the cross-section of society as illustrated by the cast, the bonding of a set of characters in the face of calamity, and the inevitable romantic subplot (342–50).

In this book we will refer to the common tropes of the disaster film as well as identify and explore others. During the course of our discussions, however, it will become clear how particular disaster subgenre conventions can be assigned without hesitation to the current Covid-19 disaster epic we have all been living through for the past few years. In addition to some of the conventions that Yacowar recognizes, we will explore, for example, the role of the female lead in relation to the male lead, the death of the Poignant Character, and whether or not a certain movie exhibits a more *proactive* or more *reactive* behavior in its confrontation of said disaster. Adhering to the paradigm of a progressive beginning-middle-end composition that serves much of dramatic filmmaking (Bordwell et al. 68), it is possible to illustrate the application of disaster genre conventions to the Covid-19 timeline and to parallel when certain real world narrative benchmarks are reached. With this in mind, we will refer to the beginning portion of our examination as Act One: The Buildup, the middle as Act Two: All Hell Breaks Loose, and the concluding section as Act Three: Out of the Woods?

"Act One: The Buildup" addresses the initial stages of the disaster scenario and what components are generally found to be present therein. In the portion of a story prior to the cataclysm that will follow, we should be able to identify with confidence who the main players are, and, barring any eleventh-hour surprises, what their relationships are to one another. Who is likely to be our Poignant Character, the individual who will meet an especially melodramatic demise? Are there kids involved? If so, what are their specific child-centric attributes that could prove vital much later in the story? If we see genre as a means of classification and if we are aware of the conventions that surround the majority of disaster films, we can project our assumptions about character, plot, motivation, etc., onto the characters as we meet them and the situations as we encounter them.

Critically, we also explore the social and/or economic conditions within which our disaster appears. What do these conditions look like as our story opens and how might they inform the protagonist's motivation that will drive him or her (this being the disaster movie, it's more often *him* rather than *her*, unfortunately) to take the lead in rescue efforts? Is there a wife or a child or children in peril? Is the protagonist an environmentalist of some sort who might take an especially keen interest in curtailing a potential environmental disaster? While I would contend that disaster movies aren't necessarily, as Keane postulates, "borne out of times of crisis" (5), I would agree with him in the sense that movies, like much of art regardless of the genre, are typically reflective of the times in which they are produced (5). These intrinsic circumstances contribute to what type of disaster the characters might experience and who might be the person or persons that make it out alive.

"Act Two: All Hell Breaks Loose" serves as the crux of the story and, arguably, the overarching reason that moviegoers buy their tickets to disaster films in the first place: it's when, as they say, shit gets real. The key spectacular set piece, the typical harbinger of the beginning of Act Two, however it is conveyed, is revealed to delighted awe from the audience. Depending upon whether we are watching a movie with a proactive or a reactive narrative thrust (both instances of which will be explored in Act Two), the disaster will occur and the core group of survivors will then struggle to get to safety or the disaster will be ongoing and the characters will use every ounce of wit and ingenuity at their disposal to prevent further peril. Regardless, in Act Two, the crisis mounts and reaches a fever pitch while characters expose their true natures (for better or for worse), and the movie mostly uncovers which stars will and which stars won't survive the disaster.

"Act Three: Out of the Woods?" is, I admit, a bit of a misnomer. This is because in a disaster movie, one is never *truly* out of the woods. Rather, one experiences a decline in severity of the disaster—for the time being, at least. Following the occurrence of the disaster, which we refer to as the Primary Disaster, there is always a trail of death and destruction left in its wake that those who have withstood the event must weather. To that end, in this section of the book we explore the concept of the Law of the Second Disaster that is present in most movies of this type. After all, disaster movies are intended to be a spectacularly thrilling form of mass entertainment, not a cheap one-and-done cash grab (though some might argue that a fair share of entertainment spectaculars do, unfortunately, deserve this ignominious label). Therefore, the audience must be provided with one final "WOW" to not only send them smiling into the night, but also to justify increasingly exorbitant ticket prices (whether in theater or streaming), not to mention the various and pricey accouterments that are part and parcel of the moviegoing experience (popcorn, soda, candy, etc.). But as with most dramatic art and in keeping with the customary beginning-middle-end narrative composition (Bordwell et al. 68), Act Three is when the story strands are (hopefully) wrapped up and conflicts are (hopefully) resolved. Thus, we explore the generic probabilities of, and reasons for, character survival.

Additionally, we take a look at the Preamble (better understood as the Prologue) and Epilogue or Coda, narrative mechanisms with which many disaster film creators choose to open and close their stories. More prevalent in recent iterations of the disaster film than in earlier creations, the Preamble and Epilogue/Coda serve as ways to, respectively, psych up the audience prior to the onset of the story proper with an opening spectacle to juice their adrenaline, and, later on, as a look into the future after the disaster has decimated the story world and forced a restructuring of society.

Throughout the explorations of the various elements of the disaster film, however, *Are We Living in a Disaster Movie?* will never lose focus on the actual disaster that is happening, in real time, as we speak. You will see the ways in which each act in this book corresponds to specific narrative beats that have been achieved in the Covid-19 pandemic disaster. By placing a discussion of the disaster film subgenre within the context of a contemporaneous, real-life disaster, the deconstruction of the disaster film will become palpable, and a more focused generic picture will come into view for audiences who aren't quite sure what to make of the current predicament.

In the chapters that follow we examine how the blueprint of the real-world disaster film we are living in has conceivably already been written by Hollywood disaster films going back decades. With this generic template in mind, we perhaps might be able to uncover the map to our future.

The Attraction of Disaster

If someone were to ask you if you had any desire to pay money to watch a film in which a group of people were trapped inside of a burning building with no way out, would you think twice about telling that person to take a hike? Who other than the most depraved person would want to see a movie like that (although, in all honesty, I am sure there's a market for it)? Or is it fair to say that you would look at a person with an expression registering the utmost concern for both their character and their sanity if they excitedly asked you to join them in viewing a movie in which a massive horde of killer bees gruesomely attacks the residents of a city? Or even better, how about if someone were to ask you to be their partner in watching a flick wherein a group of people are ensnared in the path of molten rock and creeping lava, the result of a recently exploded volcano? You might, I would imagine, envision swathes of people aflame, screaming and running wildly about as they are burned alive yet still making a futile attempt to extinguish the flames from their bodies. These are grave images, to be sure, and anyone who spends more than a fleeting moment dwelling upon them is surely a case for the psych ward at the nearest insane asylum.

Yet, it is exactly these apparently grisly scenarios that formed the basis of four prime entries in the disaster movie canon: *The Towering Inferno* from 1974, *The Swarm* (Irwin Allen) from 1978, and *Dante's Peak* and *Volcano*, both from 1997. *The Towering Inferno* was even one of the most successful movies of the year at the time of its release. The mammoth success of *The Towering Inferno*, *The Poseidon Adventure* (1972), *Armageddon* (1998), and contemporaneous films of a similar nature attest to a certain proof that the disaster movie is an enduring component of popular cinematic entertainment. However, it is exactly the psychological reason (or reasons) behind the popular success of a disaster movie that is curious. On the surface, it would appear that a movie which focuses on a specific society (or societies) as it is annihilated by a massive catastrophe (or series of catastrophes) would be nothing short of an exercise in perversion. A piece of work that paints a shiny Hollywood shellac on large-scale destruction, imminent terror, and ghastly death would seem to be something that only the most morbidly minded individual would find appealing. But this is, essentially, what forms the foundational basis for a disaster movie. It is from this horrifying scenario that the rest of the tropes in this mini genre fall into place, and the disaster movie as we know it takes shape.

I would contend that beneath all the enticing spectacle (a word that will be used frequently and liberally throughout the course of this book) and superficiality present in the modern disaster movie, there is a larger, more fundamental and primal mechanism that hearkens back to the scaffolding of our basic human biology. This would be the concept of how we, as beings in the natural world, respond to fear and the prospect of our own mortality.

People across the ages have always expressed an innate fear when confronted with the unknown. This is a natural inclination. For it is, of course, impossible to know for sure what lies beyond our earthly realm. The unknown, or more specifically the afterlife, represents, in many ways, a loss of control, a surrendering of fact and of reason for individuals. After all, it is the ability to reason, a unique attribute that human beings hold particularly sacred, that is the primary differentiator between human beings and the animal kingdom. While some people find a loss of control more stressful than others, some people need, cling to that sense of guidance, of management over their lives and their destinies. This is, perhaps, why some people turn to religion, so that they may take some comfort in knowing that if they adhere to certain structured laws and behaviors during the course of their lives, when the time comes to face the unknown, they believe they will know what to expect. But no matter a person's religious belief or the profession of "The End Is Near" rhetoric a revered clergyperson or fanatical zealot might espouse from their pulpits, the scientific truth is that the great beyond is, and will always remain, an enigma. Thus, I would argue that fear, that biological vibe responsible for anxiety as well as self-preservation, is almost always connected to the prospect of death and the moment when every being, homo sapien or otherwise, crosses over into the unknown.

Let us examine, for example, a fear shared by scores upon scores of individuals throughout the world: the common fear of heights. For some folks, the idea of ascending higher, higher, and even higher into the sky, whether through an outdoor sport such as mountain climbing or indirectly via some indoor vector such as an elevator in an urban skyscraper, is enough to send them into a state of paralyzing terror. When someone who possesses a fear of heights realizes that a meeting in which his or her presence has been requested is in a conference room on the seventy-third floor of some downtown office building, he or she is likely to get woozy at the very notion of attending. He or she might get quiet, appear anxious, or, perhaps, all color may drain from the face and a look of sheer dread may seize a normally cheerful countenance. The body may begin to tremble, the stomach tense up, or, in a drastic response, he or she might simply feel the urge to vomit. While any of these reactions might seem dramatic on their surface to someone else, they, in fact, indicate a very real, unamusing, and acute biological alarm that someone possessing a fear of heights will have at the concept of being so far off of the ground.

Now let me be clear: I am not a psychologist, nor have I ever conducted any significant or practical research on the subject concerning the root causes of a fear of heights. I am simply *suggesting* that this particular fear, routinely present in many people, might be truly manifested in an actual worry that as a result of being so high off of the ground, a greater likelihood and indubitableness of death by way of falling from such an elevated height emerges. How many times have you heard someone say that they awoke from a nightmare in which they dreamt that they were falling?

I would propose that a similar biological mechanism might be at work in someone who harbors a fear of roller coasters, for example. (The roller coaster as a motif is one that will be referred to at several points throughout this tome.) Personally, I love roller coasters and can't get enough of them. I love the excited thrill I feel when waiting in the line before boarding one of the passenger trains; I love the tense feeling of the coaster zipping along its track and feeling my stomach subtly rise and my rear end ever so slightly lift off of the train seat during the descent of a massive and unnaturally steep decline; I love feeling the need to scream and release the rush of adrenaline as the coaster train loops upside down or side-to-side, sometimes cornering on the rails of the coaster's track. There aren't many better ways of facing the prospect of death than a grade-A thrill ride such as the roller coaster.

However, I am not so naïve that I don't realize that there are others out there in the world who most definitely do not share my enthusiasm for the quintessential amusement park ride. There are some folks who are downright petrified of roller coasters and prefer to sit near the ride's exit and wait patiently while their friends go and defy death for a few minutes. And it is exactly this inflated prospect of defying death that repels some individuals from roller coasters. I might be so bold as to suggest that the fear surrounding one's riding on a roller coaster, aside from quite possibly working in tandem with one's fear of heights, may actually be more profoundly rooted in a skepticism of the safety of such amusements; the suspicion that something mechanical may go wrong on the ride—perhaps a coaster train becoming stuck on the track or even striking another train that has become stuck on the track, or a coaster car somehow derailing from the track during a sharp turn—resulting in one's death. The same skepticism surrounding the mechanical safety of the machine could also be observed in those that have, say, a fear of flying. While tragedies have, no doubt, occurred at amusement parks throughout the decades, and there are cases, rare as they are, of roller coasters malfunctioning and a passenger or passengers being injured or even killed as a result of such a mishap, this fear is most probably irrational. But as is the case with any marked fear or phobia, it is the irrational that prevails. It is extraordinarily difficult to reason one out of an ingrained fear that they have held onto their entire lives, particularly one that they cannot arguably justify.

The certain uncertainty revolving around the inevitability of death provides the underlying thematic thrust in the disaster film. Watching as recognizable marquee names, as well as some lesser-known character types, try to survive whatever the disaster might be is, unquestionably, a primary draw of the disaster film (Keane 5). The other draw being, of course, the disaster, the attraction of the spectacle. However, there is another perhaps more subconscious construction working underneath the pretension of the pictures that the audience sees moving across their screen. A disaster film, as mentioned, works easily and brilliantly by tapping into an audience's fear of their own mortality. For some, the time might be nigh; for others, hopefully, there is more life left to be lived. In the same way, perhaps, that we may slow down on the highway when we spot a traffic accident or delight in a notable celebrity that becomes entangled in an embarrassing scandal and tumbles from their superficial position high upon the pedestal of idolatry, those of us watching the disaster scenario play out onscreen, as the characters battle the elements or technology in a desperate fight for their lives, experience a morbid fascination at work in watching others confront the prospect of their own mortality. Doing so reinforces the reality that we, thankfully, are not.

What disaster movies arguably do in their own action-packed, candy-coated way is to concoct an elaborate scenario designed specifically to play on this fear of the unknown, this certain uncertainty. In contrasting a salient point concerning science fiction films that Susan Sontag makes in her seminal essay "The Imagination of Disaster," Maurice Yacowar illustrates this hypothesis in his equally seminal discussion of the disaster film "The Bug in the Rug." He posits that the disaster film "exploits the spectacular potential of the screen and nourishes the audience's fascination with the vision of massive doom" (334). In the most elemental blueprint of a disaster film, the population of a particular society somewhere in the world is confronted with an apocalyptic and cataclysmic event. Such an event is guaranteed to rain, or has done so already, untold destruction and scores of deaths upon said society if something is not done to impede it. A core group of survivors (not necessarily the *only* survivors of the disaster, but the primary characters that the film, by necessity, focuses on in order to drive the narrative) made up of a disparate group of individuals intended to, presumably, serve as avatars for the audience members, must quickly figure out how its members can work together to not only save themselves, but to somehow save the rest of the society. To impede the advancing specter of death.

The sorts of disaster scenarios that are borne from the imaginations of scenarists and filmmakers are almost infinite in nature, ranging from a cataclysmic flood (*Deluge, Flood*), destructive earthquake (*Earthquake, San Andreas*), out-of-control city bus (*Speed*), capsized cruise ship (*The Poseidon Adventure*), and rapidly spreading and deadly virus (*The Andromeda Strain, Outbreak, Contagion, The Sibylline Scourge*), among countless other horrifying scenarios. There are innumerable methods in which to throw characters against death's somber visage.

A good disaster film works easily and brilliantly by tapping into an audience's fear of their own mortality. Whether or not an individual lives with an all-consuming fear of death akin to a fear of heights and works overtime to prevent the inevitable in whatever and whichever way they are able, dictates to a large degree their response(s) to disaster in general, and the disaster film in particular. An individual who accepts the consequence of nature and understands that when the time is right and their number is called, death will come, might look at a disaster film in a more passive, more relaxed mode of spectatorship. This individual may, perhaps, view the film with more of a lilt towards the entertaining with which most disaster films are intended. Conversely, an individual who harbors a more genuine and outright terror concerning the prospect of death, while still finding the disaster film entertaining, might be more apt to internalize the disaster scenario and react with more of a frightened, apprehensive impression than their more unruffled counterparts.

What is nonetheless observable is that people gaze upon death, in fact the very notion of mortality, with a certain trepidation that borders on the reverent. It is with this level of damn awe that I view the disaster film.

Read on and join me on this voyage ... time is running out!

CHAPTER 1

The Preamble

Let us, for a moment, imagine that I am a screenwriter, about to begin a new project. I stand in the doorway to my office and look around inside. The office is comfortable, if small and basic; only a few shelves, a modern, wooden desk, an unremarkable office chair, and a two-drawer file cabinet constitute all of the furnishings. I take a deep breath and move into the room, shuffling slowly over to a window to the left of the desk and cracking it open to allow for a gentle breeze to waft in; after the early morning rain, the air is clean, dewy, refreshing. I sit down at my desk and place a nondescript coffee mug, steaming with the contents of a freshly brewed Starbucks pod, on a coaster about six inches to the right of my laptop. The laptop, your standard Mac-Book, is front and center on the desk, mocking me, daring me to flip it open. In the right corner of the desk, standing erect between two metal bookends, is a dictionary, an all-purpose notebook, and a few select books related to the entertainment industry. On the left side of the desk, a tabletop fan sits idle in the corner, properly positioned to blow air into my face should it be switched on to fan the room, which will undoubtedly become stuffy as the day goes on and the heat of the Florida summer reaches its full potential. A medium-sized bottle of generic hand sanitizer sits nearby, just in case. All is in order.

I take a sip of the still-steaming coffee and wince as the liquid burns my tongue. I flip open the laptop, enter my login information, and wait a minute as the device comes to life. I click on the Microsoft Word icon in the dock, and in a matter of seconds, a blank page appears. The blank page stares back at me, the LCD light immediately straining my eyes as the page and I engage in a duel. The white screen defies me to begin typing words, any words, onto its virtual, blank canvas. The *pas de deux* of the writer and the page has begun.

The task I have bestowed onto myself is to draft a semi-fictionalized account of the Covid-19 pandemic realized through the narrative purview of the modern disaster movie. As I review my notes in anticipation of typing the crucial first words onto that daunting blank page, I reflect upon the history of the disaster movie from cinema's storied past. At the same time,

I try to conceptualize how the events of the past few years correlate to the disaster movie's generic benchmarks, conventions that I have researched ad nauseum over the past few years. In doing so, I might begin my dramatization of the Covid-19-cum-disaster movie with a Preamble. It might look something like this:

FADE IN—EXT: WUHAN, CENTRAL CHINA—DAY

Food bazaars are a way of life in Wuhan, located in central China. In the early hours of the morning, they bustle with activity as the whole of the eastern hemisphere slowly awakens. As the morning sun welcomes mankind into the promise of a new day, a veritable potpourri of vendors stock their booths with the day's selection of fresh fruits, vegetables, meats, and seafood, creating a mad cacophony of industrial activity in the wet markets of this central Chinese city. Soon, consumers will come and go in the market and mill about the miles and miles of aisles containing produce in search of the most prime cuts of meat and the freshest, most ripened vegetables on display. Some consumers may be making their weekly—sometimes bi- or tri-weekly—sojourn to these popular markets, a more traditional alternative to the more expensive Western-type supermarkets ("Chinese Wet Market Tour" 00:03:15–00:10:24).

At some point during the hectic morning, as vendors and consumers trade cash and pleasantries, a nameless individual exploring the culinary smorgasbord laid out at the Huanan Seafood Wholesale Market in Wuhan (Aylin Woodward), possibly a tourist but certainly not a Wuhan native, purchases a piece of fish from a wet market vendor. The vendor wraps the fish in paper and hands the parcel over to the customer. The smiling customer accepts his package, makes a half-hearted and cringeworthy foreigner's attempt to say "thank you" in Chinese to the amused but appreciative vendor, and goes about his way, content with having participated in an exclusively Chinese tradition. At no point during the course of this transaction has the thought entered anyone's mind regarding the use of protective gloves as a precautionary measure against possible skin-to-fish-to-skin contact.

Meanwhile, as wet markets such as the Wuhan Huanan Seafood Wholesale Market spring to life with the day's business, work begins at the Wuhan CDC, located only a short walk from the Huanan Seafood Market (Aylin Woodward). Sporting characteristic sterile white lab jackets, research scientists set to their workday maneuvering about clinical laboratories and carefully dispensing hazardous chemicals into fragile test tubes containing liquid specimens in order to possibly provoke a chemical reaction. Other scientists in the lab may be tasked with gingerly handling precious specimens placed in laboratory centrifuges to separate their particle composition. As the hours in the day tick by like a metronome, barely any words are spoken amongst the scientists. They keep their eyes glued intently to their microscopes, separating from the ocular lens only to look to their journals and log research data.

The scientists are so totally concentrated on their work, and their eyes are so laser focused on documenting the life cycles of a myriad of infectious diseases, that it goes unnoticed when, due to the inefficacy of subpar but presumably safe enough PPE [personal protective equipment] (Aylin Woodward), a drop of specimen, microscopic in amount yet highly infectious in potency, of a novel coronavirus is accidentally shuttled out of the lab via the germ's preferred route of transmission: inhalation.

Within the etymology of the disaster film, the above-described scenario constitutes what I have termed as the Preamble (this might also be more commonly understood to be the Prologue). While certainly not a steadfast requirement for inclusion in any film purporting to be a disaster movie, the filmmakers behind many films of this type elect to include a Preamble. The Preamble oftentimes consists of an event or series of events that only we, as the audience, are aware of. As a result, the audience might be put in the position of silent witness to the events of the movie, watching from a helpless, but safely removed position, as the characters encounter the disaster. On his podcast *Kermode on Film*, film critic and scholar Mark Kermode perfectly articulates the audience's role as spectator from a safe distance and its crucial contribution to the enjoyment of the disaster movie:

> The thing that disaster movies do is this: they confront you with the spectacle of catastrophe and death and yet, weirdly enough, they make you feel very alive. I mean, partly they make you feel alive because you are a spectator and you're kind of thanking your lucky stars that you're not involved in whatever this situation is [00:32:00–22].

As you might suspect, a Preamble, if one is present, lives in the forefront portion of the movie, perhaps even before the opening credits of the film have rolled out, and prior to the occurrence of any proper narrative action. This plot device can be viewed, in various forms, in several disaster films, including *The Towering Inferno*, when at twelve minutes and forty-three seconds into the film, the circuit breaker in the control room on the eighty-first floor sparks and spews small embers into the room, igniting the eventual conflagration; *The Andromeda Strain* (Robert Wise, 1971), when at approximately seven minutes into the film, a couple of military men, on a mission to recover a satellite in New Mexico, uncover to their horror and confusion that the citizens of the small desert town they are casing have all, somehow, mysteriously perished; and in *Outbreak*, during the introductory sequence in which General McClintock (Donald Sutherland) explores an outbreak of a strange and deadly illness afflicting a military base in Zaire.

There are several reasons why a filmmaker might choose to stage a Preamble in a disaster movie, including:

- To provide an occasion exclusive of the narrative proper in which to introduce the picture's star.
- To ominously foreshadow the dire events that will, no doubt, transpire later in the film.
- To present an expository sequence, devoid of any formal introduction of a main character, in which to set the events of the film in motion.

Regardless of the method of presentation, the primary function of the Preamble is this: to kick things off and psych up the audience for the anticipated and impressive thrills that will follow. Even more, the events of the Preamble may not even have anything materially to do with the actual disaster that is guaranteed to occur later in the film. In the interest of further illustration, let's take an in-depth look at a Preamble and examine its utilization in Brad Peyton's *San Andreas*.

* * *

Preamble Sequence: San Andreas

Immediately following a bare opening title sequence, *San Andreas* opens on a young and sunshiny blonde woman (whose name, we soon learn, is Natalie) leisurely traversing a precarious San Fernando Valley mountain road (to where is not important). Natalie is enjoying a carefree drive, bouncing happily along to Taylor Swift's "Style" on her car's radio. Young Natalie commits a few moronic driving infractions, including taking her eyes off the road as she reaches behind her into the back seat to grab a water bottle and, most egregiously moronic, looking at a text as she is driving. Natalie's driving "don'ts" set the viewer up to anticipate her having an accident with two oncoming cars that suddenly appear from around a mountainous bend on the two-lane road. But alas, Natalie is, for the moment, safe … until she notices a few falling rocks, the bane of motorists on windy mountain roads everywhere.

The minor avalanche is sufficient enough to cause Natalie to swerve her SUV straight off the winding mountain road and for it to plunge down the side of the mountain. As the SUV tumbles and flips over, the soundtrack to the scene is filled with the noises of crashing metal and shattering glass underlain with a thunderous, action-movie style score. Natalie screams in terror as she is flung helplessly around the SUV as it plummets down the precipice, her belongings tousling about the car as it violently proceeds down the cliffside and Natalie's long, blonde hair, a symbol of youthful exuberance just moments ago, now representing sheer chaos as it flies wildly about her as she is tossed about the cabin. Eventually, the SUV comes to a stop, resting precariously on the mountainside. One false move from the young woman and it's lights out. And since Natalie doesn't exercise the most responsible habits behind the wheel, we have every reason to fear for the young woman's life in her current situation.

Cut to a helicopter, skillfully weaving to and fro in between the majestic mountaintops of California's San Fernando Valley. Inside the helicopter are four members of the Los Angeles Fire Department (in true Hollywood-movie fashion, these guys all look as though they might as well be on their way to a beefcake calendar photo shoot), as well as a journalist and her cameraman who are along for the ride conducting interviews for a story on the men. At one point, the journalist directs a question to the man sitting in the helicopter pilot's seat. He is Chief Ray Gaines, and as he turns his head to respond to her, the audience is introduced to the movie's star, Dwayne "The Rock" Johnson.

Soon, Gaines spots Natalie's dangling SUV, and the action-movie music picks up on the soundtrack once again. Almost immediately after Gaines opens communications with Natalie via a helicopter-to-cell phone hookup, the SUV inches a few more feet down the precipice. Time is of the essence. In order to rescue Natalie before the SUV loses its grip, the helicopter must be maneuvered in between a tight, naturally occurring squeeze in the mountains, an exciting maneuver known as "tipping the hat."

Following this fun sequence, the helicopter is now in the correct position to perform the rescue. Firefighter Joby (Colton Haynes), tasked with retrieving the girl and lifting her to the safety of the chopper, carefully repels himself down to meet Natalie in the dangling SUV. Once he is face-to-face with Natalie, she (understandably) reflexively tries to climb out of the SUV to meet Joby. He informs the terrified woman that before any rescue attempt can be made, he must secure the car. In the process of doing so, however, Joby's arm becomes stuck between the earth and the SUV, rendering him immobile. Time for our movie star to earn his movie star paycheck.

Gaines hands the reins of the chopper over to co-pilot Harrison (Matt Gerald) and gears himself up. The cameraman keeps his camera rolling, capturing everything. In no time at all, Gaines has repelled himself down to encounter Natalie, who is having just the worst day. But the SUV is losing its grip, further pinning Joby to the mountain, and its weight is putting enormous strain on the helicopter that is supporting it. The group has only seconds to safely accomplish the rescue.

As the music crescendos, Gaines rips the door from the SUV, grabs Natalie, and signals to Harrison in the chopper to release the cables supporting the car. Upon doing so, the SUV plummets to the valley below, Joby is unstuck, and Natalie is rescued, safely cradled in the arms of our star. The scene has, in effect, ended … all in under ten minutes (*San Andreas* 00:01:13–00:09:26). Furthermore, this heart-pounding chapter has nothing to do, from a narrative standpoint, with the storyline of *San Andreas*, which concerns a massive earthquake resulting from movement of the titular fault line. The Preamble is complete.

In another instance, a director filming a Preamble might elect to foreshadow the impending doom that will threaten the characters later in the film, such as Roland Emmerich does in *2012*. Or a filmmaker may decide simply to stage an exciting mini spectacle with which to hook the audience, and that has nothing to do, narratively speaking, with the story proper, as we have just explored in the case of *San Andreas*.

Understanding that juicing up the audience for the thrills to come is the primary function of the Preamble, this opening device should exploit a dazzling set piece that impresses upon the audience the scale and the grandeur of the film. The last thing any director, or playwright, or storyteller wants to do is open their story and provoke an exasperated reaction in their audience that says, "Well, this is going to be a slog."

With this is mind, the Preamble should never, ever be a bigger or more impressive episode than the focal disaster (or disasters) in the film. A director who exposes all of his or her cards too early in the film is almost certainly setting his or herself up for, ahem, disaster. It is a tricky balancing act between actively exciting the audience and reserving some element of surprise for the moment when that even more dazzling event of the focal disaster happens later in the film. How many times have you heard a frustrated moviegoer lament something to the effect of "Well, the first twenty minutes were great, but it was all downhill from there." Not good.

On the other hand, not every filmmaker behind every disaster film chooses to include a Preamble to open his or her story. Thus, a Preamble cannot be considered a defining criterion for admission into the hallowed taxonomy of the disaster film. As a matter of fact, most films in the disaster subgenre *do not* include a Preamble. In contrast with movies that utilize a very clear Preamble, such as *San Andreas*, some movies, such as the classic *Deluge*, open, more or less, directly in the throes of the disaster, sparing no screen time in getting right to the point. *Deluge* raises its curtain amid preparations for the anticipated titular catastrophe.

* * *

The Opening: Deluge

Subsequent to the opening credits (which conclude with an earnest biblical quote referencing the flood from which God tested Noah), there is a brief dialogue between two nameless meteorologists who are discussing some unconventional barometric readings. The picture then fades into a Coast Guard radio room where, over a montage of cargo ships at sea, a naval dispatcher is sending out an urgent all-points bulletin to area ships requiring that they remain in port due to an impending storm; Val Burton's score is already registering the element of suspense.

Next, the viewer watches as naval officers scurry about in full-blown panic mode as they issue orders that all ships remain docked. More importantly (plot-wise, at least), the viewer learns that a proposed record-breaking swim (through which body of water is not important) to be attempted by one Claire Arlington (Peggy Shannon) is now cancelled. Then it's back to the Coast Guard radio dispatcher sending out an order that all area airplanes currently in flight find the nearest airport and land; a montage follows of aircraft both large and small, two-seater to Zeppelin, returning to the ground.

There is then an unexplainable eclipse, and word comes down that Italy and England are experiencing incessant earthquakes and plummeting barometers. There is even worry that "the end of world is at hand, terrifying millions."

Appropriately, considering *Deluge* was released in 1933, there is the old-timey go-to montage of spiraling newspaper headlines forecasting Armageddon: "Great Calamity Predicted," "Catastrophe Imminent," "Earth Doomed." Panic in the streets ensues as preacher men espouse biblical passages regarding the End of Days and instruct the faithful to put their trust in the Lord.

The public panic, urban destruction, and societal terror continue as buildings collapse and people run for their lives until, at the fifteen-minute mark, the floods overtake Manhattan, much of which has been, by this point, reduced to rubble (*Deluge* 00:01:20–00:15:02).

A more recent example of a film excising the Preamble and diving headfirst into the disaster would be the alien invasion magnum opus *Independence Day*. ID4, as the movie's title is commonly short-handed, opens immediately with panic in the streets involving the citizens of Los Angeles, all of whom are bearing witness to strange atmospheric occurrences. Taken from a narrative standpoint, the opening moments of *Independence Day* just about parallel the opening moments of *Deluge*.

* * *

The Opening: Independence Day

After a quick shot of a travelling and menacing spaceship (we did buy tickets for this movie after all, so we know there will be space destruction), a man from an organization called S.E.T.I. (Search for Extraterrestrial Intelligence Institute) detects some weird sounds on one of his recording monitors. According to one of his scientist colleagues, the foreign bleeps appear to be coming from the Moon.

Cut to Washington, D.C., or more specifically, Robert Loggia as General Grey at Space Command, The Pentagon, as he is briefed on this strange phenomenon. General Grey examines some satellite images of an odd structure that, he is informed, has a "diameter of over five hundred fifty kilometers and a mass roughly one-fourth the size of our Moon." He immediately places a call to the Secretary of Defense.

Cut to President Whitmore (Bill Pullman), still in bed, receiving a phone call from his First Lady, Marilyn (Mary McDonnell). Still in his robe, he makes his way to the presidential breakfast nook where he is met by Connie (Margaret Colin), his Chief of Staff, who bids him good morning by way of welcoming him into a casual discussion regarding his presidential image. Then the call comes through from the Secretary of Defense. The tension is building.

The viewer is then transported to a park in New York City on a lovely morning. David Levinson (Jeff Goldblum) and his father (Judd Hirsch) are enjoying some bonding time over a game of chess. Ending the game with a checkmate, David leaves his dad and heads off to his engineering job at Compact Cable. As David arrives at work, the viewer observes that the entire office is running around in a complete frenzy. Upon David's arrival, his frantic colleague Marty (Harvey Fierstein) tries desperately to get David to pay attention to all sorts of atmospheric carnage that appears to be wreaking havoc on their network's satellites.

The film takes a few moments to introduce a lunatic crop-duster pilot named Russell Casse (Randy Quaid) and his three kids out in the desert of Imperial Valley, California. Soon however, we are back at the White House where fear is gaining momentum as officials scurry around the Oval Office trying to comprehend incoming reports of visual confirmations of the phenomenon that flood in from around the world. A newscast from Russia indicates "widespread panic."

The military is eventually called into action, the Emergency Broadcast System is enabled, and cities across the nation slowly become drenched in an encroaching and eerie darkness as the phenomenon nears and more terror ensues. Finally, at roughly the twenty-one-minute mark, the spectacle unveils itself and the massive alien spacecraft makes its first proper appearance. The eyes of the world gaze upon it in disbelief. Not for long (*Independence Day* 00:01:54–00:21:10).

In rare circumstances, it may not even be necessary for the audience to have been introduced to any of the main characters during the

Preamble. It is simply used as a device to set the plot in motion. An example of this tactic in use can be witnessed in the Preamble that opens 1977's *The Cassandra Crossing* (George Pan Cosmatos).

* * *

Preamble Sequence: The Cassandra Crossing

Succeeding a lovely opening credits sequence in which the camera glides above the glorious Swiss Alps and traces the picturesque natural beauty of the Geneva landscape, the distinctive blare of a European ambulance is heard on the soundtrack. Moments later, the ambulance speeds into the driveway of an office building which houses the International Health Organization. Two medics emerge from the ambulance and, with clear urgency, remove a stretcher from the rear of the vehicle, upon which lies what the viewer assumes to be, at the very least, an ill or perhaps wounded person, and rush it into the hospital.

Racing through the halls of the hospital to, presumably, the emergency room area, the medics encounter a roadblock in the form of a military guard. The guard informs the medics that the emergency room is, in fact, on the other side of the hospital. No matter, because this is a classic fake-out; the man on the stretcher sits up, brandishes a gun, and shoots the guard. This allows the medics (whom the viewer now understands are his cohorts) to enter into the restricted area.

But, lo and behold, the guard isn't dead! He rolls over and manages to shoot the man who was formerly on the stretcher in the back, killing him. Undeterred, the dead man's two accomplices get to work on setting up a bomb that they have smuggled into the hospital.

But wait … the guard still isn't dead! He manages to muster up just enough strength to push the button on a security alarm. Just as he does so, the two men finish installing their bomb and make a try to break into the "Bacterial and Infectious Diseases" lab. Whether they intended to enter that specific lab or whether they chose it because it was the closest door to them as they attempted to make their getaway is unclear.

However, the men are karmically thwarted by an inability to access the lab, and they frenetically begin trying to open other nearby doors. Meanwhile, two military guards, having been alerted by the security alarm, arrive on the scene with their guns drawn and at the ready. One guard immediately works to disarm the bomb while the other chases after the men. Following a brief shootout, the two men bust through a door marked "Maximum Security—Danger—Keep Out." Sage advice, this notice, because on the other side of this door is a lab which contains shelves of beakers full of, undoubtedly, hazardous and restricted materials. Within seconds of entering the lab, one of the accomplices is shot in the back. Following up with one more shot, a bullet from the guard's gun strikes a beaker on a shelf, which sends its liquid contents spraying about the room and onto the persons of both accomplices.

The unharmed accomplice is now covered in noxious biomedical goop and, identifying no other options for escape, grabs a nearby stool and tosses it through a window. As he makes his jump to freedom, the guard realizes that this man is about to leak all of the noxious biomedical goop he is covered in out of the hospital and shouts at him, "No, man, no!!"

Cut to the man, having discarded the fake medical robe he had been wearing, running across a footbridge to hopeful freedom. The Preamble comes to an end as Burt Lancaster, as Mackenzie, makes his entrance into the hospital, having been called in to assess the damage (*The Cassandra Crossing* 00:00:00–00:06:38).

In what is arguably the closest cinematic relative of *The Sibylline Scourge*, 2011's *Contagion*, a unique method is utilized in which to stage its Preamble: a method that can really only be described as "Preamble as Epilogue," an especially effective and retroactively ominous approach. Following the main events of the movie, the audience is taken back in time to the day *prior* to Beth Emhoff (Gwyneth Paltrow) leaving Hong Kong, which is when we first encounter the events of the story. In doing so, the film discloses the origins of the titular contagion: due to industrial deforestation, a displaced bat drops some half-eaten food onto a grate in a pig farm, whereby a pig snaps it up before being hauled away to a restaurant where, in preparation for a meal, the now dead animal is grossly and carelessly handled by a chef who then happily meets and shakes hands with Beth. A title card on the screen appears: "Day One," in reference to the film's day-by-day chronological structure (*Contagion* 01:39:59–1:41:26). The movie then cuts to black for the closing credits. The second that contagion is, unbeknownst to everyone, transported out of that pig farm, there is no stopping it from, in short time, grinding the world to a halt. Sound familiar?

The structural shift of disaster films from those with more of a narrative focus to those with more of a spectacular focus will be explored later in this book, specifically, in the chapter concerning "proactive" or "reactive" narrative arcs. But generally speaking, disaster films produced and released prior to the 1990s disaster cycle, which cycle I would argue began with de Bont's *Speed*, tended to focus more on the narrative progression of its stories. These movies were more interested in the interplay among the characters and the conflicts that arose among them. *Airport* was, essentially, an in-flight soap opera. Of course, these films did have a spectacular element; that's what made them exciting in many ways. But the spectacle was more in service to how it affected the relationships between the characters. The titular catastrophe served as more of a backdrop against which the drama between the characters played out according to the narrative.

Conversely, the spectacles were unquestionably central in the 1990s cycle and beyond. In the wake of media such as MTV and the proliferation of such visually oriented movies as *Tron* (Steven Lisberger, 1982) and *Top Gun* (Tony Scott, 1986), one could argue that the attention spans of audiences were on the wane in the intervening decade. Directors utilizing hyperkinetic editing techniques and flashy visuals will drive audiences to expect more bombast more often.

With regard to the disaster movie, which as we will discuss, borrows many generic elements from the action film, this meant that directors wanting to hook their audiences needed to do so sooner and with a flashy and eye-popping opening sequence. It wasn't enough to introduce their stories gradually and with a more formal introduction. As such, the Preamble, the inclusion of which we have discussed is certainly not an exclusive attribute of disaster films, does tend to appear more often in disaster films of the 1990s and onward.

In the case of the biological disaster film specifically, which Yacowar includes within the "Monster" category among his eight "Basic Types" of disaster film (337), such as *The Sibylline Scourge, Outbreak, The Andromeda Strain,* or *Contagion,* there isn't much visual spectacle vis-à-vis exploding volcanoes or precarious rescues with which to stage a Preamble. For these types of "invisible threat" movies, the Preamble might typically take the shape of an ominous build-up or foreboding scenario. For example, let's examine the opening moments of *The Andromeda Strain.*

* * *

Preamble Sequence: The Andromeda Strain

The picture opens on two Air Force men stationed near the tiny town of Piedmont, New Mexico (population, sixty-eight), where the Air Force has recently placed a satellite. While surveying the area one night, the men notice that there are buzzards hovering over the town, night being a particularly random time for buzzards to be flying. (As a sidebar, how many times is one treated to the visual of circling buzzards in movies? Props must be given to the filmmakers for this one!) The men determine that they better radio the Vandenberg Air Force Base and inform their superiors that they are moving in to retrieve the satellite. As the lieutenant at the base listens on (along with the viewer), the men proceed into Piedmont.

Upon entering the town, the men remark how spooky the town appears, how devoid of life and activity the town is.

Suddenly, one of the men notifies his lieutenant that he thinks he sees a body. The lieutenant, of course, thinks his sergeant is imagining things, hallucinating visions due to extraordinarily eerie circumstances. Director Robert Wise constructs the scene so that the only visual indicator of the lieutenant and the sergeant's fear provided to the audience are the looks of terror on the faces of the military personnel at the Air Force base as they concentrate on listening intently to the voices of the men in Piedmont emanating from the intercom. The screech of a van is heard. The men at the base anxiously lean in towards the intercom in anticipation for the reveal of the reason. The lieutenant and his sergeant see another body, this one apparently dead. The base lieutenant radios to the men requesting an update on what is going on out there. The two men exploring Piedmont indicate in horror that they can now see several bodies. The base lieutenant relays to the men that their orders are, nevertheless, to "proceed to satellite and retrieve."

As the other lieutenants at the base nervously stand about, the base lieutenant calls for the major. In the meantime, however, the men in Piedmont are indicating that there are now bodies everywhere. "They're all over the place, sir. There must be dozens of them." Again, the screech of a van. The men indicate that they seem to notice a figure in white moving towards them. The base lieutenant on the telephone connects through to the major and starts to relay to him the evening's unsettling events. Just as the sergeant in Piedmont voices to his lieutenant that they should get out of there, a primal scream is heard, and the radio receiver registers major activity. But then, nothing. A flatline. The only sound heard is the deadly, scratchy beeping of the radio receiver. Something terrible has happened to the two men in Piedmont (*The Andromeda Strain* 00:03:22–00:07:30). A brilliant opening.

We can see that in this example, Wise has engaged the audience and heightened their expectation and anticipation that something weird is and will happen during the course of the film. Using minimal special effects (only the radio receiver, really), the scene exacerbates the tension and primes the audience for the exciting tale that is sure to be told.

In the more recent *Outbreak*, the Preamble occurs in the war-torn African nation of Zaire, in 1967. At the Motaba River Valley Mercenary Camp, a camp doctor guides a military doctor around the camp to survey a scene which has seen dozens of soldiers succumb to the ravages of a mysterious illness. Something invisible and terrifying is affecting the soldiers of the camp. The unknown pathogen will apparently result in an individual's death in a very short space of time, and the camp is in grave need for the United States to intervene and distribute vital medication. The military doctor makes a promise to the dying soldiers that aid will soon be delivered on the dire scene. Not long after, however, a massive bomb, possibly nuclear in nature, is instead dropped onto the camp, decimating the entire area in an effort to eradicate the unknown pathogen from the face of the earth (*Outbreak* was released in 1995, so this particular Preamble does exhibit a certain amount of attention-grabbing spectacle in the form of a huge explosion). As the scene comes to an end, wild monkeys flee the area that was once their home in an ominous foreshadowing of the spread of the outbreak that the audience knows will transpire (*Outbreak* 00:00:25–00:03:55).

Since we, as the audience, understand that we are watching a drama concerning an invisible virus outbreak, any included Preamble will contain this element of the foreboding and ominous. We know that in the ensuing story, sickness will abound and scores of people will most likely die. In our Covid-19 drama, *The Sibylline Scourge*, the Preamble that dramatizes the early pre-outbreak days in Wuhan, China, certainly displays this same sense of foreboding. Because this film is based on a true story, the audience will be able to foretell that pain and suffering will assuredly follow, and watching as people go about their daily lives in the wet markets or in the medical laboratories of the region is guaranteed to elicit a wholly portentous and sinister undertone. The audience is smart enough to gauge that it is only a matter of time before outright chaos, fear, and hazmat suits become the norm. It is this frightening atmosphere that permeates our Preamble in *The Sibylline Scourge*.

* * *

76 Days *(2020)*

To reference a good example of a Preamble, one that could almost be seen, in part, to be the *actual* Preamble to *The Sibylline Scourge*, one should examine the pre-title sequence of 2020's Covid-19 documentary, *76 Days* (Weixi Chen, Hao Wu, Anonymous). This provocative doc traces the terror, confusion, and heartache befalling medical personnel in Wuhan during the length of that city's lockdown in early 2020. A title card opens *76 Days* that places the viewer right in the middle of a crisis that has clearly been ongoing for some time, at least in this part of the world. It reads: "On January 23rd, 2020, China locked down Wuhan, a city of 11 million, to combat the COVID-19 outbreak." We then follow a small group of hospital staff that we can only hear, but not see, due to the head-to-toe PPE that causes staff to resemble nuclear hazmat suits (which, in essence, they are), as they attempt to calm a grieving colleague. The colleague is finding it increasingly difficult to keep it together as she can only watch through a small hospital door window as fellow medical staff—her peers—remove her father from the ventilator that has been keeping him alive. She wails in agony, pleading for her colleagues to allow her to see her papa for the last time, to permit her the opportunity to say goodbye. Her colleagues genuinely sympathize but are unable to let her get too close to her now-deceased father since, in the very early days of the Covid-19 outbreak, they are unaware of how this mystifying illness is spreading. For her protection as well as their own, she must be kept at a distance.

As medical personnel wheel her father's body, now encased in a body bag, out of his hospital room on a gurney, it takes several team members to hold her back and to keep her from getting too close. Seemingly understanding the unique circumstances of the hospital staff, but nonetheless inconsolable, the daughter beseeches her colleagues to allow her to see her father. However, the situation requires that her fellow hospital workers restrain her and sympathetically try to calm her down. "Screaming won't do you any good," one attendant says to her. Her colleagues escort the grieving daughter outside so that she can stand beside the hearse that now contains her father's dead body. As the hearse begins to drive away, the daughter struggles mightily to free herself from the grip of her colleagues as she screams for her papa, desperate to say her farewell (*76 Days* 00:09–03:36).

It is a heartbreaking sequence but one which will prove common stateside in the early days of the Covid-19 pandemic. Scores of sons and daughters were placed in similarly unimaginable circumstances as the daughter in the opening of *76 Days*. This was a novel virus, never encountered in humankind before. No one knew what to expect. Was this a virus akin to pneumonia, or something far, far more deadly? These were scary times, made all the more terrifying by the universal uncertainty. If we think in terms of the Preamble to our story, we apprehend that the scene we have constructed in the Huanan Seafood Market occurred in Wuhan, China, halfway across the world from the safety of the United States. However, as is the function of the Preamble in a disaster movie, we also realize that the terror experienced by the residents of Wuhan will not remain confined to the Chinese city, that it will soon make its presence known in our backyards. The storm is brewing and, inevitably, it will make landfall.

Act One can now begin.

ACT ONE

The Buildup

CHAPTER 2

Who Are We?

One of the most dominant and recognizable features of the modern disaster film is, of course, the presence of a cast composed of all-star (or relatively all-star) faces. The disparate coterie of famous (or semi-famous) names that are gathered in one movie and the practice of playing the odds of who will and who won't survive the disaster constitute a major part of the perceived fun of disaster movies (Keane 5). If you are like me and have watched an extraordinary number of disaster films, you will probably be able to recognize the steps that the narrative treads and therefore, will, with a certain degree of confidence, be able to deduce who will and who won't be alive come the closing credits. If not, don't be alarmed! As a result of reading this book, you will hopefully amass a thorough comprehension of salient disaster film tropes so that you, too, will be capable of accurately guessing who will and who won't make it to the end of the movie. This is an acquired and remarkable skill, so be sure to use it wisely. It will either greatly impress your friends at parties or tremendously piss them off.

When we examine the assembled cast of a disaster film from the top down, it is the top-billed or most identifiable (read: most expensive) star who will, more often than not, survive the ordeal depicted. Should he or she meet their fate, it won't be until the very end of the picture. As an example, the lead character of the Reverend Scott, who is played by Gene Hackman, perishes in the final moments of *The Poseidon Adventure* when he selflessly sacrifices himself to meet a fiery death in the engine room so that the other members of the core group of survivors may access the propeller shaft, which will lead the group, hopefully, to safety. Or we can look to Michael Bay's disaster extravaganza *Armageddon*, and its leading man Bruce Willis, whose character, Harry S. Stamper, encounters a similarly self-sacrificial demise at the conclusion of that film.

In order for us to explore some of the casting rationales of filmmakers and the qualities of an actor that contribute to these tropes, let us take a deeper dive into what constitutes both the male and the female leads in a disaster film. More specifically, the male and female lead characters that we find in *The Sibylline Scourge*.

* * *

The Male Lead

When you actually take a moment to sit down and think about it, there is a very good reason why movie stars who are generally known for their appearances in action or adventure films are typically (though not uniformly) cast in the male lead roles in disaster movies. Nonetheless, like most creative endeavors, there are exceptions to generally accepted genre conventions. John Cusack, for example, is an actor who made his name playing lovable dorks in movies like the goofy *Better Off Dead* (Savage Steve Holland, 1985) and the romantic classic *Say Anything...* (Cameron Crowe, 1989). He then segued into more mature roles in features such as the Southern gothic tale *Midnight in the Garden of Good and Evil* (Clint Eastwood, 1997) and the drama *Grace Is Gone* (Jim Strouse, 2007). Cusack is not anyone's obvious choice to headline an all-action disaster movie, but apparently Roland Emmerich thought so since he cast Cusack as male lead Jackson Curtis in 2009's *2012*. Still, the movie business is just like any other business, and there stands an economic consideration in big-budget moviemaking that supports the casting of a proven bankable star in a lead role that will, presumably, attract ticket buyers and thereby, with any luck, facilitate the desired recoupment of a studio's investment. In discussing the merits of the true story tsunami film, 2012's *The Impossible* (J.A. Bayona), author Alex von Tunzelmann recounts:

> The real family on whose experiences the film is based is Spanish. Maria Bennett's real-life counterpart, María Belón, has a story credit on this production. Her husband Enrique Alvárez and their children have appeared at the film's premieres. Director J.A. Bayona has said that he changed their nationality because it was easier to secure a substantial budget with international stars [Ewan] McGregor and [Naomi] Watts on board [Tunzelmann].

I will, however, cease this discussion here since the economic complexities of film financing is, thankfully, not the focus of this book. But suffice it to say that, in general, disaster films are probably not the cheapest pieces of entertainment to produce, principally by virtue of the special effects budgets that are, with few exceptions such as the virus disaster movies of which *The Sibylline Scourge* is one, an inherent virtue of the genre. After all, there are disasters to stage and their destructive fallouts to dramatize. A massive F5 tornado that decimates an entire homestead cannot,

I would imagine, be convincingly portrayed onscreen on the cheap. *Twister*'s budget in 1996 was $92 million, approximately $160 million in 2021 ("*Twister-Box Office Mojo*"; "Inflation Calculator"). Even moderately budgeted disaster flicks, such as 2006's *Snakes on a Plane*, are pricey. *Snakes on a Plane* cost $33 million in 2006, which translates to approximately $45 million in 2021 ("Snakes on a Plane"; "Inflation Calculator").

If we consider the frequent generic overlap that action and adventure movies commonly share with disaster movies, we uncover a psychological component at play concerning both actor and role. The lead male character in a disaster movie fills (or should fill) the role, to a large degree, of the "Everyman."

An Everyman archetype is very simply defined as:

> an ordinary individual that the audience or reader easily identifies with, but who has no outstanding abilities or attributes. An everyman hero is one who is placed in extraordinary circumstances and acts with heroic qualities. While lacking the talent of the classical hero, they exhibit sound moral judgment and selflessness in the face of adversity [Ray].

The Everyman is, thus, a relatable sort and, when he is portrayed onscreen, must serve as a suitable signifier for the average audience member, even as he battles the disaster and his fortitude is tested. There is an unspoken attribute within him that makes his idolatry by the male spectator approachable, admirable, and powerful. Yet, the very masculinity of the Everyman remains unthreatening to the heterosexualized norm that constitutes the vast majority of mainstream cinema (Neale, "Masculinity as Spectacle" 2). We have just to look at some of the male leads in disaster movies throughout film history to identify men who have made careers out of appealing to audiences through the strategic use of their ingenuity, their sensitive shows of masculinity, and the swagger of their cool bravado and confidence.

Furthermore, we mustn't neglect to mention the importance of the male lead's sexual appeal, no matter how subdued, to members of both sexes. The attraction of the male lead in a disaster film is encapsulated in Raymond Mortimer's description of James Bond: "...what every man would like to be, and what every woman would like to have between her sheets." Men such as Tyrone Power (*In Old Chicago*), both Steve McQueen and Paul Newman (*The Towering Inferno*), Charlton Heston (*Skyjacked*, *Airport 1975*, *Earthquake*), Sean Connery (*Meteor*), Pierce Brosnan (*Dante's Peak*), Keanu Reeves (*Speed*), Gerard Butler (*Greenland*), and the list goes on. Film theorist Laura Mulvey addresses the psychological role of the male protagonist in the cinema in her groundbreaking essay "Visual Pleasure and Narrative Cinema." Mulvey states:

As the spectator identifies with the main male protagonist, he projects his look on to that of his like, his screen surrogate, so that the power of the male protagonist as he controls events coincides with the active power of the erotic look, both giving a satisfying sense of omnipotence. A male movie star's glamorous characteristics are thus not those of the erotic object of the gaze, but those of the more perfect, more complete, more powerful ideal ego conceived in the original moment of recognition in front of the mirror [Mulvey 720].

It serves as no wonder, then, why movie stars such as Cary Grant or George Clooney become movie stars in the first place.

In keeping with a profound and deeply prized badge of honesty which I wear proudly and seek to further profess in this book, I believe I can espouse with a healthy modicum of assuredness that most disaster spectacles are not exactly renowned for their demonstrations of acting gravitas, particularly in the more contemporaneous disaster movie. As such, in these types of films there won't be a whole lot of opportunity for actors to indulge themselves in some professional and artistic wing stretching. Many times, you will even get a more esteemed actor rarely seen in a movie that, essentially, amounts to fluff, wanting to go in the opposite direction and cut loose, have some fun. This is no doubt part of the reason why you might see actors such as Jack Lemmon (*Airport '77*), Tommy Lee Jones (*Volcano*), and Robert Duvall (*Deep Impact*) sign on to participate in a disaster movie. Of course, the sizable paychecks that big-budget disaster spectacles would probably offer aren't too bad of an incentive either. As Yacowar indicates, "Often the stars depend upon their familiarity from previous films, rather than developing a new characterization. Plot more than character is emphasized, suspense more than character development" (342).

Another characteristic of the typical leading man in a disaster film is that he is likely to be found in either a private sector or in an otherwise non-high-profile position; he would not normally be installed in such an above-the-line political role like that of president or senator or governor. This alone is a predominant reason why Andrew Cuomo, despite his nationwide visibility, particularly during the Covid-19 pandemic, cannot be considered for the male lead in *The Sibylline Scourge*. At best, Governor Cuomo must be cast in a role that would amount to the "secondary male lead," which is just a fancy way of saying that he is, basically, one step above a supporting character but not quite on the level of the lead character in the story. It's not Cuomo's fault, for even when playing a president, the inimitable Morgan Freeman, for example, acts as support to lead Robert Duvall in *Deep Impact*, not to mention Freeman's roles in the Mike Banning series of action-thrillers (*Olympus Has Fallen* [Antoine Fuqua, 2013], et al.) where he supports lead actor Gerard Butler.

Nevertheless, this non-high-profile role doesn't preclude the male lead in a disaster film from working for the government in another, less visible capacity, as in the case of Dr. Anthony Fauci as an employee of the National Institute of Allergy and Infectious Diseases. In fact, a male lead with a government-related, but non-high-profile position arguably works out better in a disaster narrative because he is tapped into the developments made in the story yet remains more accessible to the audience as an Everyman should be. In other words, he is not in such a vaulted position that denies relative audience identification and, in and of itself, denotes and demands a traditional civilian respect, such as president or prime minister.

Disaster movie male lead characters that have a prominent private sector or a government-related, but non-high-profile position and, thus, are considered to be suitable male leads in a disaster film, include: Dr. Brad Crane, entomologist and Ph.D., Institute of Advanced Study, Princeton University (played by Michael Caine, *The Swarm*); Dr. Paul Bradley, former NASA engineer (played by Sean Connery, *Meteor*); Captain Vernon Demarest, pilot, Trans Global Airlines (played by Dean Martin, *Airport*); Mel Bakersfeld, General Manager, Lincoln International Airport (played by Burt Lancaster, *Airport*); Dr. Harry Dalton, volcanologist with the United States Geological Survey (played by Pierce Brosnan, *Dante's Peak*); and Kit Latura, former chief of New York City Emergency Medical Services (played by Sylvester Stallone, *Daylight* [Rob Cohen, 1996]).

As a side note, I do realize that Linda Hamilton's character in *Dante's Peak* is the mayor of the titular town, and that Hamilton is clearly the female lead (more on female leads shortly). However, I wouldn't necessarily classify Mayor Rachel Wando (Hamilton's character) as a "government official" vis-à-vis the manner in which we are contemplating government officials in disaster movies. I would instead argue that her occupation is more a function of the movie's plot necessitating a character of a highly visible nature, regardless of occupation, in a story that involves a disaster in such a small, homey town. By contrast, the main character in 1975's *Jaws* (Steven Spielberg), for example (other than the Great White shark, naturally) is a police chief in the small, vacation community of Amity: Chief Brody, played by 1970s mainstay Roy Scheider. This, despite the notable presence of Mayor Vaughn (Murray Hamilton).

An argument could conceivably be made that a notable exception to this important character trait of the male lead in a disaster film would be the character of President Whitmore in *Independence Day*. Of course, *Independence Day* is a monster of a movie (it's directed by Roland Emmerich, after all), a blockbuster behemoth that comprises about four movies in one. So, it comes as no real surprise that this film has, debatably, three leading men who each have their own dedicated storyline: Capt. Steven Hiller (Will Smith), David Levinson, and President Whitmore.

Insofar as Smith and Goldblum can be deemed the "heroes" of the piece if we consider a hero in a very elemental sense as someone who "saves the day," I would grant them the edge in terms of how we classify the male leading roles in *Independence Day*. It might be more appropriate from a generic standpoint to identify President Whitmore, like Governor Cuomo, as a "secondary lead" (more on those later) since the characters played by Smith and Goldblum more clearly epitomize the concept of the "male lead" as we are considering it here. Both can be seen as Everymen: Steven with his non-high-profile government position, exotic dancer wife, young son, and suburban home; and David, an awkward tech-geek who plays chess with his dad in the park. Though Smith's character is a captain in the Marine Corps and Goldblum's is an engineer, neither are high-profile government officials, unlike the Pullman character's very high-profile government position (it doesn't get much higher profile than president of the United States).

So, the male lead in a disaster film is a civilian Everyman. Still, more often than not, he will possess a useful skill that connects his trade with the precarious circumstances in which he and the group of survivors find themselves. This useful skill makes him particularly suitable for leading the "Ship of Fools" to safety (Yacowar, 335–6), and especially attractive to the primarily male audience as an inspiring alpha-hero-type who will eventually save the day. We can look to the following as examples of the useful skill in action: Alan Murdock's (Charlton Heston) extensive expertise in 747 pilot instruction that permits him the ability to swoop in (more on the glaring sexism of *that* plot point in just a bit) and pilot the doomed jetliner to safety in *Airport 1975*; despite being a photographer by trade (a totally undeveloped character trait), Nick Thorne (Robert Forster) possesses a keen interest and deft expertise in environmental engineering that prompts him to sound the alarm of potentially catastrophic consequences sure to result from construction of David Shelby's (Rock Hudson) ski chalet in *Avalanche*; being a former (disgraced) New York City Emergency Medical Services chief affords Kit Latura an especially privileged understanding of the NYC/NJ tunnel system and emergency procedures, upon which he draws to lead the core group of survivors out of the Holland Tunnel to safety in *Daylight*.

You might even go so far as to posit that the character of the Reverend Scott in *The Poseidon Adventure* fits the bill. After all, the Reverend Scott is a reverend, a clergyperson, someone whose job it is to bring one closer to God through faith. The core group of survivors of the overturned S.S. *Poseidon* need to cling to faith more than anything if it is going to survive the ordeal. Even when there is dissension among the group as its members travel upwards to the hull of the ill-fated cruise ship, the Reverend Scott remains a stabilizing force who calls upon his priestly vocation to restore harmony, however short-lived, so that the group can persevere on its treacherous voyage.

Regardless of your personal opinion of him as a person or as a medical professional, Dr. Anthony Fauci, the director of the National Institute of Allergy and Infectious Diseases (NIAID) and a visible face throughout the coronavirus pandemic as a member of President Trump's White House Coronavirus Task Force, most closely inhabits the criteria as we have defined it for the male lead in a disaster film, specifically, this disaster film. If we look at the previously discussed characteristics that together combine to form the salient traits of a suitable leading man in a disaster movie, it is easy to see why Dr. Fauci fits the bill.

For starters, inasmuch as any successful doctor can be considered one (a January 25, 2021, Forbes.com article situated Dr. Fauci as the highest compensated federal employee with an income of $417,608 in 2019 [Andrzejewski]), Dr. Fauci is an Everyman, at least in the sense that we have defined the type. Much like Dr. Paul Bradley in *Meteor* or Dr. Dalton in *Dante's Peak*, Fauci holds a government-related but non-high-profile position as the director of NIAID. In fact, I would bet that many people, myself included, had never heard of Dr. Fauci prior to his involvement with the White House Coronavirus Task Force. Dr. Fauci's forthrightness and integrity have been a source of trustworthiness for a public confronted with a sea of gross politicking by elected officials and news organizations throughout the better part of this pandemic. Fauci's role as director of NIAID doesn't seem to have affected his inherent doctoral desire to simply help people either. In addition to maintaining his role as director of NIAID, Dr. Fauci continues to accommodate patients twice a week (A. Woodward). Regardless, or perhaps because of, this, and together with all of his other public health responsibilities, Fauci was still acquiescent when called into action by President Trump to combat this alien biological predator.

Of course, Dr. Fauci's training and extensive (and impressive) expertise as a medical professional specializing in infectious diseases and immunology qualifies him unreservedly with the specialized skills necessary to be on the front lines of studying the effects of a novel infectious pathogen ("Anthony Fauci | Hilleman Film"). But his mere professional qualifications notwithstanding, Fauci has developed a reputation throughout his career as "a useful bridge between the scientific community and the politicians who control the purse strings of public health" (A. Woodward). He has been able to cultivate an uncanny knack for comprehensively discussing science with politicians and budgets with scientists. It is this particular gift that Dr. Fauci possesses that proves vital when critical decisions need to be made regarding the distribution of PPE or viral testing materials.

Aside from Dr. Fauci's medical qualifications and his ability to be understood by both scientists and politicians, it is his accessibility and pragmatism that are revealed to be his most crucial skills, and that which, perhaps more than anything, makes him an ideal leading man in *The Sibylline Scourge*. When he talks to us, the scared and confused masses, during a press conference or in an interview, we understand him. He is attempting to figure this demon out just like the rest of us. We are able to take comfort in his words when it comes to obtaining the knowledge of how to keep ourselves and our families safe. The politicians that we see most of the time on the news, particularly President Trump and Governor Cuomo, have amassed such a dubious history of self-interest and playing to party politics that it is tough to trust whether or not they are being straight with us or merely looking out for themselves. In many ways, politicians, by virtue of their profession, share many qualities with good actors: they have to exhibit a public air of calm and sagacity in order to convince the people to trust them and look to their words for counsel. Much of the time in modern-day politics, this public perception just rings as hollow, an act. In the person of Dr. Fauci, a heretofore government-related, but non-high-profile public servant with whom much of the country was unfamiliar until recently, there is little to no preconception of egocentrism. In many ways, despite his distinguished career and esteem in medical circles as well as his renown concerning his controversial approaches to the field of AIDS research beginning in the initial years of the epidemic in the 1980s (A. Woodward), it is Fauci's relative public obscurity that reveals itself as his greatest advantage.

* * *

The Female Lead

As we proceed with telling the story of *The Sibylline Scourge*, one aspect that we notice is that there are not very many, if any at all, good female roles (in keeping with the gender-biased historical tendencies of Hollywood stories, some might say). However, with that being said, there is one prominent female character in this story that is, without question, the obvious representative of a true female lead: Dr. Deborah Birx, the White House Coronavirus Response Coordinator.

The female lead in the disaster film has historically been relegated as a subordinate to the male lead. It is almost incomprehensible that, in most cinematic product in this modern day and age, a woman can still be archaically perceived as meek and dependent on the powerful male figure sent to rescue her. Even though Dr. Birx is an extraordinarily smart, capable, and remarkably accomplished woman, it is Dr. Fauci who has received the lion's share of the accolades and acclaim during the course of the coronavirus pandemic. It will most likely always be Fauci's name that one associates with the voice of medical authority when speaking with regard to the pandemic. "There was also Dr. Birx" will probably and unfortunately turn out to be this brilliant doctor's pandemic legacy.

This conception in the disaster (or action) film of "woman as meek and in need of a man"—the "damsel in distress" trope, if you will—is blatantly chauvinistic and, quite frankly, outdated. More than forty years ago, in 1980's *Meteor*, we were seeing this idea flouted. Tatiana Donskaya (Natalie Wood) mentions to Dr. Bradley that her husband went up in space and never returned (i.e., died). His immediate response? "And now, is there anyone?" Classy. Thankfully, however, owing to the presence and force of many strong actresses such as Linda Hamilton, Angelina Jolie, Charlize Theron, and Jennifer Garner, the "damsel in distress" trope has been and continues to slowly evolve (or rather, devolve), taking into account a more modern, independent, and fearless woman.

Still, the male/female dynamic in the disaster film hasn't (with very few exceptions) changed to any profound degree since the early days of the genre. As one might expect from films made in the early part of the twentieth century, sexual inequity was even more pronounced than that which we see nowadays. The motion picture industry was in its infancy back then, during a time in history when mores surrounding gender disparity were downright prehistoric, especially when viewed through our contemporary lenses.

If we need an illustration that speaks to the early male chauvinism in American society on film (and, more pointedly, the disaster movie), all we have to do is take a look at *Deluge*. The majority of this movie's plot centers on who will end up in possession of Claire. Will it be the upstanding family man Martin (Sidney Blackmer) or the brutish Jepson (Fred Kohler)? Although Claire is portrayed within the context of the times that the film was made (the 1930s) as something of a tough cookie, she is nonetheless treated by the men in the movie, both good and bad, as merely a piece of property to be owned for their sole gratification. We see crude evidence of this when Norwood (Ralf Harolde) attempts to rape Claire in the shack he shares with Jepson after Jepson steps outside for a moment. Norwood attacks Claire simply because she is there. Thus, according to Norwood's caveman logic, no man can be in the presence of a woman for an extended period of time and not desire her. "It's not natural, two men to live a month in the same house as a woman and not want her," he says to Jepson (*Deluge* 00:22:19–23). But the fight for ownership of Claire is more plainly realized throughout the body of the film, which, more or less, consists of Jepson and his gang tracking her down and attempting to steal her back from Martin, who has come to Claire's rescue but has still taken her in as his own. In the 1930s, this scenario was probably viewed as romantic, worthy of a swoon. However, viewed from a contemporary perspective, it makes the more modern thinker recoil.

Later in the twentieth century, particularly in the 1970s—the golden age of the disaster movie—the Women's Liberation Movement was gaining steam. Movies such as *Klute* (Alan J. Pakula, 1971), *Network* (Sidney Lumet, 1976), and *An Unmarried Woman* (Paul Mazursky, 1978) featured strong female protagonists who seized control of their lives both professionally and personally. Yet, in the disaster film, the role of the female lead in specific and the woman in general was still governed by a very archaic, old-fashioned, male-centric model of subservience: she was still in need of a big, strong man to rescue her and keep her safe. Perhaps this is due to the fact that in the 1970s, many "baby boomer" women who were coming of age looked to their Depression-scarred parents as examples; people who had, through sheer pluck and determination, managed to barely survive the devastation of their youth. In his book *Hollywood's Last Golden Age: Politics, Society, and the Seventies Film in America*, Jonathan Kirshner observes the instance of women in films of the time:

> But the behavior of characters in New Hollywood films, men and women, as they pertain to gender, remains of their time, shaped by their witness to the experiences of their mothers and fathers, their upbringing as girls and boys, and implicitly and always of their awareness of the possibilities for and implications of various choices offered to women by society during those years [88].

If their fathers were not off fighting in World War II, then they were desperately attempting to earn enough money to keep the family afloat, using whatever means they could to do so. Their mothers, if they were not teachers, secretaries, or riveting in factories as a means of replacing their husbands who were off fighting in the war, were at home, raising the children and trying to prevent the family unit from collapsing in such uncertain times. This generational perspective was seared into the minds of the children of Depression-era parents. These children stood as mute witness to their parents toiling to ensure that their families never faltered and never had to endure the hardships they did. It was the animalistic notion of familial survival, above all else.

During the 1970s, the burgeoning emergence of women as a bona fide work force and as individuals capable of surviving just fine without the security of a provider (i.e., a man) was reflected, to an extent, in that decade's cycle of disaster films. Gwen, the stewardess (they still called them stewardesses back then) played by Jacqueline Bisset in *Airport*, was presented as an ultramodern, independent woman who, despite *wanting* a man, wasn't necessarily *dependent* on one financially or emotionally. Gwen makes it very clear to Demarest that she is aware of his status as a married man who has no intention of leaving his wife. Knowing this, Gwen is neither bitter nor jealous, and she will not descend into shopworn shrewishness and demand support from him for their unborn child. That is not Gwen's style. The implication presented by Bisset's character and that of her characterization is that a woman's body is hers, and only she can ultimately determine what to do with it. Very progressive and controversial sentiments for the time (*Airport* was released in 1970).

Proving that the *Airport* series was a particularly forward-thinking cinematic franchise, its immediate 1974 sequel, *Airport 1975*, gave us Karen Black as lead stewardess (still calling them stewardesses) Nancy. Once the men of the cockpit were rendered incapacitated by the impact of the crash into the 747 from the Baron piloted by Dana Andrews, Nancy is summoned into action to steer the plane until (male) help can arrive. Now, a female stewardess breaking through to the very male and uber-macho world of airline piloting, even under duress, was nothing short of unconscionable at this time in history, as evidenced by Sid Caesar's incredulous reaction when told Nancy was at the controls: "You mean the stewardess is flying the plane?!" (*Airport 1975* 00:53:33–34). But Nancy did fly the plane (until Charlton Heston arrived, natch), and established herself as a more than capable perpetrator of the task. No passengers were lost under Nancy's watch.

In many ways, *Airport 1975* is a particularly sexist product of its time. Murdock repeatedly refers to Nancy as "honey," and the stewardesses are constantly being ogled and accosted in what amounts to obnoxious and blatant verbal sexual harassment by nearly all of the pilots. Julio, the flight navigator played by a pre–*CHIPS* Erik Estrada, is an especially flagrant piece of machismo. Upon receiving a non-sweetened cup of coffee from comely young stewardess, Bette (Christopher Norris), he greasily remarks, "I like my coffee sweet, Mamí" (*Airport 1975* 00:23:05–07). Real subtle. Earlier, Nancy and Bette are on the "up" escalator when Julio and a man named Gary (Ken Sansom) come up behind them. Julio, ever the epitome of class, remarks from behind Nancy, "There, you see why I love my job so much?" Gary, taking a page from Julio's book of manners, responds, "Well, they sure have all the right equipment" (00:07:50–54). These guys wouldn't last five minutes in the #MeToo era. The film, taking a cue from the then contemporaneous women's movement, nevertheless places a woman into an exclusively imagined man's role of the 1970s, that of a pilot. (It is note-worthy that, in a bit of disaster movie karma, Julio dies instantly in the Primary Disaster.) Nancy assumed control, if not entirely calmly then in a very proactive manner under an extreme circumstance, and in doing so, saved the lives of everyone on board that aircraft. That is, at least until Murdock (the man) was transferred mid-air onto the plane and brought it in for a landing.

However much a glimmer of women's liberation was visible in the above-mentioned films, the imbalance between the sexes and the percep-tion of the imbalance *in capability* between the sexes as it pertained to nar-rative storylines in disaster films were still clearly and overwhelmingly in favor of the male. The tendency remained for the woman to hold a sec-ondary position to the man, both in intelligence and in competence. If we look back at the previous example of Karen Black in *Airport 1975*, we notice that, indeed, Nancy did fly the 747, for a time, and proved concretely that women were, of course, able to comprehend the complexities of jet-liner piloting. They could, in fact, be quite competent at the task. Upon closer examination, however, we realize that Nancy was only at the con-trols until Alan Murdock, the *real* pilot, arrived to take over. The sexist subtext inherent in this scenario paints a picture of Nancy as "just a girl," momentarily and accidentally thrust into a man's job due to an extraordi-nary emergency, but who should really get back to doing girl things (i.e., attending to the passengers like an airborne Clara Barton) once the man arrives to do the heavy lifting … or flying.

In another example of the flagrant sexism in disaster films, in the late-70s offering *City on Fire* (Alvin Rakoff, 1979), Diana Brockhurst-Lautrec (Susan Clark) is on a tour of the brand-new hospital of which she is a major benefactress to the tune of $3 million, in 1979 money, to boot. That translates to roughly $11.3 million in 2021 dollars ("Inflation Calcula-tor"). As Diana returns to her vehicle upon completing the tour, a reporter asks of her, "Diana, is it true you're running your late husband's publish-ing house?" Diana confidently responds, "That's right." The reporter fol-lows up with, "Does that mean there's a new man behind you?" It doesn't take a Ph.D. in Gender Studies to uncover that the not-so-subtle implica-tion here is that it is unthinkable that a woman could assume the top job at a major publishing house without a man holding her hand every step of the way. Much like Nancy before her, due to her husband's death, Diana is accidentally thrust into a man's professional domain. Only this time, the circumstance is not temporary; Diana fully intends to take the reins of the company herself. To the reporter's idiotic question about a man behind her, Diana replies like the girl boss she is with this nice piece of shade, "None that I can see" (*City on Fire* 00:39:19–26).

An especially gross and uncomfortable bit of disaster movie sexism can be witnessed in *The Cassandra Crossing*, an otherwise very good entry in the disaster subgenre. Dr. Elena Stradner (Ingrid Thulin) is presented and introduced as a brilliant doctor and scientist, her participation being crucial to the identification and containment of the clandestine pneumonic plague that has been inadvertently released from a bio lab in Geneva during an attempted heist. However, Dr. Stradner has the misfortune of working alongside Burt Lancaster's Colonel Steven Mackenzie, an obnoxious alpha male-type who is in a continual state of coercive control over Dr. Stradner. As the two begrudgingly work together to try and contain the spread of the plague across Europe (shades of Trump and Fauci during the Covid-19 pandemic do not go unnoticed), Col. Mackenzie lets it be known on multiple occasions who, he thinks, is in charge. In doing so, he subjugates Dr. Stradner with a dismissive, "I'll handle this doctor" (*The Cassandra Crossing* 00:41:36–37). As Col. Mackenzie and Dr. Stradner explain the dire situation to Dr. Jonathan Chamberlain (Richard Harris), who, along with the core group of survivors, is aboard the transnational train ferrying the plague across Europe, Col. Mackenzie even gives Dr. Stradner an unbelievably disrespectful "settle down" gesture with his hand, astoundingly demeaning to a woman (or anyone, really) with her pedigree (00:42:05).

As is probably to be expected given the attitudes towards women of the time as wives and mothers, the 1970s female leads in disaster movies, if given the situation, always provided a rather warm maternal presence. If there were children involved anywhere at all in the picture, they were the under the purview of the female lead. With this in mind, I am reminded of Faye Dunaway as Susan in *The Towering Inferno* as she tenderly comforts a child (played by Bobby Brady himself, Mike Lookinland) as they await rescue from the building's damaged elevator, which is dangling precariously from the blazing structure. The mother figure is even more pronounced in *The Swarm*, as Captain Dr. Helena Anderson (played by the delicate Katharine Ross) holds vigil by the hospital bedside of young Paul (Christian Juttner) as he recovers from an attack from the titular posse of killer bees. "Why this one? In the whole damned world, why this boy?" Dr. Anderson appeals through tears immediately following the young boy's death (*The Swarm* 01:47:16–22). It should be noted that Paul's death in *The Swarm* represents an extremely rare instance of child mortality in disaster films, especially in major studio disaster films.

Later cycles of disaster films seem to toe the line and hold the female lead to the same general secondary standard as her earlier counterparts. She is not so much a partner to the male lead, as the billing or the movie trailers might suggest. As is historically the case, she is there to offer assistance to the male so that he can use his intellect and instinctually male ingenuity to save the day. *Daylight* is, for all intents and purposes, a fantastic example of the disaster movie. However, the female lead, Madelyne Thompson (Amy Brenneman), is relegated to nothing more than a bystander in the scenario, a whiny sidekick to Stallone's Kit Latura. Madelyne offers Kit neither resourcefulness nor significant insight into the grim circumstances in which they find themselves. At least Sandra Bullock's Annie in *Speed* played a pivotal role in managing to keep the bus above fifty miles per hour while Keanu Reeves's Jack tempted fate and the fates of everyone on board the bus in his efforts to disarm the concealed bomb. Rachel Wando, the town mayor in *Dante's Peak*, while refreshingly holding a high-profile government job for a female lead in the movies at that time, essentially just tagged along for the ride like any average passenger who was lucky (or unlucky—this is a disaster movie, after all) enough to have ridden along with Dr. Harry Dalton, while he alone manfully dodged flowing lava and ash in a valiant push to escape the exploding town. Anne Heche portrays brilliant scientist (it seems as though there is no other kind of scientist in disaster movies) Dr. Amy Barnes in *Volcano*. But during the disastrous (yet cool to watch) proceedings that threaten to melt Los Angeles, she really doesn't do much more than take orders from Tommy Lee Jones's Mike Roark. Every so often she'll offer a sound piece of insight regarding stemming the tide of the lava flowing downtown. But like Dr. Birx, she is, more or less, perceived within the story as secondary, an apprentice, to leading man and society savior Roark.

As was briefly mentioned earlier, where children are involved, the female lead retains the motherly qualities of many of her cinematic ancestors. This is notably evident when considering Linda Hamilton in *Dante's Peak* or Vivica A. Fox in *Independence Day*. Though it must be said that featured children in disaster films rarely succumb to the hands of fate. No well-adjusted member of the audience wants to watch a scene where young kids painfully perish in a horrible disaster. In all of my research and in all of the disaster films that I have viewed over time, I can only recall one instance where a minor in a prominent role perished due to the disaster. That would be the fate of Paul in *The Swarm*, which I mentioned previously. When it comes to anxiety over whether or not the kids will survive in a disaster film, I always think back to what my mother said after watching the 1993 dino-blockbuster *Jurassic Park* (Steven Spielberg), "I didn't think for one second those kids were going to die." Of course, like most mothers, she was being incredibly astute. Of all the directors out there in Hollywood, there is no way that Steven Spielberg would kill off any kids in one of his movies!

With the female lead as accomplished and professionally formidable yet operating as secondary to the male lead as well as encapsulating traditional constructs of the feminine or the maternal, one can much more easily conceptualize Dr. Birx as the female lead in our story.

According to the United States Department of State website, Ambassador-at-Large, the ambassadorship appointed to her by former President Barack Obama (Pesce), and Pennsylvania native Dr. Deborah L. Birx began her career in the U.S. Department of Defense. There, she concentrated, like Dr. Fauci, on immunology and AIDS research. Throughout the remainder of her career, Dr. Birx would remain as a government and military doctor, echoing Ross's Dr. Anderson in *The Swarm*. Some of the notable positions that Dr. Birx has held prior to her appointment to the White House Task Force as the Coronavirus Response Coordinator include Assistant Chief of the Hospital Immunology Service at Walter Reed Army Medical Center, Director of U.S. Military HIV Research Program (achieving the rank of colonel), and as Director of CDC's Division of Global HIV/AIDS ("Deborah L. Birx, M.D."). It is clear that Dr. Birx is an unquestionably indomitable medical presence.

Despite her evident qualifications and stature not only in the medical community but the military, Dr. Birx was nevertheless referred to as appearing "often alongside Dr. Anthony Fauci, the nation's top infectious-disease expert" (Pesce). Like many of her contemporaries in disaster movies—Dr. Anderson (*The Swarm*), Tanya Livingston (Jean Seberg, *Airport*), Tatiana Donskaya (*Meteor*), Jennifer Chamberlain (Sophia Loren, *The Cassandra Crossing*), Annie (*Speed*), Constance Spano (Margaret Colin, *Independence Day*), among others—Dr. Birx functioned as, to use the terminology of a cinematic narrative, *support* for the male lead.

A biographical article (incidentally, written by a woman) that first appeared on MarketWatch.com in April 2020, and which was intended to familiarize Dr. Birx with a public that was perhaps encountering her for the first time, made special mention of her signature stylish scarves. Feeding a carnivorous public through the void of social media, Dr. Birx's scarves developed their own sort of cult following. Hashtags such as #deborahbirxscarves and #deborahbirxscarfqueen sprang up online (Pesce), reducing the illustrious status of a woman, regardless of her academic pedigree and accomplishments, to nothing more than a fashion plate, playing into tired clichés of the urbane, stylish woman. It is conceivable that if *Sex and the City* had still been on the air, Dr. Birx might have been cast in a cameo.

While a defining March 26, 2020, *Washington Post* profile acknowledges that "criticisms [of Birx] take aim at Birx's domesticity, her multitasking, her wardrobe—a classically tangled takedown of a powerful woman" (Bass), the same article goes out of its way to discuss Dr. Birx's splashy annual holiday [Christmas] celebration in her Northern Washington, D.C., home, even framing the profile around the event. The article is also sure to mention that "on Christmas Eve, she hosts a 24-hour buffet" (Bass). Even if we take for granted that Dr. Birx most certainly derives tremendous pleasure from throwing these yearly extravaganzas for her family and friends, the implication is that, of course, even a woman as accomplished as Dr. Birx must also be a refined and dignified hostess.

Furthermore, the *Post* profile goes to great lengths to illustrate Dr. Birx as a devoted mother and grandmother. The article makes several mentions of Birx's daughters, her grandchildren, and even includes a cute anecdote about when Dr. Birx was studying the then-novel HIV virus. "On the weekends, Birx's older daughter would sit on the floor of the lab, playing with the colored caps of sample tubes, while Birx cultured HIV" (Bass). Dr. Birx's equal attention to both her work and her family along with the obvious joy she derived from both is, without a doubt, an admirable trait. The point, however, is that when framing Dr. Birx as the female lead in *The Sibylline Scourge*, the maternal angle, a particularly narrow-focused and gendered bias, is never too far from view.

Despite the consideration of the female lead in a disaster film as both domestic and maternal, she, like her male counterpart, has advantageous skills of her own that elevate her to the status of second-in-command to the male lead. In *Meteor*, Natalie Wood's character speaks Russian and is, thereby, crucially able to bridge the language and cultural gaps between Connery's Dr. Bradley and his Russian counterpart, Dr. Dubov (Brian Keith). In reality, Wood was born to Russian immigrant parents and spoke fluent Russian ("TCM.Com"; Mason). In *Dante's Peak*, Rachel Wando's special skill was simply a virtue of her local position as town mayor. In that capacity, Mayor Wando had the ears and the trust of the town's population in a way that Dr. Dalton did not. She was one of them; he was the interloper.

In a similar fashion to Tatiana and Mayor Wando, Dr. Birx possesses a special skill that makes her role in the Coronavirus Task Force unique and strengthens her position as an ideal female lead in our disaster film. It is the foreign relations aspect of her professional life that Dr. Birx has cultivated over the course of her career, particularly as a result of her work as the U.S. Global AIDS Coordinator overseeing PEPFAR (the U.S. President's Emergency Plan for AIDS Relief). In this role, Dr. Birx notably managed not only the PEPFAR staff of over four hundred at the project's Washington, D.C., headquarters, but also oversaw more than one thousand five hundred field personnel and over forty-five global offices in Africa, Asia, the Caribbean, and Latin America ("Deborah L. Birx, M.D."). Dr. Birx has a level of international relations expertise and professional work history in the global community that would certainly be invaluable in working amidst the outbreak of a global pandemic.

I am positive that Dr. Fauci possesses his share of experience in working with a variety of foreign nations on the subject of infectious diseases throughout his storied career. But much in the same way that Dr. Fauci's laymen-speak approach allows the science of disease to be understood and accessible to the politicians and vice versa, Dr. Birx's level of international engagement, considering her work in Africa for close to six years, for example, conducting research on an HIV vaccine ("Deborah L. Birx, M.D."), is no less important when it comes to bridging the divide between the United States and its partners in the global community. Dr. Birx's State Department profile points to her success in working with foreign nations to combat the still ongoing AIDS crisis:

> Serving as the U.S. Special Representative for Global Health Diplomacy, she aligns the U.S. Government's diplomacy with foreign assistance programs that address global health challenges and accelerate progress toward: achieving an AIDS-free generation; ending preventable child and maternal deaths; and preventing, detecting, and responding to infectious disease threats ["Deborah L. Birx, M.D."].

There can be no question that Dr. Deborah L. Birx represents an ideal personification of a female lead for a contemporary disaster film, as well as a fitting partner to our male lead, Dr. Anthony Fauci.

As an exercise in illustrating what we now understand to be the key attributes of a suitable disaster film male and female lead character, let us now take a side-by-side look at how *The Sibylline Scourge* lines up with the other disaster films referenced in this book.

Title	Male Lead (including secondary leads, if any)	Female Lead (including secondary leads, if any)
Airport	Burt Lancaster, Dean Martin	Jean Seberg Jacqueline Bisset
The Andromeda Strain	Arthur Hill	Kate Reid
Skyjacked	Charlton Heston	Yvette Mimieux
The Poseidon Adventure	Gene Hackman	Pamela Sue Martin
Airport 1975	Charlton Heston	Karen Black
Earthquake	Charlton Heston	Genevieve Bujold

Title	Male Lead (including secondary leads, if any)	Female Lead (including secondary leads, if any)
The Towering Inferno	Steve McQueen, Paul Newman	Faye Dunaway
Flood	Robert Culp, Martin Milner	Barbara Hershey
The Cassandra Crossing	Richard Harris	Sophia Loren
Airport '77	Jack Lemmon	Brenda Vaccaro
Fire	Ernest Borgnine, Alex Cord	Vera Miles, Patty Duke
The Swarm	Michael Caine	Katharine Ross
Avalanche	Rock Hudson, Robert Forster	Mia Farrow
The Concorde.... Airport '79	Alain Delon, George Kennedy, Robert Wagner	Susan Blakely, Sylvia Kristel
City on Fire	Barry Newman	Susan Clark
Disaster on the Coast-liner	Lloyd Bridges, William Shatner	Yvette Mimieux
Cave-In!	Dennis Cole	Susan Sullivan
Speed	Keanu Reeves	Sandra Bullock
Outbreak	Dustin Hoffman	Rene Russo
Twister	Bill Paxton	Helen Hunt
Independence Day	Will Smith, Jeff Goldblum, Bill Pullman	Vivica A. Fox, Margaret Colin
Daylight	Sylvester Stallone	Amy Brenneman
Dante's Peak	Pierce Brosnan	Linda Hamilton
Volcano	Tommy Lee Jones	Anne Heche
Titanic	Leonardo DiCaprio	Kate Winslet

Title	Male Lead (including secondary leads, if any)	Female Lead (including secondary leads, if any)
Deep Impact	Robert Duvall	Téa Leoni
Armageddon	Bruce Willis, Ben Affleck	Liv Tyler
The Core	Aaron Eckhart	Hilary Swank
The Day After Tomorrow	Dennis Quaid, Jake Gyllenhaal	Sela Ward, Emmy Rossum
Snakes on a Plane	Samuel L. Jackson	Julianna Margulies
2012	John Cusack	Amanda Peet
Contagion	Matt Damon	Kate Winslet, Jennifer Ehle
San Andreas	Dwayne Johnson	Carla Gugino
Geostorm	Gerard Butler	Interestingly, no true female lead. Based upon the script, I'd say Alexandra Maria Lara. Abbie Cornish is more prominent, but she's Jim Sturgess' story counterpart.
Greenland	Gerard Butler	Morena Baccarin
The Sibylline Scourge	Dr. Anthony Fauci	Dr. Deborah Birx

A Case Study in Gender Reversal: Twister

The traditional masculine/feminine character binary in a disaster film is subverted in a much more explicit manner in 1996's *Twister*. Dr. Jo Harding (played by Helen Hunt and a most rugged sounding name if I ever heard one) is given what would traditionally be the male lead role. In this film, Jo is perceived as very mannish in nature, capable and stalwart. Jo's estranged husband, Bill Harding (Bill Paxton), inhabits what would, in the majority of disaster movies, be seen as the more feminine, sidekick role, even though he is a much more active and contributing participant in the storm chasing that drives the picture. Jo is the one who is married to her job. So much so, that in the movie's early scenes, Bill is introduced while he is hounding Jo to get her to sign their divorce papers. She is strenuously avoidant of anything concerning a relationship, until the final scene of the movie, of course, when she aggressively initiates a kiss with Bill. Conversely, Bill is anxious and excited to get remarried and settle down with his new love, Melissa (Jami Gertz). Melissa, for her part, also emasculates Bill to a certain degree. She is written and portrayed as a neurotic psychologist, career-focused and pushy, who has somehow managed to cajole Bill away from a life and a lifestyle that he is clearly meant to live in order to walk in her shadow.

After a few near-death experiences that constitute a normal day-to-day for tornado seekers, Melissa, brilliant (there's that word again) psychologist that she is, realizes Bill's natural inclination for the hunt and selflessly accepts that he could never be happy living a more subdued (read: domesticated) life. Melissa takes charge as a person with her natural disposition would, assesses the situation, and dumps Bill, despite his whining, er, protests. Bill's feminized character is such that he is much more likely to passionately express his feelings than act in a manner resembling assertiveness. Late in the film, Bill beseeches Jo to let go of her past (the death of her beloved father in a massive tornado, duh) and look at what's right in front of her (i.e., him) (*Twister* 00:00:00–01:53:00). That sort of sentimental profession of love is not something that one would typically expect from the male hero, particularly in a disaster film where the action genre tropes are so overwhelmingly present and, for the most part, so rigorously defined.

* * *

The Secondary Leads and Supporting Cast

Much of the appeal of the modern disaster film, particularly in its heyday in the 1970s and aside from the more contemporary focus on the spectacle, is in watching has-been or rarely-seen-on-screen actors working their way through the tumult in the hopes of surviving the disaster. The very nature of the large cast in a disaster film lends itself to offering opportunity for actors or actresses who are, perhaps, past their prime (Jennifer Jones & Fred Astaire in *The Towering Inferno*; Myrna Loy in *Airport 1975*; Vanessa Redgrave in *Deep Impact*), actors who have notably worked in television or musicians seeking to expand their appeal in motion pictures

(Amy Brenneman in *Daylight*; John Corbett in *Volcano*; Freddy Rodriquez & Fergie [Stacy Ferguson] in *Poseidon*, Wolfgang Petersen's 2006 remake of *The Poseidon Adventure;* Helen Reddy in *Airport 1975*), or people of dubious celebrity seeking to cash in on their current notoriety by way of some good old-fashioned stunt casting (Marjoe Gortner in *Earthquake*; Charo in *The Concorde.... Airport '79*) to grab what will, most probably, be a nice, hefty paycheck.

Every film has a protagonist and an antagonist; that's the blueprint of narrative conflict. The populous name casts present in the disaster film are such that not all of the above-the-line actors and/or actresses merely act as supporting characters (as there are in most stories) to the male and the female lead, but as characters more prominent in nature that might even be qualified as "secondary leads," such as Remy (Ava Gardner) in *Earthquake* and President Whitmore in *Independence Day*. These secondary leads, which can be construed as offshoots of the supporting cast, have more narrative eminence than what we might consider true supporting characters to possess. For example, if we are to refer to the films that were just mentioned, we would encounter Richard Roundtree or George Kennedy in *Earthquake* and Harry Connick, Jr., and Judd Hirsch in *Independence Day* as exemplars of true supporting characters. The secondary leads do not hold the same prominence as the true lead characters driving the picture, and their characters are not designed to be the focus of the story for the audience in the same way that the true male and female leads are. The secondary leads live in the white space between the lines on the page, but a perceptive viewer can usually identify them when they are present in a story.

In the manner in which Rock Hudson in *Avalanche* or Bill Pullman in *Independence Day* can be considered secondary leads, in the case of *The Sibylline Scourge*, there are two very clear characters that stand out, that we can classify as bona fide secondary leads: President Donald Trump and Governor of New York State Andrew Cuomo.

True to disaster movie protocol and as has been discussed previously in this chapter with respect to how characters whose work is in an especially high-profile political or governmental position that commonly places them in secondary or supporting roles, Trump and Cuomo certainly do not possess the Everyman quality that is essential for the leading man role in a disaster film to carry. These two men live in much too privileged and rarefied a world to be even remotely accessible and identifiable (as much as they would like to think they are) to the average person. There is simply no credible way, given their respective backgrounds and family histories, that Trump or Cuomo could even begin to relate on a substantive level to the ninety-nine percenters.

But still, characters holding high-profile political or governmental positions, such as that of president or mayor, are oftentimes present in disaster films for the sole reason that these types of positions are conducive to relaying information about said disaster to a large number of people en masse; witness Mayor Ramsey *(The Towering Inferno)*, Mayor William Dudley *(City on Fire)*, President Whitmore *(Independence Day)*, President Beck *(Deep Impact)*, and President Thomas Wilson *(2012)*. Specifically, presidents have the unique authority as an effect of their position to make and enact decisions regarding mobilization of military forces and dissemination of federal resources in response to the public need. This authority is most visibly utilized in times of crisis and disaster (the mobilization of FEMA in cases of natural disaster, for example).

This trope continues to hold true for *The Sibylline Scourge*. Love him or hate him (and it is not the function of this book to cast any assumption upon this controversial figure), there is no denying the fact that President Donald J. Trump (or more accurately as of the writing of this book, former President Donald J. Trump) is a central figure in the account of Covid-19. Trump was the elected leader of the American people, not to mention the leader of the free world, when the pandemic erupted onto the global stage in early 2020. With less than a year to go on the first term of his presidency, among many executive actions he instituted was the assembly of a task force (inclusion on which thrust Dr. Fauci and Dr. Birx onto the national stage) to confront growing concern surrounding the virus, the imposition of travel restrictions for those travelling to the United States from China and Europe, and the authorization of stimulus checks (based on income) to be distributed to those individuals and households that were experiencing extreme economic hardship as the United States economy tanked in the thick of the pandemic (Al Jazeera).

Film being a visual medium, it would seem to certainly be the aim of the cinematic arts to tell stories in a particularly ocular fashion. In this manner, *The Sibylline Scourge*, as a mainstream disaster film, would probably need to exhibit a modicum of creative license and/or conceive of some visual mechanism with which to dramatize Trump's famous use of and favorite method of communication to the American people: Twitter. The former president was, in this respect, something of an innovator since no other president had before utilized such uninhibited and incessant use of social media to directly speak to his constituents. Regardless, the narrative thrust remains uncannily the same with other disaster movies. There is oftentimes a presidential address to the people written into the narratives. As examples, look at the addresses of some of Trump's presidential peers in disaster movies: President Whitmore, President Beck, and President Thomas Wilson.

The role of the president, in real life and in disaster films, goes hand-in-hand with a first lady, even though she may or may not be as prominent a character as her husband. First Lady Marilyn Whitmore was a supporting character, for sure, but not nearly prominent enough in the story to be considered a female lead. Her character is not established enough nor presented in enough of a melodramatic fashion for her to even be considered the Poignant Character (I would argue that that honor in *ID4* goes to Harry Connick, Jr., but more on the Poignant Character later). However, she is a presence in the story, even though the circumstances of the narrative dictate that she is not at her husband's side, even when she ultimately passes away.

However, Marilyn Whitmore could be considered an anomaly because first ladies and/or the wives of prominent authoritative characters in disaster movies, if developed as characters at all, have historically not been presented in the most flattering of lights. Mostly, they have been written as whining obstacles that get in the way of the male doing his job of saving the world. Witness Cindy Bakersfeld (Dana Wynter) in *Airport*, Remy (Ava Gardner) in *Earthquake*, Dr. Melissa Reeves (Jami Gertz) in *Twister*, or Karen Wallace (Lee Grant) in *Airport '77*. When we look at *The Sibylline Scourge*, Marilyn Whitmore's counterpart, First Lady Melania Trump, is present in the narrative, but her role doesn't have much of an impact on the story at all. In fact, Mrs. Trump was hardly ever seen or mentioned during the prime months of the coronavirus pandemic. It can be argued that Mrs. Trump's sole defining characteristic during the pandemic (or, arguably, her husband's presidency) was that of an ice queen who was complicit in her husband's perceived misgoverning of the country. In *The Sibylline Scourge*, we may even be reluctant to attribute any lines or significant screen time to her, so inconsequential was her relevance to the story.

It's not so much the technical position of each of these real-life government VIPs that is laterally equitable to a character in a disaster film. Rather, it's more about the *prominence* and the *authority* of the VIP's position that makes the transfer into a disaster narrative. For example, if we look at a film such as the disaster movie progenitor *Airport*, we are able to recognize several characters of authority whose roles aren't counterparted *exactly* to *The Sibylline Scourge* but are nonetheless equated in authority and prominence within the diegesis of *Airport*.

We have already established that the characters played by Burt Lancaster and Dean Martin in *Airport* (Mel Bakersfeld and Vernon Demarest, respectively) hold non-political high-profile and private sector positions that, at least professionally, denote both of them as acceptable male leads. Both Bakersfeld and Demarest are at the top of their official hierarchies;

Bakersfeld is the General Manager of Lincoln International Airport and Demarest is a pilot for Trans Global Airlines. Both men are in positions that require *operational* and *functional* skill, rather than the softer "people skills" that are the provenance of the female leads in *Airport*, Gwen Meighen as the lead stewardess on board the Golden Argosy and Tanya Livingston as a customer service representative for Trans Global Airlines.

The narrative of *Airport* clearly concerns plotlines revolving around Bakersfeld and Demarest. Therefore, the characters that support them, while each may exist at a certain level of prominence in their own professional designations, must maintain positions in the story that serve only to bolster the narrative surrounding the lead men. In this respect and in addition to Gwen and Tanya, we have the top engineer for TWA, Joe Patroni (George Kennedy), whom Bakersfeld calls upon to rescue the stalled aircraft that has gotten stuck in the snow, blocking a major runway; Commissioner Ackerman (Larry Gates), with whom Bakersfeld must contend regarding protestors that are creating a nuisance at the airport; and, of course, D.O. Guerrero (Van Heflin), the bomb-smuggling passenger aboard the Golden Argosy whom Demarest must diffuse lest the bomb Guerrero is carrying explode and threaten the safety of the aircraft and its passengers.

Similarly, to illustrate an example from a more recent (though still more than twenty-year-old) disaster film, the narrative thrust of *Armageddon* surrounds the pressing need to prevent the impending planetary impact of a colossal asteroid on a collision course with Earth. Specifically (because this is, after all, a movie and we need a storyline), this deed falls to lead character, deep core oil driller Harry S. Stamper (Bruce Willis), whom the government has called in to assist based upon Harry's reputation and expertise as the best man around on an oil rig. Once Stamper is installed as, what amounts to, the savior of mankind, everyone else's role in the film comes into sharper focus as the means with which to support him. In all honesty, this really shouldn't come as much of a surprise to the viewer. One did purchase a ticket for a movie in which Bruce Willis was advertised as the clear headliner; obviously Willis will be the main character. All of the functions of the other characters will be of service in assisting Harry in his mission. This includes Harry's men from the oil rig—Bear (Michael Clarke Duncan), Max (Ken Hudson Campbell), Rockhound (Steve Buscemi), Oscar (Owen Wilson), Chick (Will Patton)—Executive Director of NASA Dan Truman (Billy Bob Thornton), General Kimsey (Keith David), and even the one character that is almost always present in disaster movies—the President of the United States (played here by Stanley Anderson). The character of A.J. Frost (played in the film by Ben Affleck) is the one team member who is arguably an exception to the purpose of the supporting cast, mainly because Frost can be considered a secondary lead, a character tier located between the lead and supporting cast (see President Whitmore in *Independence Day*). Frost is the one person whose functionality in the film is, no question, primarily to service Harry's mission. But Frost is also on hand to force the realization for Harry that his daughter, Grace (played by Liv Tyler), of whom Frost is the romantic interest, is all grown up—and an adult in her own right—a common learning curve for any father of a daughter to have to endure. The rest of the cast members all behave as sheer support for Harry and the mission to save the world which he has been tasked to oversee.

The notability of a person or character such as Governor of New York State Andrew Cuomo (or more accurately as of the writing of this book, former Governor Andrew Cuomo) as well as his high-profile political role makes him an ideal secondary male lead. He is in the presence of our narrative to support the directions of the lead, Dr. Fauci, who, as the Director of the National Institute of Allergy and Infectious Diseases (a government-related, but non-high-profile position), is guiding the nation on the biology of the pathogen as well as safety protocols. In the sense that the state (in this case, New York State) takes its direction from the federal government, Cuomo is acting in a capacity to administer the directives of Fauci (and, by extension, Trump, as Fauci's boss). Of course, that is not to say that Cuomo and Trump have not had volatile (and numerous) public disagreements, similar to Bakersfeld and Commissioner Ackerman, with regard to public safety, urban economics, vaccine rollout, etc., over the course of the pandemic year 2020.

In constructing the core group of survivors that will forge together as one in a valiant effort to withstand the disaster, directors and screenwriters will normally make an attempt to depict a representative cross section of the actual and contemporaneous society in question. This practice works particularly well in the disaster film, especially when one considers the generally large cast of characters typically present in an average disaster movie. "The entire cross section of society is usually represented in the cast" (Yacowar, 342). This cross section isn't necessarily defined solely along racial and ethnic lines, although those identifiers can certainly be observed and are valid within the plotlines of these stories, especially in the more current iterations of the disaster film. Within the filmic society created by the disaster film, we may find characters that are young (children, as previously discussed, are oftentimes present in the narrative, though rarely die in the course of the film) as well as senior, those with distinctive body types or different religious affiliations, etc. *The Poseidon Adventure* and *The Towering Inferno*, for example, both exploit a wide spectrum of character ages in significant roles: from kids (Susan and Robin in *The Poseidon Adventure*; Phillip in *The Towering Inferno*) to seniors (The Rosens in *The Poseidon Adventure*; Harlee and Lisolette in *The Towering Inferno*). *The Poseidon Adventure* digs deeply into religious adherences with the character of the Reverend Scott and the exploration of his crisis of faith, and the stereotypical old Jewish couple depicted in Mr. and Mrs. Rosen (Jack Albertson and Shelley Winters). Contrastingly, in *The Towering Inferno*, there is a more subtle insinuation of socio-economic class consideration in the rich and powerful Jim Duncan (William Holden), the moneybags who reigns supreme over the Glass Tower and whose concern above all else is to see that his well-heeled guests at the building's dedication gala are entertained and kept free of worry, regardless of the potential threat to their safety and their lives. Meanwhile, everyone who works under Duncan is running around behind the scenes (especially once the inferno is ignited) in a feverish attempt to ensure that the evening runs smoothly and all of the guests remain blissfully happy and unaware of the crisis. "The material concerns—and our differences—of daily life are supposed to pale in the shadow of death cast off in disaster films" (Yacowar, 343).

But as is the case with any component in an artistic genre piece, there is ample accommodation for modification and for reexamination. Of course, it makes sense that many generic conventions vis-à-vis specific casting requirements relative to the reflection of society would tend to shift over the years. This contemporary casting context is evident in more recent examples of the disaster film, such as *Dante's Peak* or *2012*, both of which employ a wide range of multiculturalism in their casts. While in both films, as well as in the vast majority of disaster films regardless of era, *The Sibylline Scourge* included, the male and female leads remain White (Pierce Brosnan and Linda Hamilton, John Cusack and Amanda Peet, respectively), there is nevertheless more of an effort made in later instances of the disaster film to ethnically diversify the supporting cast. People of color in earlier disaster genre cycles, for example, were almost unilaterally relegated to supporting roles, or even worse, used as a means of stunt casting. Need proof? Just look at the casting of O.J. Simpson in both *The Towering Inferno* and *The Cassandra Crossing*. Or Richard Roundtree in *Earthquake*, Robert Hooks in *Airport '77*, or either Roosevelt Grier or Leslie Uggams in *Skyjacked*. Or either sax-playing Jimmie "JJ" Walker or English-mangling Charo in *The Concorde.... Airport '79*.

Not much can be said to have changed, unfortunately, in later genre cycles, at least not in terms of the lead characters. In fact, it wasn't until 1996 when Will Smith was cast as the (co-)male lead in *Independence Day* (and in the process, carved out a mini niche for himself for a brief time as the undisputed king of the Fourth of July holiday weekend blockbuster release with that film, *Men In Black* [Barry Sonnenfeld, 1997], *Wild Wild West* [Barry Sonnenfeld, 1999], and *Men In Black II* [Barry Sonnenfeld, 2002]). Even still, at the very least, the supporting casts in disaster films managed to experience more of an intersectional shake-up in the last decade of the millennium. In *Dante's Peak*, for example, Harry Dalton's supporting team of scientists is comprised of Stan (Tzi Ma, Asian), Nancy (Arabella Field, female), Terry (Kirk Trutner, schlubby), and Greg (Grant Heslov, of outwardly ambiguous ethnicity. Heslov is actually of Ashkenazi Jewish heritage [Stlucas]). With a larger cast, *2012* is comprised of even more of a diverse cast, including, in addition to Cusack and Peet, President Thomas Wilson (Danny Glover, Black), Laura Wilson (Thandiwe Newton, female, biracial), Adrian Helmsley (Chiwetel Ejiofor, Black), Dr. Satnam Tsurutani (Jimi Mistry, multiracial), Harry Helmsley (Blu Mankuma, senior, Black), and Tony Delgatto (George Segal, senior, White).

As we move forward in the twenty-first century, it's anyone's guess when we may see another disaster genre cycle appear on the horizon. Nevertheless, as filmmakers strive to reflect current society more accurately with more diverse and inclusive casting, including lead character casting, it should follow that we find this trend reflected in more and more disaster movies that barrel down the pike. One of the most bankable marquee stars in the world, Dwayne "The Rock" Johnson, an actor of mixed heritage (Black and Samoan [Editors, TheFamousPeople.Com—Dwayne Johnson]), has made his share of disaster or quasi-disaster movies, including 2015's *San Andreas* (a film discussed at length in this book), and *Rampage* (Brad Peyton) and *Skyscraper* (Rawson Marshall Thurber), both from 2018. We, thankfully, witness this trend in other popular genres across the board as well. For example, one of the most recognizable and culturally iconic franchises of all time, the James Bond films, has recently retired its heretofore White, male Agent 007 character made famous in the series of books by Ian Fleming, in favor of a modern take on the character in the casting of Lashana Lynch as a new Black, female Agent 007. I look forward with keen interest to what will assuredly be a fascinating socio-cultural study in undertaking and examining how this multicultural integrating of characters in mainstream Hollywood narratives progresses, particularly in the disaster film.

CHAPTER 3

Where Are We?

The start of the second decade of the millennium was shaping up to be a very busy year. For one thing, the 2020 Summer Olympic Games were scheduled to be held in Tokyo, Japan. The Olympic Games, always an occasion for national unity and pride as the world's premiere athletes strive for the gold, might be just what the country needed to bring it together after the tumult of the past four years. Legends are made in real time, but there are just as many dreams that are promptly dashed in the Games' arenas.

Over in the entertainment space, the guilty verdict in the rape trial of former Hollywood movie mogul Harvey Weinstein was announced in February. International cinema came to the fore as Bong Joon Ho's Korean nightmare, *Parasite* (2019), cleaned up the 2020 Academy Awards ceremony. The film was awarded the top prize of Best Picture as well as Best International Feature Film, the first film to accomplish this feat ("*Parasite* [2019]"). And tragically, celebrated actor Chadwick Boseman, the Black Panther of *Black Panther* [Ryan Coogler, 2018], passed away in the prime of his career following a battle with colon cancer (Salo).

Supreme Court Justice Ruth Bader Ginsburg passed away, and accused Jeffrey Epstein accomplice Ghislaine Maxwell was finally apprehended in New Hampshire after a celebrated manhunt. Then, of course, who can forget the hordes of murderous hornets that descended upon the nation in a seemingly concerted effort by Mother Nature to ensure that 2020 clinched the title as the "Worst Year Ever" (Salo)?

But most importantly for many Americans, 2020 was a presidential election year. Now, presidential election years are always somewhat nerve-wracking, even for the most politically disinclined, such as me. I have always thought of political elections to be not unlike one big summer camp Color War competition, as the red (Republicans) battle the blue (Democrats) in a series of Beltway competitions to see which side's candidate will assume the highest office in the nation and clinch the title of Leader of the Free World for the next four years. And as is the case every four years when the presidential election cycle comes around, the year or so prior to Election Day, the first Tuesday of that year's November—in this case, November 3—is a non-stop barrage of twenty-four-hour news cycles, debates, town halls, and bipartisan muckraking. This bombardment of political messaging is even more obnoxious in the digital age wherein everyone with a smartphone deems themselves to be a crack political pundit in one form or another. The primary news sources of the modern era, Twitter and Facebook, were aflame with dogma and scathing vitriol for the other side in the lead-up to the 2020 election, with opinionated musings from anyone and everyone savvy enough to hit "retweet" or "repost" within their chosen apps. Think back, dear reader. I am sure that most of your friends and family at some point weighed in on the importance of this "historic" election which, it was popularly thought, could bring some sanity back to the White House. The outcome of this election would either bring a cause for celebration and a welcome reprieve from the madness of the previous four years for some, or more madness for others. Yes, this was definitely gearing up to be no ordinary presidential election year, but an especially *consequential* presidential election year.

The White House, standing as that grand icon of American democracy at 1600 Pennsylvania Avenue, and what it represents has always been fodder for public controversy, much of it fruitful but just as much of it only a distraction from more serious topics. Countless hours upon countless hours have been spent on discussion, dissension, and even political satire from the pulpits of late-night talk show hosts and political newsmagazine commentators, each, some might argue, more insufferable than the last. Regardless of each of the talking heads angling to be the breakout media star of the election cycle, the reason why the 2020 election was seen by the nation as particularly "historic" is because former reality TV show host Donald J. Trump had been in occupancy at the hallowed Oval Office and was up for re-election. (As an aside, I continue to use quotes around the word "historic" because, for my money, it currently holds the title for the most overused word in recent linguistic memory.)

Now, casting aside whatever personal judgments you might hold pertaining to Trump as a political figure, social figure, or private citizen, there is no disputing the fact that he is conceivably one of the most (if not, *the* most) polarizing personalities ever to occupy those sacred halls of government. From the moment he took the oath of office following his stunning defeat of presidential favorite Hillary Clinton in 2016 (whose victory would have made her the first woman to hold the highest office in the land), Trump's presidency has been fraught with controversy, at times undoubtedly deserved and at other times, likely overblown. His politics relating to issues concerning the LGBTQ+ community, taxes, and immigration, to name a few hot-button issues of the day, including his infamous and signature dictum that was the construction of a wall along the southern border of the United States intended to curb illegal border crossings, quickly bisected the nation in such a dramatic manner that many people had never experienced before. This was a man who, before holding the nation's highest office, was known more for his ostentatious displays of wealth and hard-nosed business acumen. Prior to his spearheading of the hit reality show *The Apprentice*, Trump had written several bestselling books that capitalized on his image as a Master of the Universe, including *The Art of the Deal* and *The Art of the Comeback*. He had had three stunningly beautiful wives (Ivana, Marla Maples, and Melania) and fathered children with each of them (Donald Jr., Ivanka, and Eric with Ivana; Tiffany with Marla Maples; Barron with Melania). No question a business savvy and intelligent man, he had been a fixture in Manhattan high society for decades, holding court from up on high in Trump Tower.

More than anything, I suppose, the divisiveness prompted by the election and subsequent administration of Donald Trump could be seen as rooted in that of which Trump represented to those who opposed him as a candidate: a rich, adulterous, more than likely corrupt, White guy with, prior to his 2016 election, no political experience or adeptness who epitomized Fifth Avenue privilege and excess. Here is a man whose sole mission in the White House might have been perceived as to enhance the coffers of the already wealthy at the expense of the average Joe and Jill American. Trump was seen by many as a sort of megalomaniac, an evil mastermind who reigned over his global empire from his Fifth Avenue penthouse lair in Trump Tower, like some sort of real estate Lex Luthor, or from his sprawling Palm Beach compound, Mar-A-Lago. It could be argued that Trump's most identifiable trait for many voters in 2016, particularly teenagers who were voting for the first time, other than his weird flyaway hair, was his signature catch phrase from *The Apprentice*: "You're fired."

Donald Trump, as an incoming president following the highly respected Barack Obama's two tenures as president of the United States, was likely too much for some people to comprehend. It was almost laughable in its improbability. Trump had none of Obama's magnetism, humanness, and goodwill; not to mention any of his predecessor's years of political experience, something that one would think would be of particularly critical value prior to holding such a highly esteemed office as president of the United States. "[Trump has] no regard for alliances at all," Kim Beazley, a former Australian ambassador to the U.S., said of Trump in 2016. "A totally crackpot presidential candidate," mused President Mauricio Macri of Argentina prior to Trump's election, per the Argentine press. And in a particularly apropos quote for the subject of this tome, the former Danish foreign minister, Martin Lidegaard, avowed prior to Trump's election victory, "If he becomes president, it will be a disaster" (A. Taylor, "83 Not-Very-Flattering Things Foreign Officials Have Said about Trump"). Clearly Trump was not only seen as a potentially worrisome candidate to the constituents who would ultimately be responsible for electing him, but for a myriad of world leaders as well.

So, for better or worse and for all the good as well as the bad, Trump's presidency was, in a word, "historic." There were obviously individuals from all over the country, though notably, not many hailing from the coastal elitist hot zones of California and New York, who were drawn to Trump and his religiously American proclivities. Trump's popular campaign slogan, "Make America Great Again," was a rallying cry to those citizens who deemed themselves forgotten by the cultural and political elite and who were concerned for American perseverance and prosperity. Trump cozied up to these folks, understood them from a deeply economic and patriotic perspective. The media spoke of the "Cult of Trump," those whose dedication to Trump and his cabinet was so unequivocal that it teetered on the sycophantic.

So, this was the social climate in which our narrative was set in early 2020, the United States awash in the heat of a political fervor. It was all but inescapable. The crowded field of candidates hoping to unseat Trump was massive and their faces were ubiquitous in the run-up to March 3, 2020 (Super Tuesday), when the Democratic Party candidate would, effectually, be decided. In the running included former Vice President under Barack Obama, Joe Biden; California Senator and former State Attorney General Kamala Harris; Massachusetts Senator Elizabeth Warren; former presidential candidate and Vermont Senator Bernie Sanders (running for the second time); New York City Mayor Bill de Blasio; South Bend, Indiana, Mayor Pete Buttigieg (the first openly gay candidate to run for the office of president of the United States); among numerous other less high-profile hopefuls. All of them threw their hats into the ring for the chance to lead the United States and to usurp the man who had so thoroughly and viciously bisected the nation during his term in office.

Citizens throughout the fifty states endured months and months of debates, news articles, twenty-four-hour television coverage, and incessant and childishly petty back-and-forth between the candidates. This political insanity finally and mercifully came to an end on Super Tuesday. Going into that fateful day, it looked as though the fight for the Democratic presidential nomination was going to come down to two candidates: Joe Biden and Elizabeth Warren. Warren, if she won the nomination and then the election, would become the nation's first female president, a truly historic event (former Secretary of State Hillary Clinton was the first female presidential *candidate* when she won her party's nomination during the 2016 election cycle). But when the election results finally came in and the votes were tallied, history would have to wait. Joe Biden was declared the individual with the most overwhelming likelihood of obtaining the Democratic Party nomination for president of the United States. Warren quickly thereafter dropped out of the race on March 5, 2020, after realizing her chances of victory were now, effectively, over. This "historic" race for the presidency and the ostensible fate of the nation would come down to Democrat Joe Biden versus Republican incumbent Donald Trump.

It was the topic of politics that unquestionably remained front and center in the popular American social consciousness in those early months of 2020. But something more sinister than politics was slowly creeping up on the horizon. People were beginning to hear the rumblings of a strange and mysterious virus peeking through news stories from across the globe.

In late February of 2020, I was in Albuquerque, New Mexico, attending the Southwest Popular/American Culture Association Conference and happily removing myself as much as possible from the bubbling political cauldron that everyone seemed to be drinking from. As someone who has always been a student of life and who has possessed an inquisitive eagerness to learn about subjects that I knew little to nothing about, a conference like the SWPACA represented the proverbial candy store, and I was the kid. An expansive table of contents were on display, all of them about popular culture in one form or another, including animation, game studies, rap and hip-hop culture, occultism, even Grateful Dead studies. I certainly wouldn't be able to attend all of the sessions I wanted to, but I was determined to get as much out of the 2020 SWPACA as I could.

The module in which I was slated to present at the 2020 Southwest Popular/American Culture Association Conference involved theses surrounding the concepts of apocalypse, dystopia, and disasters (it sounds worse than it is). I had never thought of myself as much of a scholar with regard to the first two topics, but disaster was certainly something on which I could speak. The paper I had authored, and was there at the conference to present, drew a comparison between the disaster subgenre in film, which reached its popular and cultural zenith in the 1970s, with the genre's subsequent cinematic revival in the late-1990s. How had the genre evolved, if at all, between the success and popularity of films like *The Poseidon Adventure* and *The Towering Inferno* to offerings such as *Twister* and *Dante's Peak*? What generic conventions had changed, and which ones had, more or less, remained the same? What were the cultural shifts that had taken place in the intervening years that had informed such changes in cinematic disaster stories? What could the viewer learn about mankind and social evolution from the ways in which disaster films were presented in the 1970s juxtaposed with the ways in which their cousins were presented in the 1990s?

As you might expect from someone attending his first academic conference, I was pretty jazzed to present. I had been revising and tweaking my paper, psyching myself up ever since I received the notification that my paper was accepted to the conference. I wasn't so deluded to think that the Southwest Popular/American Culture Association Conference was a gathering on the scale of something like South by Southwest, for example, but it was nonetheless a momentous honor for me to be asked to present, as I'm sure it was to every presenting student, scholar, and professor.

Yet, before I had even passed through the TSA checkpoint and boarded the plane for Albuquerque, I had become aware of circulating news reports that concerned a baffling flu-like virus that was apparently working its way through the Wuhan region of China. In fact, in late January, the word had come down that heightened security measures were being implemented at New York City's JFK Airport (and other major U.S. airports) for passengers arriving into the U.S. from the afflicted Chinese region. Luckily, I suppose, my return flight was scheduled to fly into Newark, an airport unaffected by these new security measures. But once you hear about extra security measures being enforced at any of your city's area airports, your innately human defensive radar springs into action.

Not long after the airport security measures went into effect, thousands of passengers aboard the cruise ship *Diamond Princess* were quarantined in Yokohama, Japan, after one of the passengers, who had disembarked the cruise ship in the Japanese port city on January 25, had tested positive for the virus (Yamamitsu and Dooley). Shortly after that, on February 7, Dr. Li Wenliang, an ophthalmologist who had tried to warn the world about the coronavirus in its early stages and about the very real possibility of widespread infections if the outbreak was not brought under control in China, passed away from its effects (Taylor). Upon his death, Wenliang immediately became a tragic symbol of the need for immediacy of action in the face of a potential biological crisis. The more I read, the more the knot in the pit of my stomach tightened. Similar to the disaster movies I had been studying prior to Albuquerque, I noticed an ominous snowball effect beginning to take shape. And it was strengthening in size.

According to a running *New York Times* timeline of the pandemic, on February 23, 2020, Italy was forced to take action and issue lockdowns for entire towns in its northern Lombardy region as positive tests for the novel coronavirus exploded throughout the area. Soon thereafter, several nations across continents were reporting positive coronavirus cases, including the Middle Eastern nation of Iran, which was identified as a hotbed of coronavirus activity, as well as the Latin American country of Brazil. Following the virus's official entry into the United States and with the coronavirus death of a Seattle man on February 29, 2020, school closures, arena closures, event cancellations, border closings all started to become commonplace (Taylor). I am certain that I echoed the thought many people in various municipalities around the globe were having in this moment (as well as the denizens of the societies in every disaster movie ever made) when I thought to myself, "What is going on? Is Armageddon real? And if it is, is it actually happening?" People could hardly believe what they were reading in the news or on social media: a real-life doomsday scenario was, unbelievably, taking shape. The world was shutting down!! The terror and the uncertainty of this unfathomable situation, fueled by a lack of consistent information from authorities coupled with rumors spread over the Internet, was gripping society on a global level. To make matters even scarier, events were unfolding with lightning speed. As soon as one piece of information came out, there was another piece of information piggybacking on it. Hospitals were slowly becoming overwhelmed. It truly seemed as though the End of Days were upon us, and it had been just about two months since the first reported cases had come out of Wuhan.

Now at the conference, I was at the same time thrilled to be in the same room as so many other students and professors and scared shitless for the same reasons. Having just earned my master's degree in cinema studies from New York University's Tisch School of the Arts just under a year prior, I was very much anticipating the opportunities to exchange ideas and to be introduced to subjects and fields of study to which I had, heretofore, experienced minimal, if any, exposure. As confident as I was in my paper and my self-perceived ability to dazzle a crowd, I was still working through a bit of good old-fashioned stage fright. What if no one attended my session? What if someone asked a question that stumped me and made me look foolish in front of these esteemed students and professors I so desperately wanted to impress? What if my laptop ran out of juice and I was unable to run the kick-ass visual presentation I was so proud of? Rookie concerns.

Nevertheless, I was ecstatic to, once again, find myself in an academic environment, even if that academic environment was, in fact, the conference room floor of the Albuquerque Hyatt Regency. It was invigorating to be amongst people with similar interests, however tangential, to my own. I soaked up as much atmosphere as I could and attended as many sessions as my brain could tolerate, spending my off moments in the common area outside the session rooms browsing the vendor booths. My inherent thirst for knowledge was being quenched to the point of overflowing. I recall thinking to myself, "Wow, I have truly found my element here."

As wrapped up in popular culture bliss as I was during those enlightening days at the Southwest Popular/American Culture Association Conference, I was always maintaining a keen eye on the news. How is it possible for one not to, given the physical attachment many of us these days, me included, have to our phones? Every day we are subjected to the constant dings of reminders and push notifications from news sources that barrage our mobile devices in a seemingly steady and endless flow of information. Nowadays, people have to *try*, and try hard, to be kept in the dark.

The conference eventually came to an end. After spending a few extra vacation days exploring Albuquerque as well as neighboring Santa Fe (cities I never expected to see in my lifetime), I left the American southwest and returned to the freezing urban landscape of the northeast that I called home. I had only been back at my cozy studio on the Upper West Side for a few days when the afterglow of my first academic conference was cruelly shattered. The so far mythic and hyperbolic doomsday scenario hit home. On February 29, 2020, the inevitable happened: word came out that the United States had reported its first coronavirus death, an unnamed man in Washington State (Taylor). Washington would soon thereafter become the state with the most coronavirus infections in the United States, until it was surpassed on March 9 by New York State, where a particularly concentrated number of cases in the Westchester County suburb of New Rochelle had been reported (Impelli). Doomsday was no longer a scenario: it had arrived.

In the viral plague story that is *The Sibylline Scourge*, we notice that the biological threat started small and removed, by oceans and continents. Since the threat was distant and happening in faraway foreign countries and we, the future filmic society, only became aware of the looming crisis via news stories, the general observation among the society at home in those early days was, "Isn't that horrible what's happening in China/Italy?" Indeed, it was. But after a brief, solemn moment of consideration, everyone appeared to resume their daily lives, bathed in the relative ignorance of the calamity to come. Members of the society made jokes about Corona, the particularly unfortunately named brand of beer which, in the early days of the virus's spread, some knuckleheads genuinely thought was an actual avenue of transmission for the bug. Humorous memes and tweets from Internet "comedians" made the viral rounds online. A mystifying overseas biological threat was hovering about in the news, enjoying a terrifying sweep overseas. But stateside, political messaging remained first and foremost in the minds of most Americans. While the present threat of the coronavirus had now become front-page news, the two lead stories in the March 3, 2020, *New York Times*, to cite an example, were of a political bent. One headline read, "Buttigieg and Klobuchar Endorse Biden, Aiming to Slow Sanders," and the other read, "How the Democratic Establishment Stumbled as Sanders Surged." Two stories concerning the coronavirus were relegated to the right-hand side of the page ("The New York Times in Print").

It is in this uneasy environment in which we find the filmic society of *The Sibylline Scourge* during Act One of our story. In many ways, American life is business as usual. Businesses operate, movie studios regularly release their slates and prepare their upcoming spring and summer tentpoles, public transportation shuttles riders around urban centers as they normally would, rents are renewed, workout junkies across the nation get their sweat on in gyms and fitness centers, restaurants are packed on weekend nights, and people imbibe bottomless mimosas at Sunday brunches throughout New York City. Athletes from all over the world continue to train with characteristic passion and vigor, the hope of realizing their dreams of winning gold medals for their countries at the Tokyo Olympics later in the year never too far from their sights. Perhaps the only indication of an impending viral invader, at least in New York City at that time, was the installation of hand sanitizer stations that began to regularly pop up in restaurants and in retail stores. However, since hand sanitizer is something that I had learned long ago that residents of New York City should have on hand at all times anyway, these stations just seemed like a good idea.

As we have addressed in the Introduction to this book, the first act of a typical disaster film is primarily devoted to establishing the societal structure within the narrative. The first act should answer the questions: Who are we? Who are the main characters? What are their relationships to one another? Who are the potential villains (there is always at least one)? What are some of the special skills that certain characters hold? And so on and so forth. However, just as crucial to the development of the dramatic thrust of the story is the creation of the societal *mood* at the story's outset. The concept of creating an appropriate mood goes well beyond simply establishing the setting of the story (a city, a cruise ship, an airplane, what have you). In the portion of the film that precedes the emergence of the Primary Disaster, it is necessary for the viewer to gain a keen observation of how people are behaving. Some of the questions we might want to ask ourselves as both audiences and as filmmakers of disaster movies include:

- Where is the attention of a character focused?
- What are the character's general attitudes towards safety, both for themselves and for others? Many times, disaster films are set in an environment where, to an average person, safety might be of paramount importance, such as an airplane, a passenger train, or a town built around a volcano (even if it's dormant).
- Further to the above questions, are some members of the society aware of the *possibility* of a calamitous event or catastrophe? If so, how are they preparing or working towards warning others about the catastrophe, if at all?

- Will the disaster take *all* members of the society by sheer surprise or just those that are unprepared?
- As the story opens, is the whole of the society in the film presented as one that exudes, among other facets, excitement, fear, solemnity, jubilation, or frenzy?

All of these elements work together to inform not only how the disaster will affect the society once the disaster strikes, but they will also be key pieces in contributing to the reinforcement of the larger narrative themes that will predictably emerge throughout the course of the story.

As a matter of illustration, let's take a detailed look at the construction and the mood of the filmic society in *The Towering Inferno* in the portion of the film leading up to the Primary Disaster, the moment when the blaze violently bursts forth onto the eighty-first floor.

* * *

The Society: The Towering Inferno

The opening shots of *The Towering Inferno* follow a helicopter belonging to Duncan Enterprises, as it whirrs over the azure coastal waters of the Pacific Ocean. The seascape footage is idyllic, stunning on this beautiful, crystal-clear day. As the helicopter travels on, the natural scenic beauty of the California coastline eventually gives way to the urban skyline of San Francisco. The Duncan Enterprises helicopter at last approaches its destination: the rooftop of the Glass Tower, a magnificent architectural structure that soars above the "City by the Bay" like a giant watchtower. The music playing on the soundtrack complements these introductory images with a pleasant score that indicates hope, progression, and optimism for the future.

The helicopter lands atop the Glass Tower and from it emerges Doug Roberts (Paul Newman), the skyscraper's chief architect and a guy who just oozes cool (not unlike the actor who portrays him). Doug is greeted by the company's namesake, Jim Duncan (the character played by William Holden), the sort of man who resembles every other suspiciously smarmy executive in movies of the 1970s. It is apparent that Doug is returning from a business trip to somewhere much less urban than San Francisco. Somewhere in which, despite the skepticism of Duncan who knows Doug deep-down to be a "city boy," Doug will be accepting an unspecified but evidently much less stressful job and one which will allow him to enjoy a much more laid-back and peaceful lifestyle. There is an invigorating aura circling about Doug and a noticeable resolve in his decision to exchange the big-city rat race for a life more tranquil. Much like the Glass Tower he designed, Doug Roberts is representative of a new future, his new future, moving forward into a new age with confidence and enthusiasm.

Doug and Duncan take an elevator from the rooftop to the sixty-fifth floor of the building, on which is housed the executive offices of Duncan Enterprises. Here, nothing appears to be out of the ordinary; it is presumably, business as usual. Secretaries tend to their work at their desks, miscellaneous office personnel go on about their day, visitors patiently wait to be seen. Status quo. Still, the viewer can sense that there is a perceptible buzz about the office, a feeling that something momentous is about to occur. This sense of anticipation turns out to be due to the fact that the occupants of the Glass Tower are looking forward to the glamorous building dedication ceremony and black-tie gala, events scheduled to take place that very evening. The people who will be on hand at the gala, or otherwise working within the building during that time, will constitute our filmic *society*.

After a short while, Doug leaves Duncan and heads up a few floors to his own office, which is situated amongst the rest of the building's architectural staff. On the architect's floor, it is, once again, busy business as usual. Architects bustle about, drafting tables are strewn with papers and instruments, and Doug's subordinates welcome their boss back by immediately harassing him with questions. We can tell that Doug is clearly an esteemed and well-respected foreman among his men. (Well, mostly men. It's the early 1970s and these are architects … just accept the inherent sexism of a certain period in history and move on.)

There is a brief homecoming episode in which the audience is introduced to female lead (and Doug's love interest) Susan (the character played by Faye Dunaway). The scene then cuts to a taxicab as it pulls up to the plaza outside the Glass Tower. A man (Fred Astaire) emerges from the cab, pays the driver, and proceeds to briskly walk across the building's plaza to the revolving door entryway. Along the way, the man passes through a preparation zone where an event crew is erecting velvet ropes and where red carpets stand at the ready to be unfurled for the VIPs attending the dedication ceremony that evening. The man pauses for a moment and tilts his head upwards, gazing in absolute wonderment at the majesty of the Glass Tower. Once he regains himself, he enters the building's lobby, which looks much like the lobby of any modern luxury hotel. Soft ambient music plays in the background as people mull about the expansive space and an elevator descends gracefully to the ground floor. This could be the lobby environment on any normal day in any Four Seasons or Hyatt Regency.

Another cut, and the viewer is introduced to Jennifer Jones as Lisolette, a sort of in-house art teacher/day care provider at the Tower. Lisolette is clearly a kindly woman who takes great care in her position at the Tower and enjoys an extremely cordial relationship with her young charges as well as with their parents. Indeed, as she bids good night to one of her young students, the girl's deaf mother asks (via her daughter) if the teacher will join them for dinner. Lisolette politely declines, mentioning to the girl that she is attending the party in the Tower that evening. As the girl and her mother walk away, Lisolette, in her very grandmotherly way, offers to remove some of the paint from the young girl's dress. It's a happy scene.

We are now able to infer after meeting some of the story's characters, that our filmic society includes seemingly well-adjusted and polite children, older members of the population, and most that seem to fall somewhere in between. The mood that is being established in the film, so far, appears to be one of merriment and straight-up joy, similar to what a businessperson might experience come five o'clock on a Friday afternoon.

The scene then moves to a utility room of the Glass Tower, one of those non-public facing spaces that always seem to have an underscore of incessant humming about them, where the inner workings of the building are kept and maintained. In this rather sterile environment, engineers of various levels (again, all men) check panels, test generators, flick switches, and turn knobs. A few of the men concernedly turn their attention to one of the generators after an electrical spark shorts a panel.

In the next scene, we witness a real estate agent emerge from the elevator on the eighty-first floor, escorting a pair of prospective tenants. We learn in this moment that the Glass Tower, like many urban skyscrapers, is not the exclusive provenance of an office building, but that it also contains residences. From what we have seen of the building thus far, we can deduce that the residential society of the Glass Tower will more than likely be populated with affluent, primarily older individuals. I mean, really. Who else prior to the tech boom would have been able to afford a condo in a luxury skyscraper in the heart of downtown San Francisco?

Also present in our filmic society are members of the building security personnel, principally represented by Jernigan, the character played by O.J. Simpson (he's in a bunch of movies around this time period, including another disaster movie discussed in this book, *The Cassandra Crossing*). In the main control room, Jernigan and the other security personnel are keeping busy checking the numerous monitors, generally making sure that all is safe and sound in every corner of the Glass Tower. Then an interesting thing happens. Suddenly, an alert comes through on one of the security monitors that something has malfunctioned in one of the circuit breakers in the main utility room. Simpson mobilizes to check it out. (Of course, we, as the audience, are aware from the previous scene that a fuse box in the eighty-first floor storage room has, in fact, blown open, exposed a live wire, and ignited a small fire. A small fire that will eventually swell in size and ferocity and mature into an inferno.)

The prerequisite sense of foreboding that is expected of a true disaster movie bubbles to the surface once Doug is notified about the shorted generator and discovers that the wire covers are not conduit, per his specifications. This is an issue Doug and his deputy, Giddings (Norman Burton), will take up with Duncan. The jubilant and hopeful mood among the group, stimulated by the grand opening of their structural masterwork, has now turned into one of distress and concern as the potential ramifications of the faulty wiring in the building are addressed.

Following a rather contentious visit at Duncan's mansion (whereupon we also meet Duncan's daughter, Patty, played by Susan Blakely) with Duncan's son-in-law, Roger Simmons (Richard Chamberlain), a man we just know will turn out to be a sleazeball since he was the person charged with ensuring the electrical systems for the building were in order, it's finally time for the dedication ceremony. The atmosphere on the plaza of the Glass Tower is not unlike that of a gala movie premiere. There is a palpable sense of grandeur hovering about this festive scene, which is comprised of a massive crowd of spectators, reporters, photographers, cameramen, and floodlights. The emcee of the event even spells it out for us when he remarks, "Ladies and gentlemen, this is a gala evening. The entire city is in the holiday mood." The VIP members of the filmic society pull up to the event in chauffeured limousines and dramatically materialize onto the plaza swathed in elegant evening gowns and tuxedos. The spectators cheer as various luminaries, including the Honorable Gary Parker (Robert Vaughn), Chairman of the Federal Urban Renewal Commission, and Mayor Robert Ramsay along with his wife (Jack Collins and Sheila Allen), step out onto the glamorous scene. Some even shake hands with the commonfolk. (Although if you ask me, it's one thing to be hanging out with the fans, clamoring for autographs, at the Academy Awards. It's quite another if you're hanging out with the fans, clamoring for handshakes from the Chairman of the Federal Urban Renewal Commission.) In any case, once Mayor Ramsay cuts the ceremonial ribbon formally dedicating the Glass Tower the "Tallest Building in the World," the switches are hit and the entire crowd congregated on the plaza observes in a collective moment of awe as the Tower gloriously illuminates the San Francisco night sky, a beacon of technological achievement that telegraphs capitalism and futurism in its magnificence. The Glass Tower is absolutely a wonder to behold. And to be fair, it looks pretty darn cool.

At this point following the dedication ceremony, the entire filmic society is accounted for and the party up in the Promenade Room, the pinnacle floor of the Glass Tower, can commence. Everyone in attendance is in a celebratory state of mind. The "Tallest Building in the World" has just been christened and they have been invited to the exclusive grand opening … what is there not to be excited about? Even the Chairman of the Federal Urban Renewal Commission is there! Drinks are flowing, the band is playing, and all of the attendees are dressed to the nines. (As a side note, this movie's anthem, "We May Never Love Like This Again," is sung by Maureen McGovern, who seemed to be the go-to crooner for disaster movie anthems of the 1970s with this tune as well as her previous cover of "The Morning After" from *The Poseidon Adventure*. Both songs won the Oscar for Best Original Song ["The Towering Inferno—Awards," "The Poseidon Adventure—Awards"] in their respective award years.) The indicators are in place for a magical and memorable evening for all. Of course, because this is a movie called *The Towering Inferno* and not *The Towering Party*, we, as the audience, know that this evening will surely be a memorable one all right … though not necessarily because the guests will be nursing a hangover the next morning.

So, while most of the members of the movie's filmic society are being fabulous and enjoying cocktails in the Promenade Room, Doug and Giddings are busy investigating the source and cause of the mishap with the circuit breaker. Upon checking on some wiring on the eighty-third floor, Doug notices that the wires are too hot. "This can't be right," he says. This telegraphs to the audience that the storm clouds are rolling in; something is very wrong in the Glass Tower, and we shift in our seats. A few minutes later back in the control room, security guard Bill (William Traylor) sees on one of the monitors that smoke is emitting from the storage room on the eighty-first floor (*we* know what it is). "There's something on eighty-one," Bill advises Jernigan. The proverbial (and literal) flames are getting larger. Jernigan notifies the San Francisco Fire Department at once and they immediately spring into action, proceeding to hightail it to the Tower. The pace is quickening; disaster is imminent. Meanwhile, the party progresses, and the majority of our society remain happily oblivious to the dangerous situation unfolding only a few floors below them.

On eighty-one, a fire alarm is sounding. A confused security guard stationed on the floor moves to investigate. Seconds later, Doug and Giddings emerge from the elevator on the eighty-first floor. At this point, the investigative security guard notices the smoke wafting through the ventilation space between the bottom of the door to the storage room and the floor. Ominous, low music starts up on the soundtrack and the audience is cued that this is the big moment. While Doug attends to the fire alarm, Giddings hears something, movement, down a nearby hallway. As he rushes to check out the noise, he spies the security guard about to unwisely open the door to the storage room. Instinctively, Giddings calls out to the security guard, "Hey!" Just as Giddings tackles the guard to remove him from harm's way, the door bursts open, and a conflagration violently spews forth from the storage room and engulfs Giddings in flames. This, ladies and gentlemen, is our Primary Disaster. Act Two of *The Towering Inferno* has now begun (*The Towering Inferno* 00:00:00–38:39).

The Act One narrative mechanism we have just detailed in *The Towering Inferno* we also witness in *The Sibylline Scourge*. In many disaster films and disaster stories, there tends to be a period of buildup in order to garner the necessary anticipation for the disaster among the audience as well as to lay the groundwork for the narrative that follows. This buildup may be handled in a variety of ways, depending upon how the story is structured and the choices made by the director and the screenwriter(s). For example, Steven Soderbergh's *Contagion* opens its story on what is technically Day Two of the disaster, manifested as the viral outbreak—the contagion—that will soon envelop the globe. But even though this particular film opens in what could be argued as the beginning of Act Two, there is still a period of buildup before the portion of the story where all hell breaks loose. There are scenes in which characters that we, as the audience, know nothing of yet, cough and stumble as they attempt to go about their daily lives, assuming that they are simply under the weather. Even Beth Emhoff, coughing in the first scene of the movie, assumes that she is "just jet-lagged" (*Contagion* 00:01:28–32). One instance in Kowloon, Hong Kong, one instance in London, one instance in Minneapolis, etc. (00:02:00–04:32) Seemingly unrelated instances that, while troublesome to those individuals involved and those that are in contact with them—friends, family—are not a reason in and of themselves to be concerned for something that might resemble a catastrophe. Nevertheless, Soderbergh constructs his Act One as a series of isolated instances that immediately involve the audience in an atmosphere of anxiety and dread. The sense is created that if things start off on this ominous a note, there is nowhere for this story to lead but to inevitable disaster.

And that it does. Soderbergh provides normally benign shots of handlebars and of notebooks, commonly touched surfaces that are easily transmissible avenues for even the mildest of viruses. Since we, as an audience, can presage the outbreak that will soon follow, these shots assume an especially threatening overtone in this context. A child goes home from school early with a fever. Beth Emhoff, who only a few scenes earlier was preparing to board a flight from Hong Kong to Minneapolis, suddenly collapses with seizures and, shortly thereafter, passes away (*Contagion* 00:06:42–08:59). The momentum is building, and in short order, occurrences of this mystery illness begin to multiply. Then there are the quarantines, followed by school closures and contact tracing. Starting to sound familiar?

Right on schedule, at around the movie's half hour mark, the Primary Disaster makes its presence known. In an eerily portentous piece of dialogue that could have been written for *The Sibylline Scourge*, Dr. Ellis Cheever (Laurence Fishburne) vocalizes the disaster, a commonplace but non-visually spectacular spectacle that we will address more thoroughly in the later chapter covering the Primary Disaster: "So we have a novel virus with a mortality rate in the low 20s. No treatment protocol and no vaccine at this time" (*Contagion* 00:29:18–25). When you take a minute to think about it in retrospect, it's no wonder that *Contagion* was seen by some government agencies as somewhat of a serendipitous template for the Covid-19 disaster ("Contagion [2011]").

The buildup segments that we have discussed which appear in *The Towering Inferno* and in *Contagion*, not to mention the vast majority of disaster films, we see paralleled in *The Sibylline Scourge*. This is a period that is best described as "ignorant vulnerability," the state in which one's guard is at a weakened level, whereby people take their everyday circumstances for granted, no matter how frenzied they might behave in the moment. Griping about PTA meetings, for example, or going grocery shopping or to the gym or even to work. The mundanity of civilian life is viewed through an entirely different lens when the disaster strikes in a disaster film, and all of these everyday comforts are eliminated in an instant. The society in a disaster film, once confronted with said disaster, is forced to immediately evaluate their mortality, something which the average person probably doesn't pay too much heed to day-to-day. When faced with disaster, the views and attitudes of that society in the front-end moments of the disaster film are stripped away as a new, possibly permanent, reality emerges and must be contended with by the society. In the disaster film, this new reality is, most prominently and dramatically, experienced by the core group of survivors.

All Hell Breaks Loose

CHAPTER 4

The Primary Disaster

Picture it:

An enormous wall of water slowly but easily capsizes the cruise liner S.S. *Poseidon* in a marvelous, pre-CGI sequence of awesome terror and destruction. In a matter of minutes, the entire ship is turned upside down and rendered helplessly floating somewhere in the middle of the ocean.

Or this:

The pilot of an ultra-luxurious, private 747 flying under the radar in extremely foggy conditions is having difficulty gauging the airplane's altitude, resulting in the jetliner's wing fatally grazing an oil rig. This causes the airplane to make a spectacular crash water landing in the Atlantic Ocean.

Or, maybe, this:

A long dormant volcano located high up in the mountain wilderness suddenly erupts with a thunderous, explosive bang. The eruption causes the earth to shake and incites the residents of the nearby town into a full-blown and dangerous panic.

In most generic disaster films, the Primary Disaster is the focal, visual spectacle of the film. This event should be the centerpiece attraction, justifying why the audience has bought a ticket to the movie in the first place. Whether produced with old-fashioned trick photography, special effects, or more modern computer-generated imagery, the Primary Disaster is what sells the movie, and it should deliver the goods.

But let's, for a minute, put the visual spectacle aside and assess the sequence of events in a disaster film from the perspective of a narrative flow. Referring to the "beginning through middle to end" structural narrative timeline that Bordwell et al. indicate (68), we can, more or less, recognize that the Primary Disaster will tend to punctuate the end of Act One. To further simplify this idea, this means that one can reasonably expect the Primary Disaster to appear at, roughly, the movie's one-third mark (Shaer, *"Poseidon Protocol"* 4). However, as we have previously discussed, in most art forms, particularly in genre films, there will be variation or overlap. Depending upon the specifics of the movie and how the filmmakers choose to construct their story, this one-third mark time-line is certainly not always strictly adhered to. In 1972's *Skyjacked* (John Guillermin), yet another disaster film starring Ben-Hur himself, Charl-ton Heston, whose proficiency in disaster movies of the 1970s might have made one reconsider whether they wanted to be in the same room with him for fear that something calamitous might happen, the realization that a bomb has somehow been surreptitiously smuggled on board a passen-ger airplane occurs at fourteen minutes, thirty-four seconds into the one hundred and one-minute movie. By contrast, even though there is panic in the streets at the outset of 1996's *Independence Day*, the first proper alien attack of the film occurs at forty-six minutes and thirty-five seconds into the movie's one hundred and forty-five minutes, roughly one-third of the movie's running time (Shaer, *"Poseidon Protocol"* 4–5).

Regardless of when in the movie's life span it occurs, following the appearance of the Primary Disaster, all hell will break loose in Act Two, when the voyage to rescue ensues. Act Two is the portion of the narrative in which the bulk of the action and plot elements are fleshed out. Theoreti-cally, Act Two will take up most of the film's running time. For it is within Act Two that the Reverend Scott and his shipwrecked flock embark on their perilous journey to the top, or rather the bottom, of the overturned S.S. *Poseidon* in the hope of finding salvation. Act Two contains the sequences of the film when the city bus, driven by Annie, must remain in constant motion at a speed of no less than fifty miles per hour, while Jack valiantly attempts to diffuse the bomb rigged to detonate should the bus fall below that speed, and thus killing everyone on board. Act Two is when the people on South Pacific Air Flight Number 121 use every means they can to get the hell out of the way of those troublesome poisonous snakes that have some-how gotten lose on that plane (Shaer, *"Poseidon Protocol"* 5)!

In the table that follows, we can see when the instances of the Primary Disaster transpire in the selection of disaster films we are examining in the book. It is after each of these occurrences, including that of the Primary Disaster in *The Sibylline Scourge*, that the narrative moves into Act Two, when the majority of the disaster film will play out and all hell will break loose.

Title	Primary Disaster
Airport	airplane stuck in snow
The Andromeda Strain	oddity in Piedmont, New Mexico
Skyjacked	discovery of bomb on airplane

Title	Primary Disaster
The Poseidon Adventure	cruise ship capsizes
Airport 1975	collision between the 747 & the Baron
Earthquake	major earthquake
The Towering Inferno	fire on 81st floor
Flood	dam breaks
The Cassandra Crossing	Mackenzie notifies Chamberlain that there is a plague on board
Airport '77	plane crashes into water
Fire	Mrs. Malone sees smoke in the woods
The Swarm	swarm of bees attacking 2 helicopters
Avalanche	avalanche
The Concorde.... Airport '79	drone target is changed to target Concorde
City on Fire	leaked gasoline in water ignites from sparks, causing major explosions
Meteor	notification that a major piece of the asteroid Orpheus is approaching earth
Disaster on the Coastliner	south bound train doesn't switch tracks to avoid the north bound train
Cave-In!	Kate becomes trapped in the cavern after a cave-in
Speed	Jack notified that there is a bomb on bus
Outbreak	notification of mysterious virus outbreak
Twister	first proper tornado sequence
Independence Day	first alien attack
Daylight	car crash in Holland Tunnel

Title	Primary Disaster
Dante's Peak	volcanic eruption
Volcano	first eruption
Titanic	ship strikes iceberg
Deep Impact	announcement of comet hurtling towards Earth
Armageddon	notification of enormous asteroid heading towards Earth–18 days to destroy it
The Core	notification that the earth's core has stopped spinning
The Day After Tomorrow	notification of polar icecaps melting
Snakes on a Plane	snakes burst forth into cargo hold
2012	California faultlines collapse
Contagion	vocalization of novel virus with no treatment and no vaccine
San Andreas	earthquake in LA due to fault splitting
Geostorm	Hong Kong gas main explosions
Greenland	fragment of comet Clarke makes impact
The Sibylline Scourge	the novel coronavirus infiltrates the New York City metro area

I paid attention at that conference in Albuquerque back in February of 2020 as the events surrounding what would become the Covid-19 pandemic slowly unrolled in faraway countries. And as is the case with any invasive species, the virus started to spread, not so little-by-little, outside of China, then to Italy, to Brazil, to Iran, finally to the United States, until BAM…global pandemic!

As we discussed in the previous section, in *The Sibylline Scourge*, like in most disaster dramas, there is an obvious first act, a clear buildup. Rumblings out of Wuhan regard an enigmatic coronavirus afflicting the region; perhaps resulting from one of the area's famous wet markets, or perhaps surreptitiously trafficked out of the Wuhan Institute of Virology. On this, the answer was not clear (and depending upon which news source you attend to or to which pundit you listen, it still isn't). Concern begins to grow as the passengers aboard the *Diamond Princess* cruise ship are quarantined after a disembarked passenger receives a positive diagnosis for the coronavirus (Yamamitsu and Dooley). There is further unease when Italy issues strict lockdowns, as the Mediterranean country becomes the European epicenter of an erupting global health crisis. Then, more concern abounds as countries as polar as Brazil and Iran turn into unwitting hotspots of infection (Taylor). The previously mentioned U.S. airports tighten security protocols. The novel coronavirus pops up in Washington State.

But as far as I was concerned, and speaking only from my individual experience, although it was difficult to imagine that it was too far removed from the prevailing thoughts of my fellow New Yorkers at the time, the coronavirus was still somewhat remote from my life. Sure, heightened security measures had been implemented at JFK, SFO, and LAX Airports for passengers arriving from the affected Chinese region since late January ("Public Health Screening"), but for the most part, people in my immediate orbit were going about their lives, albeit maybe in a higher state of alert than normal. Things were happening in Washington State, a far cry from my corner of the world on West End Avenue and Ninety-Second Street in Manhattan.

Not for long, though. Washington State would initially be the location with the largest number of coronavirus infections in the United States, until March 9, when it was surpassed by New York State (Shaer, *"Poseidon Protocol"* 5). On March 3, 2020, it was announced that a middle-aged man in the New York City suburb of New Rochelle had tested positive for the novel coronavirus (Lombardi). Finally, the virus was confirmed to have infiltrated New York City, one of the most populated and dense cities on the planet. Containment at this point would almost definitely have been a non-starter.

It is at this juncture, dear disaster reader, that we enter into Act Two of *The Sibylline Scourge*. Once large corporations and governments around the world realized that the pathogen's tentacles were growing and widening with no signs of slowing down, and sparing no one in their devastating wake, drastic measures were swiftly enacted in the name of public safety. In short order, businesses were shuttered, large-scale multi-day events including the popular South by Southwest Festival in Austin, Texas, were cancelled, countries around the globe began to close their borders to foreigners as strict travel restrictions were enforced, and states of emergency were declared. The United States government, the institution to which the public should be looking to for guidance and reassurance, fed bewilderment and fear with sporadic and inconsistent information (although to be fair, this particular coronavirus was new to everyone, even scientists and health professionals, so no one knew for sure the ultimate effects it could and would have on anyone, especially the elderly and the infirmed). Still, misinformation abounded online and in other forms of media, creating panic and confusion and decreasing confidence in the nation's leadership (there hadn't really been that much there to begin with, but that's beside the point). While there were some messengers of misery that reared their heads and espoused what amounted to hysterical sermons touting the End of Days, many people were still not sure how they should and shouldn't behave, whether to mask up or not to mask up. Even President Trump was perceived as minimizing the severity of the germ and of downplaying concern for the coronavirus (or the "China Virus," as he xenophobically referred to it), carrying on with his presidential duties and maintaining his social calendar as normal (Collins and Liptak).

Conjecture and rumor about this novel coronavirus expanded throughout New York City and the country like frustration caused by a subway signal malfunction. Increased demand for cleaning products such as hand sanitizer, Clorox Wipes, and, interestingly, toilet paper, fueled by a disaster phenomenon known as "panic buying," heightened to such an extent that convenience markets and corner bodegas could barely keep these items stocked. The inventory on e-tailer Amazon.com consistently seemed to be in a state of "currently unavailable" (Shaer, *"Poseidon Protocol"* 5–6). Driven by the intense demand, food delivery and personal grocery shopping services such as Instacart, experienced extraordinarily long wait windows, sometimes extending several days in advance. This, combined with mounting fears of contamination by riding the subways or in taxis or Ubers, contributed to momentary food shortages and further terrified an already frightened public. It truly was, in New York City at least, the "panic in the streets" scenario writ large.

Having lived in New York City for the majority of 2020, I think I can, with a certain degree of truthfulness, speak to the impact of the Primary Disaster in *The Sibylline Scourge*. At least I can from an especially personal point of view. Now, let me acknowledge that I was not a first responder and have never been a medical professional in any capacity at any time whatsoever. Nor was I working in an industry deemed "essential," such as in a pharmacy or a grocery store. So, my experience of living through the Covid-19 outbreak in New York City is vastly, *vastly* different from those individuals. As such, I viewed the unfurling of the 2020 disaster from the safety of my cozy, Upper West Side studio apartment on the seventeenth floor. From this relatively safe and detached perspective, I observed the breakdown of the "City that Never Sleeps" as the pandemic swept through the usually bustling metropolis like The Blob. I can still vividly recall looking out of my apartment window, dumbfounded, as fleets of ambulances traveled uptown on Broadway, sirens blaring; a grim visual memory that is forever burned into my subconscious. I watched and listened as fear and confusion overtook my friends and neighbors, all trying to maintain a positive outlook while at the same time the news reports disseminated bleaker and bleaker statistics, and as our beloved city became the epicenter of a burgeoning viral outbreak.

Proclamations were issued from the Centers for Disease Control and Prevention (CDC), recommending that the public avoid gatherings of more than fifty people (Taylor). As the situation worsened and the storm of doom gained strength, it quickly became commonplace for more and more people to opt to work from home out of a newly realized germaphobia and generalized fear of encountering an infected individual. Let's not forget, conventional wisdom at the time indicated that symptoms, if they were even to be apparent, were unlikely to appear until roughly fourteen days after exposure to the virus; all the while an infected person was still, in fact, contagious. In New York City in the spring of 2020, Broadway shows ceased to operate; restaurants were forced to reduce their capacities and modify their operations to take-out or delivery services only, devastating some businesses in an already tough industry; schools shut down; the city paused (Adcroft and Toor, Warerkar). Amid this backdrop of alarm and chaos and demonstrating truly scumbag ideals, unscrupulous price gougers began to crop up, despite the warning given down by authorities that those practicing price gouging would face steep consequences if apprehended. A March 2020 article in *The New York Times* chronicled instances of gross price gouging in those first anxious weeks of the pandemic. Scores of morally daft people across the United States picked up on an opportunity to make a profit from the desperation of others by hoarding hand sanitizer, face masks, and other bacteria prevention necessities (Nicas; Shaer, *"Poseidon Protocol"* 6).

The ensuing public pandemonium and mass confusion following the commencement of the Primary Disaster characterizes much of Act Two of a disaster film. Within this atmosphere of frenzy, actions are taken and judgment calls are oftentimes made that, for better or worse, shape the outcome of the course of events. In *Twister*, for example, the team that is led by Bill and Jo is simultaneously competing in a storm chasing drag race with their rival team of storm chasers led by Jonas (Cary Elwes). Both teams are chasing an extraordinarily ferocious twister. When Bill realizes that the twister is suddenly turning on an unexpected trajectory, he and Jo attempt to warn Jonas that the twister is now headed directly into the path in which he and his team are travelling. Jonas just assumes that Bill and Jo are simply trying make a play to get to the storm first, and he makes the choice to ignore them (*Twister* 01:31:54–33:48). This act of hubris on the part of Jonas leads to his death as well as those of his team members (Shaer, *"Poseidon Protocol"* 6).

In the much earlier example of *The Andromeda Strain*, Dr. Jeremy Stone (Arthur Hill) realizes to his anger and frustration that a potentially devastating judgment call has been made by the president of the United States concerning the puzzling and deadly outbreak he and his team are researching. A motion known as Directive 7–12, in which an atomic bomb would be dropped on the initial outbreak site of Piedmont, New Mexico, should have been enacted by the president. The purpose of the bomb would be, of course, to decimate the town and, hopefully, abort the spread of the pathogen. Seeking answers as to why this directive was not implemented, Dr. Stone reaches out to Dr. Robertson (Kermit Murdock), a scientific advisor to the president, who ensures Stone that Directive 7–12 hasn't been vetoed as of yet, just stalled for the moment. Stone and his team angrily push back, reinforcing to Dr. Robertson and his colleague, Grimes (Richard O'Brien), that the longer they wait to drop the bomb, the likelier the virus will escape. A potentially global outbreak could be on the horizon if Directive 7–12 is not carried out immediately (*The Andromeda Strain* 01:43:00–48). Not too long after, in the movie's Second Disaster (more on those later), Dr. Stone and his team uncover the true nature of the viral cell and come to the realization that carrying out Directive 7–12 could, in fact, exacerbate the problem and multiply the pathogen. Luckily for them, while the president has now agreed to carry out Directive 7–12, he hasn't pushed the button yet. It turns out that the president's judgment call to hold on carrying out Directive 7–12 was the right call all along. Grimes snidely remarks, "The boss'll be pleased to know that he made the right decision on 7–12 in the first place" (*The Andromeda Strain* 1:49:04–08).

We have already explored how in the early stages of *The Sibylline Scourge*, facts were scarcely available, much less verified. To boot, some facts *still* aren't proven even at this point in time. In those first few months of the outbreak, the supply of beds couldn't keep up with the number of Covid-19 cases being admitted to hospitals. Life-saving ventilators quickly became a premium commodity. It is essential for one to also keep in mind that just because Covid was garnering all the press and heart-rending images of worn-out and exhausted doctors, nurses, and other first responders were plastered all over the news, it's not as though all other illnesses simply took a break for the time being. Hospitals still had to admit patients for any number of reasons: injuries, pregnancies, other diseases, etc. It was simple math: the supply of patients was overwhelming the demand for hospital beds and ventilators. Realizing this, the federal government dispatched the United States military hospital ship, the U.S.N.S. *Comfort*, to New York Harbor in late-March of 2020. The naval hospital ship was dispatched to New York with the express purpose of admitting *non*-coronavirus patients to the ship's wards in an effort to free up overtaxed hospitals that needed to admit and treat patients with the novel coronavirus (Cooper and Gibbons-Neff). While the intention of this action was unquestionably good, the execution wasn't entirely successful; the ship remained largely vacant following its arrival in New York. A *New York Times* article published on April 2, 2020, stated, "On Thursday, though, the huge white vessel, which officials had promised would bring succor to a city on the brink, sat mostly empty, infuriating executives at local hospitals. The ship's 1,000 beds are largely unused, its 1,200-member crew mostly idle. Only 20 patients had been transferred to the ship, officials said, even as New York hospitals struggled to find space for the thousands infected with the coronavirus" (Schwirtz).

It is within this pressure cooker of an environment that secondary male lead Governor Andrew Cuomo made his fateful March 25 issuance requiring nursing homes across New York State to admit those individuals who had confirmed or suspected cases of Covid-19 from the overtaxed hospitals. This proved to be a pivotal mandate that was widely viewed as having contributed to thousands of Covid-related deaths (Villeneuve and Peltz; Shaer, *"Poseidon Protocol"* 6). "No resident shall be denied re-admission or admission to the (nursing home) solely based on a confirmed or suspected diagnosis of COVID-19" (Lewis), read the official directive issued by the New York State Department of Health. For the remainder of his term in office, which would end in disgrace with his resignation in August 2021 amid a barrage of sexual harassment charges, the controversy surrounding Cuomo's disastrous nursing home proclamation would adhere to him like a malignant tumor.

The bewildering pace at which the rapidly evolving information was disseminated from public authorities with regard to how this virus was spread led, in part, to a situation where people were apprehensive about leaving their own homes. Once restaurants, bars, gyms, movie theaters, Broadway theaters, and other social venues started to shutter up, the scene became even more frightening (Shaer, *"Poseidon Protocol"* 6). On March 13, the other secondary male lead, President Donald Trump, officially declared a national state of emergency (Taylor and Sullivan). In late spring of 2020, the local governments of most states in the nation started to issue stay-at-home advisories or downright orders to residents that they not leave their homes except in the most necessary of instances (Mervosh et al.; Shaer, *"Poseidon Protocol"* 6).

It was full-scale alarm as an anxious citizenry found itself residing in some sort of dystopian landscape, with no choice but to stand by, remain docile, and obey the rules. There was no option but to surrender one's health and safety to one's local leaders, some of whom might have been (not so discreetly) perceived as enjoying their newfound executive powers a little too much. "Cuomo's approach to leadership has all of the worst components of a nanny state—heavy-handed regulation, complicated rules and intrusions into private life—without any of the benefits," read one *New York Post* article with the apt headline, "You're not my dad, Gov. Cuomo—and please stop pretending" (Rogers). The party attendees in *The Towering Inferno* faced similar circumstances as they nervously waited for assistance in the Promenade Room and deliberated over when and if they might be rescued from the incendiary prospect of death (Shaer, *"Poseidon Protocol"* 7). They had no choice but to surrender to those members of the society who assumed authority over their circumstances at the time (Chief O'Halloran and Doug Roberts, principally, as well as the firemen).

In an effort to construct a narrative for the disaster film, some measure of buildup preceding the Primary Disaster must be included. After all, most disaster movies exhibit a certain degree of the thriller genre that is inherent in these types of life-or-death scenarios. The buildup is the accrual of anticipation to a momentous event (i.e., the spectacle, be it earthquake, tidal wave, virus release, etc.). When the spectacle finally arrives in the form of the Primary Disaster and the cast of characters finds itself having to hastily devise a plan with which to escape a life-threatening peril, it's almost as though the audience is given an opportunity to release its pent-up anxiety. The stack has been blown. The audience now has a reason to think, "The disaster is here and it's awesome. Let's see how this (earthquake, tidal wave, virus release, etc.) beats the hell out of (the cast of characters) and how they manage to confront it head on or let it beat them." As indicated by Keane as one of the main pleasures of the disaster film, the game can now begin (5).

The disaster film, like any other piece of work in a film or literary genre or subgenre, encompasses certain identifying characteristics, generic traits, that comprise its biology and identifies it as part of the genre. We are already aware that many genre types overlap and share characteristics with one another, especially with such an obviously hybridized genre as the disaster film. The majority of the time, evidence is clear that the disaster film, as we have been examining it in this book, is a broadly constructed entertainment that includes salient elements of the action film more than any other genre: imminent danger, massive explosions, widespread destruction, characters skirting death utilizing any method or methods that they can, a villain or villains trying their level best to thwart the success of the core group of survivors, etc. Because the generic components of the action film run dominant over the other subordinate genre tropes existent within the disaster film, such as the melodrama, the family drama, or the romance, I will confidently posit that the disaster film is, on the whole, more accurately described as a *subgenre* of the action film, rather than a bona fide literary or cinematic genre all its own.

With that being said, there remain unique generic traits that specifically characterize a disaster film, the majority of which are being discussed in this book. These include the Poignant Character, the characteristics of the male and female leads, the breakdown then reunification of the society, etc. Of course, there comes a moment in every disaster film when the titular disaster finally establishes its presence and the characters in the story must begin their fight for survival. I refer to this standout moment as the Primary Disaster (the qualifying word "primary" will become clear later on).

* * *

The Primary Disaster

First off, the obvious. It will come as no great revelation to learn that the Primary Disaster must be a major spectacle. After all, what have viewers bought tickets to other than to see a great, big disaster catastrophe? Whatever type of disaster the movie might present, it must give the audience its money's worth. For audiences in 1933, when filmmaking was arguably still in its adolescence, the tidal wave sequences in *Deluge* must have delivered the requisite spectacular thrills. Likewise in 1936, when audiences were no doubt awestruck by the destruction caused by the depiction of the 1906 earthquake in *San Francisco,* and then two years later, by the blazing fire scenes simulating the Great Chicago Fire of 1871 in *In Old Chicago.* The Primary Disaster is the centerpiece attraction, the awesome promise of which, more so than any particular star attraction, drew the viewer to purchase a ticket. And tickets, as anyone who has seen a movie in the theater in recent years or purchased a first-run day-and-date ticket on a streaming platform can attest, ain't cheap!

New York Times film critic Manohla Dargis sums up the showstopping effect that the Primary Disaster should invoke in the opening lines of her review for the 2015 Norwegian disaster movie smash *The Wave* (Roar Uthaug):

> The flashy number in "The Wave" rolls in like a star. You know it's coming, just not when. (Fanning the crowd's anxiety is crucial to making a great entrance.)

Once it arrives, the crowd gawks and freezes, mesmerized by the spectacle of so much ferocious power [Dargis].

In 1974's *Earthquake*, for example, the titular disaster doesn't occur until approximately halfway through the film, almost an hour into its two-hour, two-minute running time. It hardly matters because when it arrives, it is an impressive spectacle of intensity and destruction that demonstrates the wrath of which Mother Nature is capable (at least in Hollywood-ized fashion ... the film is *not* a documentary). Without a doubt, audiences in 1974 were certainly given their money's worth with an earthquake sequence that lasts for just over eight terrifying, earth-shaking minutes of screen time (although a cameo by Walter Matthau as a besotted barfly who clearly doesn't give two shits about the carnage transpiring all around him practically steals the scene, if not the entire movie).

Furthering the audience's bang for its buck, at the time of the movie's release, *Earthquake* was presented along with a pioneering immersive experience called Sensurround, a gimmicky sideshow-type attraction developed by audio engineers Cerwin-Vega in conjunction with Universal Pictures. Sensurround was a short-lived, yet influential innovation that involved custom-made sound woofers that were specifically constructed into movie theaters and developed to emit ultra-low frequencies. These frequencies were designed to allow a person's body to tangibly *feel* the sound. In the case of *Earthquake*, the intention was to mimic the physical effects of withstanding an earthquake. Sensurround was used only a handful of times throughout the remainder of the 1970s—notably in 1976's *Midway* (Jack Smight) and 1977's *Rollercoaster* (James Goldstone)—before innovations in audio engineering, not to mention the expense required for its maintenance, rendered Sensurround basically untenable (Mouttet).

In the years since *Earthquake* and Sensurround shook cinemas across the nation, the science of audio technology has, of course, continued to develop and expand. Among other innovations, an example of advancement in audio technology is the development and proliferation of Dolby sound, prevalent these days in cinemas throughout the world. So, for the next disaster film genre cycle in the 1990s, contrivances such as Sensurround were not only no longer feasible, but were simply no longer necessary. Audiences weren't likely to be wowed by gimmicks such as Sensurround when advancements in special effects technology including audio, but most notably, computer-generated imagery (CGI), had become widespread, allowing for an audience to experience the world of a film on more of a sensory plane, rather than a physical one.

Twister whipped audiences into its mighty wind in the spring of 1996 with several jaw-dropping tornado-sequence spectacles that alone justified the price of admission (no one was buying a ticket to *Twister* for the story). While *Twister* employs a good example of the Preamble sequence discussed in Chapter 1, the first proper disaster sequence (i.e., the Primary Disaster) occurs at roughly a half-hour into the one hundred thirteen-minute movie (just about one-third of the way through, conforming to the true disaster movie standard). As exes Jo (Hunt) and Bill (Paxton) bicker, their team, travelling behind them in a separate vehicle, radios to the two exes that they are, in fact, giving chase to a rampaging funnel wreaking havoc on the nearby Midwestern plains. Jo and Bill attempt to get ahead of the twister, but in no time flat, the tornado picks up and, unbelievably, appears to actually be *chasing* Jo and Bill! The two take the closest and most stable refuge they can identify under an overpass that bridges a ravine. But alas, the two are able to do nothing more than hold on for dear life and watch as the twister turbulently swirls above them. (Let me just mention that the amount of wind in *Twister* is so fierce and so powerful that I wouldn't be surprised if Hunt and Paxton didn't experience some sort of medical-grade windburn after shooting this movie.) The tornado, of course, destroys everything in its path, tossing around infrastructure, land, debris, and even a Jeep, like toys cast about a room by an itinerant child throwing a tantrum. The soundtrack accompanying the scene booms with wind sounds that cancel out all other noise and reduces shouting speech to no more than a mere whisper (*Twister* 00:26:59–33:25). It's an unquestionably awesome sequence that announces to the audience that the filmmakers are not taking their spectacle lightly. De Bont's *Twister* is mid–90s Hollywood disaster movie blockbuster filmmaking at its finest and most bombastic.

We refer once again to theorist Tom Gunning's "cinema of attractions," as perfect a reason for the existence of the disaster film as I have found. "…the cinema of attractions directly solicits spectator attention, inciting visual curiosity, and supplying pleasure through an exciting spectacle—a unique event, whether fictional or documentary, that is of interest in itself" ("Cinema of Attractions" 73).

At the risk of appearing to contradict myself with regard to the visual spectacular of which the Primary Disaster should be comprised, there are also instances wherein the Primary Disaster might, in fact, *not* be a visual spectacle at all. Though this does not necessarily make the impact of the Primary Disaster any less visceral, however. Sometimes, a disaster film will simply vocalize the disaster. In other words, a character will spell out explicitly that a particular disaster is apparent, and the society present in the film, whether that be the core group of survivors or the society at large, will be vocally notified that a disaster has either struck or will imminently strike. While a certain amount of portent is often espoused by characters in a disaster film (disaster films are generally in the thriller mode, after all), such as during a Preamble sequence, the notification method of a Primary Disaster will be conveyed more as a dire emergency, not merely a warning. For example, in Michael Bay's *Armageddon*, Dan Truman, the Executive Director of NASA, is briefing the president of the United States on the asteroid that is hurtling towards earth. When Truman is queried by the president on the size of the asteroid and the potential consequences for the people of earth, Truman responds that the asteroid's collision with earth will mean "the end of mankind." Just then, a staff member on Truman's team bursts into the conference room where Truman is teleconferencing with the president, and out of breath, he proclaims, "We have eighteen days before it hits earth" (*Armageddon* 00:10:51–11:52). This notification to the present filmic society that disaster is more or less imminent can be construed as *Armageddon*'s Primary Disaster.

However, it is more often the case that this method of vocalization or notification of a disaster is witnessed in disaster movies of the biological type, or virus-related movies, like *Outbreak, Contagion*, or our own, *The Sibylline Scourge*. This makes sense since, in a disaster movie where a virus is the main catalyst for the narrative, the disaster is, naturally, invisible. By virtue of the silent, invisible nature of the disaster, there can be no visual spectacle. Yet, the realization that a potentially deadly virus outbreak is on the horizon is no less frightening or alarming in magnitude than an asteroid heading toward earth or a swarm of killer bees. In *Outbreak*, for example, Col. Sam Daniels (Dustin Hoffman), a scientist with the United States Army Medical Research Institute of Infectious Diseases (USAMRIID), is peacefully going about his non-working day, playfully and lovingly soaping up his two dogs. He receives an urgent phone call from General Billy Ford (Morgan Freeman) in which Ford notifies Sam that there is a suspected Level 4 outbreak in Zaire. He needs Sam on the case (*Outbreak* 00:07:05–59). Now, the audience has learned, via a beautifully executed opening credits tracking sequence through the USAMRIID, courtesy of famed director of photography Michael Ballhaus (00:04:09–00:06:41), that Biosafety Level 4 contains the most deadly, incurable infectious agents: pathogens such as Ebola, for example. Knowing this information, coupled with the fact that we have bought a ticket for a movie called *Outbreak*, we can deduce that Ford's notification of the Level 4 outbreak is the movie's Primary Disaster.

In order to introduce the Primary Disaster in any disaster movie, there must be a "tipping point" moment in which the cataclysm becomes a reality for the society and in which the characters understand that their circumstances are now irretrievably dire. This situation may, in fact, be the Preamble. Or it may occur shortly after, as in the case of *Outbreak*, in which the notification of the Primary Disaster takes place at just seven minutes and forty-five seconds into the movie. Even with the Primary Disaster occurring so near the front end of the film, when we consider, as has been suggested previously in this chapter, the disaster film in a traditional narrative sense and refer to an Act One, Act Two, and an Act Three dramatic chronology, it makes sense that Act Two, which contains the meat of the film following the Primary Disaster, would occupy the majority of filmic and expository time. Regardless, and as we have also mentioned in this chapter, it helps when deconstructing the disaster film to think of the incidence of the Primary Disaster as typically occurring at or about the one-third mark, give or take, in filmic time.

However, most often in disaster films there has been some concentrated and significant buildup in the story that serves to prime the viewer for the anxiety and terror that erupts with the Primary Disaster. As soon as a prisoner working on a crew in the woods in the 1977 Irwin Allen-produced TV movie *Fire* (Earl Bellamy, 1977) casually tosses a lit cigarette that, of course, isn't completely extinguished, we know that disaster is not far off. Sure enough, a brush fire breaks out which the crew works to smother and believes to have done so. Smoke advisories are subsequently called off. Later, Mrs. Malone (Donna Mills) drives into in a clearing near the woods in question along with her elementary school-aged pupils for a field trip. We, as the audience, know it can't be good when little Judy wanders off shortly thereafter. All of this buildup culminates in the moment when, in the Primary Disaster at a few minutes under the twenty-minute mark into the ninety-seven-minute movie, Mrs. Malone notices suspicious smoke rising above the trees from the nearby patch of woods into which she suspects little Judy has gotten lost (*Fire* 00:06:46–17:50).

To use another example from a movie that packs a lot of buildup into a short amount of time, following brief introductory sequences that introduce the characters that will compose our core group of survivors in *Daylight*, we watch as a trio of thieves straight out of *Mad Max* violently hijack a car and speed frenzied through the streets of Manhattan. The driver loses control (as any maniac driving like him would), and, at just over fifteen minutes into a one hundred and fourteen-minute movie, the car crashes into a truck that is shuttling explosives en route to New Jersey. This inciting incident results in the massive combustion (the fiery Primary Disaster spectacle) in the Holland Tunnel, which leads to scores of deaths and incredible destruction (*Daylight* 00:11:11–15:32).

I have mentioned several times thus far in this book that any artistic endeavor, whether disaster movie, abstract painting, or science fiction novel, can be subject to reimagination or generic modification when creators of different influences and backgrounds (filmmakers, screenwriters, authors, etc.) become involved. You might have heard the term "creative license?" Well, this is what it means. Creators play with a template and adjust it in an effort to infuse a generic project with their own individual, creative imprint. Many times, creative license in the disaster film takes its shape in the presentation of the Primary Disaster. Filmmakers and other creative personnel behind different sorts of disaster films choose to stage their Primary Disasters in a variety of imaginative, eye-catching, and thrilling manners.

So, while like any form of art, the disaster film may be prone to creative license, the disaster film still has established conventions that dictate, to some degree, how the stories should be told. Since the disaster film is a subgeneric off-shoot of the action film, there are telltale characteristics that are universal across each piece of work that, consequently, help to define the disaster film as a distinct subgenre. Specifically, we can identify two dominant disaster tropes: the "panic in the streets" motif that occurs once the Primary Disaster gets underway, and that of the "breakdown then reunification of society," which affects the diegetic society that the film has created within itself in the immediate aftermath of the Primary Disaster. Once we look at a few examples of each disaster convention, it will be clearer for the average viewer to understand just how the Covid-19 pandemic story dramatized in *The Sibylline Scourge* fits squarely within this framework.

Panic in the Streets

When one sees or hears the words "panic in the streets," it is understandable for one to imagine hordes of frenzied people running chaotically throughout the streets of a town or city as they scream and flail their arms in hysteria. The mouths of the citizens agape in disbelief and their eyes wide in abject horror is a scene reminiscent of some sort of 1950s sci-fi moment. Susan Sontag articulates this possible scenario in "The Imagination of Disaster":

> There is an obligatory scene here of panicked crowds stampeding along a highway or a big bridge, being waved on by numerous policemen who, if the film is Japanese, are immaculately white-gloved, preternaturally calm, and call out in dubbed English, "Keep moving. There is no need to be alarmed" [235].

However, the "panic in the streets" leitmotif can actually take on any number of contexts depending upon the type of disaster movie we are watching as well as the overall tone of said film. For example, we find that sometimes this moment of panic manifests as a quiet, more introspective form of all-encompassing dread, such as in the case of *Meteor*.

Panic in the Streets: Meteor

In the scenario of this film, the Sean Connery character, Dr. Paul Bradley, has just arrived in Washington, D.C., for an informational briefing with Harry Sherwood (Karl Malden) at NASA regarding the asteroid Orpheus. During the meeting, Sherwood explains the possibility of Orpheus's impending collision with the earth (the disaster). Later that evening as Dr. Bradley lies in bed, staring at the ceiling, he recalls Sherwood's words: "There's a chunk of Orpheus heading towards earth, a pretty big one. There're a lot of little pieces coming along with it and in front of it, but it's the big one we're worried about. The figures haven't been worked out yet, but six days from now we *could* be hit." Then, as an expectedly ominous score is heard on the soundtrack, the camera tracks along Orpheus, allowing the audience to gauge its immense size and every jagged edge of the speeding space rock (*Meteor* 00:05:25–16:03).

The "mounting dread" scenario, such as that experienced in *Meteor,* can be described as a **soft panic**. There is no observed pandemonium. No looting. No throngs of people fleeing, feverishly trying to escape the path of destruction and certain death. There is only one man, unpacking the grievous news he has just received concerning a looming, and potentially cataclysmic, event. This news is his to process.

On the other end of the spectrum, however, there exists a scenario in a film like 2020's *Greenland* (Ric Roman Waugh, 2020), in which the panic is presented as much more explicit.

Panic in the Streets: Greenland

This motif as used in *Greenland* takes the form of utter public chaos and violent rioting and looting (what most people envision when they hear the word "panic"). When John Garrity (Gerard Butler) arrives at Robins Air Force Base along with his wife, Allison (Morena Baccarin), and young son, Nathan (Roger Dale Floyd), the scene that greets them is one of mass confusion and deafening commotion caused by an enormous crowd desperate to gain entry onto the base. The crowd resembles rabid fans at a Justin Bieber concert. The soldiers charged with guarding the entry gates attempt to keep the onslaught of shouting extras at bay in order that those specifically selected for relocation, like the Garritys, are able to pass onto the base. The soldiers don't say much other than "keep moving" as they herd the multitudes of anxious and perplexed people onto a fleet of planes, while the Garritys proceed in a dumbfounded daze through the relocation aircraft boarding process.

Soon (and inevitably, otherwise we wouldn't have much of a movie) there is a perimeter breach. This is not completely surprising when you consider what might happen when hundreds of terrified, screaming people attempt to force their way into a restricted area. The downright tumultuous atmosphere that surrounds the base's tarmac is made all the more tumultuous as a massive swath of people rush the grounded planes that are still in the process of boarding passengers. The ambush results in both civilians and military alike opening fire on the other and prompting a fuel leak that, when ignited by the gunfire during the confrontation, combusts in a monstrous and thunderous explosion. So, we observe in this chaotic scene, a fiery combination of a mass of screaming, confused people, running for their lives, being shot at by the military, and eventually finding themselves having to dodge a tremendous fuel explosion. Sounds like a "panic in the streets" scenario to me if there ever was one!

It is not long after this tense scene that Allison and Nathan, having both been denied boarding on the relocation airplane due to Nathan being a diabetic, venture out in search of a pharmacy where they hope to stock up on Nathan's diabetes medication. (Nathan's meds were inadvertently left in the family car upon arrival at the base. John then left his family for what he assumed would be a quick errand and went back to the car to retrieve the meds. During his absence, Allison and Nathan were, unbeknownst to John, denied boarding on the plane, and the family was subsequently separated.) Allison and Nathan eventually spot a drugstore, which, establishing shots inform the viewer, is in the process of being ransacked and looted. But as soon as Allison finds the critical medicine that will save Nathan's life, a potentially dangerous situation abounds. Gunshots ring out in the store, deployed by a gang of drug-crazed thugs who wish to abscond with the unclaimed and unmanned drugs located in the store's pharmacy. Allison and Nathan do eventually make it out of the drugstore, but not before crawling on their hands and knees towards the exit to avoid detection by the murderous gang, and only by being waved through by a (plot necessary) sympathetic gang member to whom they plead for mercy while he holds them at gunpoint (*Greenland*, 00:27:54–45:25).

While we can observe *Meteor* as clearly more of a soft panic, *Greenland* represents its polar opposite: a much more vivid depiction of the violent and chaotic aspects of the "panic in the streets" motif. Conversely to *Meteor*, *Greenland* might be referred to as a full-on **hard panic**. Yet, much in the same way that I think most people politically reside somewhere between the far reaches of the left and the opposing right, I would argue that most disaster films present a "panic in the streets" situation that falls somewhere on the spectrum in between the soft and hard panic extremes.

Breakdown, Then Reunification, of Society

The "breakdown" or "fracturing of society" exists in any disaster film after the disaster has occurred and has thrust the greater society in the film into a state of chaos. There may be one or more manifestations of the breakdown, including organizational, class or racial, or public. Many disaster movies will even include isolated instances of a character having a mental breakdown of sorts. This is, more or less, to be expected since it's likely that any person who unwittingly finds themselves in the midst of any type of disaster, particularly the types of disasters that we have examined in this book, would be subject to a mental breakdown. I know I certainly would be.

Organizational Breakdown

An organizational breakdown may appear as one in which leadership is challenged, such as in *The Poseidon Adventure*. In this instance, the Reverend Scott seeks to compel those in the ballroom of the S.S. *Poseidon* following the ship's capsizing to trek upwards (downwards?) to the hull of the ship. However, he is challenged by the ship's purser, who argues with the Reverend Scott in favor of staying put in the ballroom until help arrives (*The Poseidon Adventure* 00:38:40–39:00). We all know by now which side wins *that* argument.

Class or Racial Breakdown

An example of class or racial breakdown might be similar to that which is observed in *Volcano*. Here, Kevin, a Black man, begs a cruelly dismissive fireman for assistance in curbing the destruction of homes caused by the flowing lava in his nearby neighborhood. A White police officer, clearly presented as a racist as well as a classist figure, intervenes, and assumes that Kevin is behaving as a nuisance, immediately placing him in handcuffs. "Oh great. Mark Fuhrman," Kevin remarks, referencing the former Los Angeles police detective famous for both his pivotal role in the O.J. Simpson murder case of the early 1990s as well as for his common perception as an alleged racist (*Volcano* 00:56:03–22; Editors, TheFamousPeople.com—Mark Fuhrman).

Public Breakdown

We have already discussed in detail an example of a public breakdown, such as that seen in *Greenland* at the entrance to the military base, as the desperate masses try, and eventually succeed in, swarming the gates. The public breakdown calls to mind a scene of mass chaos, wherein all notions of decorum are tossed aside in favor of an "every man for himself" group mentality. As Dan Truman advised Harry S. Stamper in *Armageddon*, when briefing him on the urgency of the disaster and its guarantee to decimate the earth in a little over a week's time, "If news like this got out there would be an overnight breakdown of basic social services worldwide. Rioting, mass religious hysteria, total chaos as you can imagine. Basically, the worst parts of the Bible" (*Armageddon* 25:16–28). Yup, that pretty much sums up the dramatic concept of the public breakdown, I would say.

Mental Breakdown

A mental breakdown doesn't normally take the form as a substitute of an organizational, class or racial, or public breakdown. Furthermore, you can't really consider Randy Quaid's Russell Case in *Independence Day* or Woody Harrelson's Charlie Frost in *2012* as examples of a mental breakdown since those characters start out if not totally crazy, then dubiously sane. It's weaved into the biology of those characters. Rather, a mental breakdown might better be understood as a by-product of one of the other forms of social breakdown in the disaster film. In this case, there would typically be a character who simply can't compose themselves under the circumstances and, essentially, loses their cool, requiring another character or characters to calm them down. We can cite Eve Clayton (Brenda Vaccaro) in *Airport '77* in the immediate aftermath of that film's Primary Disaster. Upon learning that that the airplane has crashed, Eve is clearly in shock, in disbelief that they have crashed and is barely holding herself together. Don Gallagher (Jack Lemmon) firmly takes her head in his hands and forces her to look him straight in the eye as he reinforces the fact that the two of them more than anyone (she as the head stewardess, he as the pilot) must remain calm, lest there be full-blown chaos. Don's pep talk helps, as Eve comes to understand the situation and responds to Don that she will try her best to assist the injured and frightened passengers (*Airport '77* 50:28–51:01). We can also look to the character of Nonnie Parry (Carol Lynley) in *The Poseidon Adventure*, in the lower key but just as mentally shattered instance where she simply freezes in total and complete terror on the ladder immediately following Acres's (Roddy McDowall) plummeting to his death. "I'm sorry, I can't move. I can't," she ekes out in fractured breaths when prompted to continue climbing by James (Red Buttons). Unable to move, it takes James gently reminding her, despite Mike Rogo (Ernest Borgnine) shouting at them from below, to keep her eyes on the ladder and climb one foot at a time (*The Poseidon Adventure* 1:10:08–12:05).

The mental breakdown subset of this leitmotif is probably best exemplified in a film we haven't much mentioned in this book, 1980's classic disaster movie spoof *Airplane!* Anyone who has seen this film (and that arguably includes more people than have seen the films that *Airplane!* actually parodies) will remember Mrs. Hammen (Lee Bryant) completely losing her shit mid-flight and screaming, "I've got to get out of here" over and over as fellow passengers get in line to smack (or otherwise weaponize) some sense into her.

The "breakdown, then reunification, of society" leitmotif is primarily present in the disaster film in order for the viewer to witness disparate groups within the society (the core group of survivors) as they endure the disaster, which will "break down" their individuality, thus rendering them all on equal footing. Then, once the Primary Disaster subsides for the moment, the group can assess the situation they now find themselves in and come together as one, "reunify," and develop a plan of action with which to defeat the virus, monster, what have you, or construct a route of escape, and eventually rebuild their society. Much like the "panic in the streets" motif, the "breakdown" or "fracturing of society" can assume a variety of forms in the disaster film, encompassing the organizational, class or racial, or public breakdowns, depending upon the type and the size of the society in the narrative.

Both 1974's *Earthquake* and 1997's *Volcano* provide good examples of this concept of the "breakdown, then reunification, of society" in action. The society in both movies, quite literally and structurally, breaks down. The earth shakes violently in the former which causes the society's infrastructure to collapse and the society to bear witness to the massive destruction and disruption of their city; in the latter, the earth physically splits open and, in the process, allows hot molten lava to spew forth from its depths and project lava bombs that attack the society, rendering buildings, streets, and the entire urban infrastructure ruinous. It may or may not be worth mentioning that in both *Earthquake* and in *Volcano*, the society in question happens to be Los Angeles, but you get my point.

While both *Earthquake* and *Volcano* obviously present a clear literalization of the breakdown of society motif in the disaster film, both films illustrate this idea within their narratives in manners in which a little more reading (or watching) between the lines to comprehend might be worthwhile. First, let us take a bit of a deeper dive into this trope and look at the case of *Earthquake*.

Breakdown, Then Reunification, of Society: Earthquake

Once the titular disaster has struck and Los Angeles has been brought to a crippling standstill, supermarket manager/all-around weirdo Jody

(Marjoe Gortner) sees an opportunity to seize his moment amidst the ensuing chaos and looting. Jody also serves as a squadron sergeant in the city's special forces, assigned to maintain law and order following the disaster. Being the military aficionado that he is, Jody quickly abandons his rather banal role in society as supermarket manager and reinvents himself unrestrained as a sort of megalomaniacal leader, taking full advantage of the breakdown of the society and the lawlessness that has overtaken Los Angeles in the wake of the disaster. (Fun fact: this role exploits some smart stunt casting by the filmmakers given Gortner's own notoriety at the time as a real-life religious charlatan and evangelist.)

Jody proceeds to delight in asserting almost dictatorial authority over his troops. Relishing the hyper-macho new guise that he has assumed in this strange, new, anarchic Los Angeles, Jody essentially kidnaps the beautiful Rosa (Victoria Principal), with whom he has held a not-so-indiscreet lust for in the previous reality. Jody holds Rosa hostage with the lecherous expectation that she will find him irresistible. Of course, this being a big-budget, mainstream, commercial movie produced in the socially shifting but still relatively repressed 1970s, Jody must suffer for his crimes. Interrupted by police officer Slade (George Kennedy) while attempting to rape Rosa, Jody is fatally subdued by a bullet from Slade's pistol. Upon his death, Jody is removed from the society, that it may now reunify and move the story forward towards the finish (*Earthquake* 1:39:18–41:52).

Jody's attempt at commandeering his group of adherents in the wake of the anarchy that has gripped Los Angeles in the aftermath of the earthquake represents an *organizational* breakdown of society. In the way that Jody is forcibly assuming control of his troops, with an eye on reigning supreme over a new society of his own, he is challenging the dominant leadership that has emerged in the story in the form of the Charlton Heston and George Kennedy characters, whose sole missions following the massive quake is to ensure that everyone in the society is safe and out of harm's way.

Breakdown, Then Reunification, of Society: Volcano

As discussed above, *Volcano* presents an explicitly *class or racial breakdown* of society in the form of the benevolent Black man's altercations with two blatantly racist and disregarding White police officers. After being placed in handcuffs at the hands of the White police officer, the now-restrained Kevin has little to do but to wait and watch, with thinly disguised glee, as the police officer and his partner attempt in vain to move a concrete barrier into position to help contain the flow of lava. "You know what they say. No pain, no gain," Kevin admonishes the police officers. At this point, one of the officers stands up and forcefully confronts Kevin, who assumes he is about to get a beatdown. He announces, "Here it comes. I'm about to get the volcano version of Rodney King." In reality, the police officer removes the handcuffs from Kevin and tells him to just go home (*Volcano* 01:06:42– 1:07:05). The police officers have more important things to do than babysit a man who is providing no assistance other than to be a general pain in the ass to those first responders that are in the midst of crisis control. The Rodney King reference here is a timely allusion to the 1991 beating of a Black man in Los Angeles by four, mostly White police officers, the acquittal of which a year later incited five days of rioting and civil unrest throughout Los Angeles in what commonly became known as the L.A. Riots (Sastry and Grigsby Bates).

Now freed, Kevin takes a minute to observe the chaos surrounding him as firefighters, policemen, and other rescue personnel urgently work to construct the lava dam. In a moment that signals the reunification of this class or racial breakdown, the Black man offers up his considerable size and strength to assist the White police officers, the same officers who had been obviously telegraphing their racism only a few scenes earlier, in moving the concrete barrier. Just before they lift the barrier, there is a shot of Kevin and his tormenter looking straight at each other, signifying their unlikely union in accomplishing the goal of moving the concrete barrier into place (*Volcano* 1:07:12–42). Later, after the lava has effectively been corralled, the White police officer asks the fire chief to mobilize his resources to Kevin's neighborhood in order to finally address the structural damage the Black man had asked for assistance with in the first place (01:15:30–39).

So, having successfully accomplished a common goal and, in the process, having had their class and racial differences broken down to the same level, the Black man and the White police officer have reemerged as hostile compatriots. Each has a mutual, albeit wary and tenuous, earned respect for the other. In *Volcano*, this instance can be construed as the reunification of the society.

In Act One, the society created at the outset of the disaster film is going to be depicted as relatively stable, even in circumstances when the movie opens during the initial stages of what is, in truth, the Primary Disaster, such as *Independence Day* or *Contagion*. Sure, certain characters might have minor tensions; in *2012*, for example, it is clear that Jackson and Kate are contentious exes and Jackson harbors a visible resentment towards Kate's new husband, Gordon (Tom McCarthy), and his positive relationship with Jackson's kids. However, these surface tensions may be regarded as standard (some might say lazy) character buildup and not necessarily distinctive to the disaster film. Obviously, every piece of narrative fiction, or nonfiction for that matter, must first establish the relationships between the characters in order to introduce a measure of conflict and to maintain any interest for the audience in the remainder of the drama. Who wants to watch a movie (or play or read a book) where everyone in the piece starts out blissfully happy and remains blissfully happy throughout the course of the story, never encountering any dissension in their everyday lives? That was the supposed premise of Bryan Forbes's 1975 film *The Stepford Wives*, based on Ira Levin's novel. And that was a horror movie!

Expanding upon this character buildup, in Act One, a viewer will also learn of any brewing romantic subplots that may be developed throughout the course of the narrative. Typically, these will be romantic entanglements that will be tested in some way as a result of the disaster. For example, a character may begin the film with overt or veiled antagonism towards another. But by the film's end, such antagonism will have morphed into a mutual respect and admiration or even love, such as with Jo and Bill in *Twister*, or Jackson and Kate in *2012*. In other films, there might be an estranged couple who couldn't manage to cohabitate legally as husband and wife, but nonetheless maintain a cordial relationship and forever carry that torch for one another, such as Dr. Jonathan Chamberlain and his estranged wife, Jennifer, in *The Cassandra Crossing*. Such a scenario sets up a supposed "partnership" between the male and female leads in combating the disaster (although we've already discussed how normally gender-imbalanced this male-female "partnership" typically turns out to be). There also may be instances in disaster movies wherein one character, trapped in a loveless marriage, carries on an extramarital affair with a younger, more desirable, more amenable character. By the conclusion of said film, the adulterous character will discover, in spite of themselves, where their romantic loyalties truly lie. Such is the case with the Capt. Demarest, Sarah Demarest (Barbara Hale), Gwen triangle in *Airport*, or the Graff (Charlton Heston), Remy, and Denise (Genevieve Bujold) entanglement in *Earthquake*.

But most importantly, Act One, specifically, the conclusion of Act One, is when, according to the sketched-out narrative timeline that we have established, we will expect to encounter the Primary Disaster. It makes no fundamental difference when the precise instance in the timeline of the narrative this moment occurs, whether it is nicely and neatly situated in the narrative at the one-third mark or occurring only a few minutes into the film. Whether the Primary Disaster is conveyed via a visual spectacular or relayed through a grim and dramatic pronouncement, this is the essential moment when the spectacle unveils itself as the showstopper it is (or should be). The Primary Disaster should be the moment in a disaster movie in which audience members shift in their seats and silently acknowledge that the lives of the characters that occupy the filmic society are about to change forever.

As a connoisseur of disaster cinema, I would contend that there is one consummate exemplar of the Primary Disaster in all of the disaster movies made and released to date, the standard by which all others are judged. At approximately twenty-eight minutes into *The Poseidon Adventure*, the enormous tidal wave is fatefully spotted, albeit too late, by Capt. Harrison (Leslie Nielsen) and the rest of the captain's deck. The imposing wall of water slowly upturns the S.S. *Poseidon*, to the bewilderment and horror of the cruise ship passengers celebrating in the ballroom. We, the audience, watch mesmerized as the spectacle unfolds, as partygoers desperately cling to anything they can grab—tables, chairs, decorative columns—to avoid falling to the ceiling of the overturning ship and, in the case of one unlucky passenger, crashing through it. We marvel at the technicality and the awesomeness of this sequence as place settings that had been set for the evening's New Year's Eve dinner slide off of their tables and loudly shatter as they crash into the ceiling. Bodies toss and tumble as the lives of everyone on board are, in a very literal sense, overturned. On the soundtrack, the audience hears nothing except for people screaming in horror over the ship's alarm, shattering glass, and crumbling infrastructure as the ship's passengers tumble about the ballroom as easily as though they are wet clothes in a dryer, arms flailing, many to their deaths. Every so often, the audience will get a wide shot of the tidal wave as it continues to flip the ship, emphasizing the magnitude of the situation as much as the hopelessness of the circumstance engulfing the S.S. *Poseidon*, isolated as it is in the ocean with no one around to bear witness to the carnage taking place. Eventually the electricity goes out and people cease being thrown about the ballroom. The glass stops shattering and the screaming, for the moment, subsides. The surviving passengers register their situation in disbelief as they come to, paralyzed in a state of shock and disorientation concerning what has just transpired around them (*The Poseidon Adventure* 00:27:59–32:30). The entire capsizing scene only lasts for approximately four minutes, but it is a scene of equal parts pure mayhem and unbridled exhilaration. The Primary Disaster sequence in *The Poseidon Adventure* is a grade-A, wondrous spectacle, gloriously staged on a massive scale by director Ronald Neame.

And it is this brilliant staging that is so spectacular about the capsizing scene in *The Poseidon Adventure*. Firstly, all of the characters (main, supporting, extras ... the society) are in the ballroom in the joyous throes of celebration immediately following the ringing in of the New Year. Once the tidal wave is spotted, the portentous music kicks in on the soundtrack, and Capt. Harrison reacts with a stunned and horrified "Oh My God!" He instantly, but tragically, too late, sounds the alarm, interrupting the festivities and throwing the passengers into a state of utter confusion. Gradually, the ship begins to tilt, and the audience prepares for what we know is about to happen (after all, we bought a ticket for a movie about a capsized ship). Sheer panic sets in among the passengers as the reality of what is happening starts to manifest. One by one, the passengers lose their balance and scream as they fly into walls and over banisters. As we watch the scene unfold from the safety of a cinema (or home, wherever), the hairs on the back of our necks stand up as we settle in for the money-scene. We sit back in anticipation of the glorious destruction. This is what we came for, baby (*The Poseidon Adventure* 00:27:59–31:48).

CHAPTER 5

The Poignant Character

Nick Cordero was, as they say, living his dream. In the years since the Canadian native's 2012 Broadway debut in the hit jukebox musical *Rock of Ages*, Nick had amassed an impressive and award-winning resume trodding the boards in musicals such as *Bullets Over Broadway* (creating the role of Cheech in 2014), *Waitress* (in the role of Earl in 2016), and *A Bronx Tale: The Musical* (creating the role of Sonny, also in 2016). An opportunity for Mr. Cordero to star in a new Los Angeles production of *Rock of Ages* prompted him and his family, which consisted of wife Amanda Kloots, an actress and fitness trainer, and infant son, Elvis, to make the move from New York City out west ("Nick Cordero—Obituary").

But the anxious enthusiasm generated by a cross-country move along with the young couple's rite of passage of purchasing their first home (Kloots, "New Home"), was cruelly curtailed by the vicious hand of fate. In late March 2020, while people around the world were wondering aloud in confusion about this unexplainable illness that was seemingly blazing a trail across the globe, Nick began to experience difficulty with his breathing; he was initially diagnosed with pneumonia (Frishberg; Henderson). On March 30, Nick was admitted to Cedars-Sinai Hospital in Los Angeles (Truitt; Wu). A short time after that, it was discovered that the initial pneumonia diagnosis had been incorrect; Nick had, in fact, contracted the dreaded novel coronavirus (Henderson).

Doctors placed Nick in the ICU, where he was quickly put on a ventilator (Frishberg). His situation critical, Nick was subsequently placed into a medically induced coma, where he would remain for six weeks (Wu). All the while, Amanda remained steadfast in her conviction that her husband, a heretofore healthy and vibrant young man with no underlying medical conditions that might hinder his recovery (Wu), would soon come back home to her and little Elvis.

Yet, aside from some brief moments of marginal improvement, Nick's condition did not substantially improve. In the course of Nick's bout with Covid-19, he experienced a myriad of severe ancillary complications,

105

including two mini strokes, an episode of septic shock, a lung infection, the introduction of a temporary pacemaker, and a tracheostomy (Frishberg; Kelley). As if Nick's ordeal wasn't harrowing enough already, blood clots had formed in his right leg, the result of his reliance on an ECMO (Extracorporeal Membrane Oxygenation) machine, a complex device which removes carbon dioxide from a person's blood, then repumps freshly oxygenated blood back to the individual (Stump; Mayo Clinic Staff). This blood clotting eventuated in a drastic and especially heart-breaking development considering Nick's talent as a multi-hyphenate actor, singer, and dancer: in order to save Nick's life, doctors had no choice but to amputate his right leg (Stump).

Throughout this period of excruciating tribulation and unconscionable heartache that would surely be enough to test the resolve of people with even the strongest of constitutions, Amanda prayed for a miracle and held out hope in her darkest hour that Nick would return to her. She "spoke" to her husband in the language that both of them fluently understood and which intrinsically bound them together: music. She sought solace by dancing to one of Nick's songs that he had recorded, "Live Your Life," because she knew it was a subliminal lifeline to her beloved husband. Amanda also tapped into the power of social media in an effort to release her grief into the world, looking to her multitudes of "friends" who might provide a shoulder for her to cry on. Who cares if such a shoulder was virtual? She provided updates to her scores of Instagram followers regarding Nick's journey, posting frequent videos and progress reports. This being the age of Twitter, a hashtag was soon created that united everyone everywhere in their support for Nick: #WakeUpNick. Viral blessings for Nick, Amanda, and Elvis poured in from around the world as well-wishers across continents began to dance to "Live Your Life" every day at three o'clock in the afternoon, which represented a sort of moment of unified pleading for Nick's rehabilitation.

Many of the cast members of A Bronx Tale joined in a video prayer for their sick brother-in-arms (Kloots, "A Bronx Tale Cast in Prayer for Nick"). Nick's colleagues from the Broadway musical Waitress produced a touching testimonial in which they recorded a cover version of "Live Your Life" (Kloots, "Waitress–'Live Your Life'"). A GoFundMe campaign was quickly created in mid-April in order to assist the family with Nick's medical expenses (Nugent). Scores of people living in the ether, unknown to Kloots, uploaded videos of themselves dancing to "Live Your Life" in solidarity with the family in crisis. #WakeUpNick had transcended a mere call for support for an infirmed actor and his family and became a collective anthem for all those individuals who were hospitalized or otherwise suffering from this novel, frustrating, and terrifying illness and for all of the heroic medical personnel that were on the frontlines to care for them.

As the Covid-19 pandemic raged throughout the spring and summer of 2020, Nick remained encamped at Cedars-Sinai fighting for his life. As his complications with Covid continued, his prognoses were sometimes good, sometimes not so much. Yet the global community united and rallied in support. In a time of political and social upheaval, it didn't matter where on the socio-political spectrum you lived; everyone wanted Nick to get better and go home to Amanda and Elvis. This illness wasn't supposed to happen to someone like Nick. He was a man in the prime of his life: healthy, happy, with everything to live for. We begged for Nick to wake up and return home to his wife and young son. We grieved with Amanda and marveled at her unwavering strength and inhumanly positive attitude in the face of such an overwhelming crisis. We needed Nick to recover, in part, because in the back of all of our minds, if Covid could happen to someone like Nick Cordero, it could happen to absolutely anyone. Nick was all of us.

Finally, on July 5, 2020, Amanda Kloots posted the following message, in part, to her Instagram feed:

> God has another angel in heaven now. My darling husband passed away this morning. He was surrounded in love by his family, singing and praying as he gently left this earth [Kloots, "Nick Cordero"].

Nick Cordero was forty-one years old.

Within the narrative of the disaster film, Nick Cordero would occupy the position of what I refer to as the Poignant Character, a character whose death constitutes a particularly emotional and tragic point within the story. Disaster films are certainly not the only genre or subgenre in cinema in which there exists a character whose death might be seen as occupying a similar narrative role; Shelby in *Steel Magnolias*, a comedy-drama, might be considered an example. In some ways, it might seem as though a perceptible moment of schmaltz or syrupiness doesn't belong in a disaster movie, a type of entertainment, as we have previously discussed, that owes much of its cinematic heredity to the action and thriller genres. And after all, the studio marketing and promotions departments responsible for developing a movie's marketing plan most often focus on the spectacular elements of the disaster film: the special effects, the Primary Disaster, the thriller aspects. It is the promise of an impressive and exciting, one-of-a-kind spectacle, first and foremost, that studio powers that be are hoping will attract ticket buyers.

Let's take a look at the Poignant Characters, if present, in the disaster films we are studying here.

Title	Poignant Character
Airport	D.O. Guerrero (Van Heflin)
The Andromeda Strain	n/a
Skyjacked	n/a
The Poseidon Adventure	Mrs. Rosen (Shelley Winters)
Airport 1975	Scott Freeman (Dana Andrews)
Earthquake	Royce (Lorne Greene)
The Towering Inferno	Lisolette (Jennifer Jones)
Flood	Alice Cutler (Teresa Wright)
The Cassandra Crossing	Kaplan (Lee Strasberg)
Airport '77	Martin Wallace (Christopher Lee)
Fire	Doc Bennett (Lloyd Nolan)
The Swarm	Paul (Christian Juttner)
Avalanche	Mrs. Shelby (Jeanette Nolan)
The Concorde…. Airport '79	n/a
City on Fire	Nurse Harper (Shelley Winters)
Meteor	General Adlon (Martin Landau)
Disaster on the Coastliner	n/a
Cave-In!	n/a
Speed	Harry (Jeff Daniels)
Outbreak	Casey (Kevin Spacey)

Title	Poignant Character
Twister	Meg (Lois Smith)
Independence Day	Jimmy (Harry Connick, Jr.)
Daylight	George (Stan Shaw)
Dante's Peak	Ruth (Elizabeth Hoffman)
Volcano	Stan (John Carroll Lynch)
Titanic	n/a
Deep Impact	Oren Monash (Ron Eldard)
Armageddon	Max (Ken Hudson Campbell)
The Core	Braz (Delroy Lindo)
The Day After Tomorrow	Frank (Jay O. Sanders)
Snakes on a Plane	Grace (Lin Shaye)
2012	Harry Helmsley (Blu Mankuma) & Tony Delgatto (George Segal)—the pair counts as one
Contagion	SPLIT: Dr. Mears (Kate Winslet) and Dr. Hextall (Jennifer Ehle)
San Andreas	Dr. Kim Park (Will Yun Lee)
Geostorm	Cheng (Daniel Wu)
Greenland	Dale (Scott Glenn)
The Sibylline Scourge	Nick Cordero

The Poignant Character is a defining characteristic of any standard disaster film and should be included within the narrative in order to truly attempt to qualify as such. I have found throughout my research that there really are only a handful of disaster films that can get away with being called a disaster movie that do not include even the most nominal Poignant Character. These movies include: *The Andromeda Strain, Skyjacked,*

The Concorde.... Airport '79, Disaster on the Coastliner, Cave-In!, and *Titanic.*

With this in mind, there are a few salient characteristics that ought to be met (though naturally, there will be variations, as there always are) in order for a story character to be deemed the Poignant Character. These characteristics, described in more detail further in this chapter, include the following:

- The Poignant Character must be a notable and prominent character, though crucially, not an identifiable lead character or primary protagonist.
- The Poignant Character's death should ideally be in the service of an extreme self-sacrifice in order that the other members of the core group of survivors have a better chance of making it through the disaster alive.
- While the specific cause and/or manner of death does not need to be conveyed in any particularly spectacular fashion, the incidence of the Poignant Character should have its own stand-alone scene. The character's death needs to elicit marked sorrow from a majority of the core group of survivors, reminding them of their own mortality and incentivizing them to push through the disaster and make it out alive. In doing so, they honor the memory of the Poignant Character.

Let's take a moment and examine these three criteria in more detail.

Prominence

I have previously indicated that a qualifying mark of a Poignant Character is that he or she cannot be the main protagonist in the story. As a supporting character, the Poignant Character has specific motivations and flaws that must draw identification and/or sympathy from the audience; the audience must always be on the side of the Poignant Character. It follows that the Poignant Character can, thus, never be the villain of the piece. Unless, of course, it is perceived that underneath the nefariousness, the villain is really a good person and his or her character arc reveals the same, as in the case of General Adlon (Martin Landau) in *Meteor.* But such circumstances are rare.

The main protagonist in any disaster film would be, of course, the largest role in the movie. With most commercial filmmaking, this role is typically played by the most recognizable (and, more often than not, most expensive) marquee name in the cast: Charlton Heston, Gene Hackman,

Bruce Willis, Dustin Hoffman, etc. Even so, there are instances in disaster films wherein the filmmakers flip the script and in which the main protagonist, the lead, meets their fate. So, while the lead actor may, sometimes, perish in the picture, their death won't be until the very end if they do (Heston in *Earthquake*, Hackman in *The Poseidon Adventure*, Willis in *Armageddon*). The protagonist is the tendon that holds together the connective tissue of the film; the person who, whether they live or die, must endure the proceedings all the way through to, just about, the finish.

Oftentimes, a major movie star will come to a film carrying negative personal baggage or backstage drama reported in the press or tabloids that might sway a viewer's opinion of them too far one way before the picture even begins. As a result, the requisite sympathetic allegiance that must be formed with the Poignant Character might risk being compromised, thereby rendering the star-as-Poignant Character casting ineffectual (for example, Gwyneth Paltrow in *Contagion*). In most cases, the Poignant Character is therefore played by an actor that is either (a) moderately recognizable; they have been in a few, perhaps many, projects but hasn't yet booked that breakthrough role that will catapult them to the level of superstar (Kevin Spacey, in *Outbreak*, for example*), or (b) a popular character actor that has carved a career out of being a character actor; a character role that is, by definition, not intended to be filled by someone with name recognition but who is definitely recognizable from other projects (Elizabeth Hoffman in *Dante's Peak*), or (c) an actor that is well past their prime but is, perhaps, eager to be a part of the project and would be recognizable, particularly by a certain age demographic of the audience, from popular past projects (Jennifer Jones in *The Towering Inferno*). This particular person might also be understood as contributing a touch of class to what is, when you really break it down, a piece of mainstream popcorn entertainment (Helen Hayes in *Airport*, Lee Strasberg in *The Cassandra Crossing*, Olivia de Havilland in *The Swarm*). By denying a current major box office name casting in the role of the Poignant Character, filmmakers remove the potential of incoming preconceptions of a performer and any actor's off-screen association remains clean in order to allow for the crucial audience sympathy that the Poignant Character must engender.

---

*At the time of the release of *Outbreak* in 1995, Spacey had appeared in supporting roles in major films such as *Working Girl* (Mike Nichols, 1988), *Henry & June* (Philip Kaufman, 1990), and *Glengarry Glen Ross* (James Foley, 1992). Immediately prior to *Outbreak*, Spacey appeared in what remains one his most famous projects, *The Usual Suspects* (Bryan Singer, 1996), for which he would win an Oscar for Best Actor in a Supporting Role, although *Outbreak* was released first. Spacey would eventually win an Oscar for Best Actor in a Leading Role a few years later, for Sam Mendes's *American Beauty* (1999) ("Kevin Spacey").

Self-Sacrifice

While it is not always the case, the death of the Poignant Character should ideally be framed as a self-sacrifice that the character is undertaking in order that the other members of the core group of survivors have a greater chance of survival (John Carroll Lynch as Stan in *Volcano* or Lin Shaye as Grace in *Snakes on a Plane*). For this reason, the death of the Poignant Character cannot be in vain; the core group of survivors and/or the filmic society at large must see the Poignant Character's death as a reason, a motivation to keep moving through to their hopeful and eventual rescue. In *Daylight*, tunnel security guard George (Stan Shaw) lies incapacitated with a broken neck in the exploded-out Holland Tunnel once he is rescued from becoming trapped underneath an overturned vehicle. Realizing that, due to his incapacitation, any attempt to tow him to safety will cause significant burden on the core group of survivors, George advises Kit Latura that the only prospect Kit and the others have of survival is that they leave him behind and forge ahead without him, leaving him to perish alone in the tunnel. George's final words to Kit, "Get them to daylight. Don't let them die in this place. Tell them I'm gone" (*Daylight* 01:24:25–33).

Even if the self-sacrifice is in the service of the character's job description (for instance, if the character is a police officer or a fireman), it can nonetheless be regarded as self-sacrifice. Here, the Poignant Character is sacrificing his or her safety just as they might on any other day. Except that in this instance, they will make the ultimate sacrifice with the intention of somehow quelling the disaster. For example, in *Speed*, Harry (Jeff Daniels) is a cop attempting to make a bust when the house he is searching, having been booby-trapped by the story's villain, Howard Payne (Dennis Hopper), instantly explodes, killing him as well as several other cops participating in the siege.

The selflessness of the Poignant Character also works towards fostering the necessary audience sympathy towards the character. When George asks Kit to take the bracelet he is keeping for Grace (Vanessa Bell Calloway) and gift it to her once Kit is safely rescued (and he is, presumably, dead), he divulges with labored breathing that he never got the chance to tell Grace that he loved her. In a supremely melodramatic moment, George reflects upon the things in life that he wishes he had accomplished, a common and extremely relatable lamentation for anyone contemplating their own mortality (*Daylight* 1:23:36–24:22).

Stand-Alone Scene

The Poignant Character's death should have a dedicated scene. Since it will, theoretically, elicit a tremendous amount of audience sympathy, it stands to reason that the Poignant Character's death scene should garner an especially melodramatic episode unto itself. It works against the concept of managing audience sympathy for a supposedly compassionate character to have their big scene be staged as nothing more than a throwaway episode. If Paul Durant had been left alone in his hospital room to die, rather than accompanied by an extraordinarily sorrowful Capt. Anderson holding vigil, the audience would have no identifier against which to measure their grief. Similarly, if George in *Daylight* had simply been allowed to unceremoniously drown in the tunnel, there would have been a fatal dearth of humanity in the film. Furthermore, and more basically, the movie would likely have appeared rushed, moving rather perfunctorily towards the conclusion. While a frantic race might suffice as an ostensible marketing tagline for an action movie (we've already discussed how the disaster film engages elements of action-adventure), without a necessary moment of deceleration like the Poignant Character death scene, the narrative thrust into the final act would be castrated.

In order to provide this desired lull in the narrative prior to the third and final act, and to provoke maximum sympathy from the audience, the scene in the disaster film in which the Poignant Character expires must be staged for optimal melodramatic effect. In accomplishing this, a filmmaker might choose to stage this as an old-fashioned "died in my arms" scene, such as that of Mrs. Rosen's death in *The Poseidon Adventure*. Or rather, a filmmaker might elect to stage a smaller scale version of the slow build prior to a massive explosion (or other such catastrophe) wherein or through which the character dies (Harry's death in *Speed*, Stan Olber's death in *Volcano*).

The sole purpose of the Poignant Character within the context of the disaster film is to allow for a feeling and an instance of melancholy and melodrama in the course of the proceedings. While the entire film is predicated around a disaster in one form or another—environmental, biological, etc.—and as such, many, sometimes hordes of people must perish, the Poignant Character evokes a unique sort of sympathy in the cast of characters as well as from the audience. The audience should be able to say to itself, "Oh no, not So-and-So." A tremendous sense of loss and grief must be felt when this particular character's death comes. *The Towering Inferno*, *Volcano*, and other bona fide disaster movies will always have an identifiable Poignant Character. In *The Towering Inferno*, this trope can arguably be personified by the Jennifer Jones character, Lisolette, whose motherly instinct snaps into action to protect the little girl she's holding from plummeting to her death when the elevator they are in is blown from its tracks. In sacrificing her safety so that the little girl can live, Lisolette falls to her own death and cements her status in the film as the Poignant Character. In

Volcano, the Poignant Character is obviously Stan, who intentionally sentences himself to a particularly horrendous death by melting in order to save the life of the anonymous and unconscious subway driver before he surely perishes. And in our own *The Sibylline Scourge*, this character trope presents itself in the form of Broadway actor Nick Cordero, who put up one hell of a fight while battling Covid-19, before succumbing to this novel and contemptible disease in July of 2020, leaving behind a grieving widow and young son.

Like most templates, within the scopes of each individual criterion, there is room for customization. Depending upon the size and breadth of the disaster film in question, for example, there may be more than one character that qualifies as a potential Poignant Character (*The Swarm*, *Independence Day*, *2012*, all employ several possible candidates for the role of the Poignant Character). This isn't necessarily a filmmaker trying to reinvent the genre; it's more a matter of relative numbers. When you consider the larger cast of principal characters in a disaster movie, the more people there are to die. Ultimately, it's all about giving the audience its money's worth of spectacle.

In another variation on the trope of the Poignant Character, we may come across instances in which two separate characters taken together as a whole embody the three marked criteria that I have outlined above in reference to an ideal Poignant Character. Such is the case with *Contagion*.

Lastly, the seemingly paradoxical choice might be made by the filmmaker of a disaster film to include a Poignant Character that doesn't, in fact, perish. This character may encounter such severe hardship or, perhaps, be dealt such a crippling, but not fatal, blow that such an event in and of itself might change their physical makeup or alter their character irreparably, eliciting the required audience sympathy. This occurs with the character of Oren Monash (Ron Eldard) in *Deep Impact*.

Let's take a closer look at the circumstances surrounding the Poignant Character in both *Contagion* and *Deep Impact*.

Two Characters That Together Form a Poignant Character: Contagion

In this film, we are presented with the character of Dr. Erin Mears (Kate Winslet), an epidemic intelligence service officer, sent by the Centers for Disease Control and Prevention (CDC) to investigate the outbreak of the mysterious and rapidly intensifying illness affecting the city of Minneapolis. Mears is all business, dedicated to documenting the outbreak and determining the best course of action to take in mitigating its spread. She is not presented as someone who is at all "warm and fuzzy," although that certainly may be a component of her character in the world outside of the immediate story. As it stands, Mears is not by any means a malicious presence, but she is, nonetheless, on the scene to do a job, and do it quickly with as little interference as possible in order that lives may potentially be saved.

Concurrently, we encounter Dr. Ally Hextall (Jennifer Ehle), an epidemiologist with the CDC whose job involves working closely in tandem with Dr. Ellis Cheever, the head of the CDC. Dr. Hextall, like Dr. Mears, is nothing but business, intent on researching the origins of this mysterious bug and, once uncovered, formulating a vaccine with which to prevent it from taking hold in a host. While Dr. Hextall, again like Dr. Mears, is not exactly what one would term "warm and fuzzy," she is presented in a slightly softer light than Mears. This is especially pronounced in a moment late in the film where she has a tender heart-to-heart with her ailing father.

Both Dr. Mears and Dr. Hextall each possess certain traits that, if they were to be combined as one character, would make an ideal Poignant Character in a disaster film. For example, while no one in this film can be considered a true "lead" (it's too much of an ensemble piece to fairly designate a male or female lead, though Matt Damon and Kate Winslet come closest, I suppose), both Dr. Mears and Dr. Hextall each have the prominence required of the Poignant Character. Each is a substantial supporting character with specific motivations and functions within the diegesis. It would be a tremendous loss for and create great sympathy within the filmic society if either character were to perish.

Which is the fate that eventually befalls Dr. Mears. She winds up contracting the illness and, while quarantined in a makeshift medical ward housed in a cavernous hangar, slowly succumbs to its effects. To that end, one could assume that, in a traditional sense, Dr. Mears's death would qualify her by virtue of her death to be an appropriate Poignant Character. Except for the fact that there is no melodramatic core surrounding her character. There is nothing for the audience to emotionally connect with in the character of Dr. Mears. She is a good doctor and wants, like all of the doctors in this story, to get to the bottom of this illness. However, other than being a good and diligent doctor, there is no sentimental characteristic for which the audience can cling to in sympathy should the character perish.

So, while Dr. Mears has the stand-alone death scene, Dr. Hextall has the instance of self-sacrifice. Knowing that clinical human trials of the newly developed potential vaccine would take months and occupy an extraordinary amount of time that no one can spare as the disease rages on, Dr. Hextall makes the fateful decision to use herself as a guinea pig and injects herself with a dose of the potential vaccine. Dr. Hextall is very clearly electing to sacrifice her own life for the cause of stopping the devastating effect this illness is having all over the world. She realizes that she could, in fact, die should the vaccine be ineffective. Or even worse, cause some sort of side effect that results in her death. There are all sorts of sound reasons to not use oneself as a guinea pig in a clinical trial such as that which accompanies the development of a vaccine. But Dr. Hextall knows that the world is running out of time. In her mind, using herself as a test subject makes the most sense (*Contagion* 01:15:33–16:12).

Following the scene in which she injects herself with the proposed vaccine, Dr. Hextall goes to visit her father in the hospital, where he is laid up with the illness. Knowing that this may potentially be the last time she sees him, she sits down at her dad's bedside and removes her face covering, much to her dad's dissent. This is a tender scene between father and daughter. She softly explains to him that she has given herself the shot, and the two sentimentalize about old times in a scene reminiscent of countless of other similar scenes between a dying parent and child or dying child and parent (*Contagion* 01:16:12–18:09). In the case of Dr. Hextall, however, she survives and the vaccine for the illness is rendered effective. She has saved the world.

The selfless attitude and occasion of self-sacrifice, along with the moment with her father referenced above, allows the audience to connect with the character of Dr. Hextall on quite an emotional level.

The point is that the emotional connection absent in the character of Dr. Mears is present in the character of Dr. Hextall. More than any other aspect of the Poignant Character, the emotional component is, perhaps, the most important. It is the clear sympathy that the audience is directed to feel for the Poignant Character and their melodrama that makes them "poignant" after all. Apart, neither Dr. Mears (prominence, stand-alone death scene, no sacrifice or emotional connection) nor Dr. Hextall (prominence, sacrifice or emotional connection, no stand-alone death scene) can truly be designated as *Contagion*'s Poignant Character. If the characters of Dr. Mears and Dr. Hextall were to be combined as one, however, we would have a dynamite Poignant Character.

However, in rolling up both Dr. Mears and Dr. Hextall into the role of the Poignant Character, we encounter a problem. Now, I would argue that Winslet and Ehle both share the female leads in *Contagion*. Thus, in this way, the movie violates a major tenet of the disaster film as we have so far defined it in this book: the leading character (male or female) cannot be the Poignant Character. Be that as it may, I'm not intending to state that Soderbergh's rendering of his story to not include a black-and-white Poignant Character is somehow a bad or misdirected attribute of his movie.

Rather, his and screenwriter Scott Z. Burns's project simply harkens back to what I have said previously with regard to there being room available for creative editorialization in disaster films (or any film, for that matter). The inclusion of both characters and their fates is a creative choice that provides a unique interpretation of the role of the Poignant Character.

The Poignant Character That Doesn't Die: Deep Impact

In *Deep Impact*, the first of 1998's two summer blockbusters orbiting around a space rock on a collision course with the Earth (the other being *Armageddon*), an obstacle has arisen for the crew tasked with rescuing the Earth from an impending and fateful date with a comet. A drilling unit known as a mole, affixed with a nuclear explosive, is being used to tunnel down into the comet. Once in place and upon detonation, the mole will blow the comet to smithereens. However, as it is burrowing deeper and deeper into the rock, the mole becomes stuck in the wall of the comet. Unfortunately, the device hasn't drilled far enough down to make any significant impact should it be detonated at its stuck depth. Somehow, the mole must be wedged free from the comet wall so that it can continue to pore deeper and blow the comet up. Assessing the time-sensitivity of the crisis, Oren volunteers to rappel into the channel that has been burrowed thus far by the drill with the intention of physically freeing the mole from its stuck position. A risky venture, to be sure, but Oren can see no other way with which to remedy the situation.

This plan is all well and good in theory, except for the life-threatening fact that Oren and his fellow astronauts on the drilling expedition have an extremely finite amount of time with which to get the drill into its position and then skedaddle back to their ship before the sun comes up. If they're still working come sunrise, they will, quite literally, be toast.

Oren dives in, and as soon as he reaches the stuck mole, he begins to yank and pull and even jump up and down on it in an effort to loosen it from the comet's wall. Of course, *Deep Impact* being a PG-13 disaster piece of mainstream entertainment requiring some tense moments to keep the audience on the edges of their seats, the time that Oren expends on his mission to free the mole comes right down to the wire; the approaching horizon encroaches upon the group with the finality of subway doors closing as you run to make it onto the car in time. An indicator on the ship that is counting down the moments until the sunrise hits speeds closer and closer to the zero hour as another screen flashes, "Horizon Approaching."

Finally, Oren is able to loosen the mole and he moves to hightail it out of the crevasse, but it appears to be too late. The horizon is closing in on the group. The indicator screen now flashes "Horizon Bridged." The group is out of time. The team applies its sun-blocking face visors. Alarms are now sounding as the countdown timer flashes 00:00:00 and the "Horizon Bridged" screen furiously follows suit. Oren bursts past the threshold of the comet's surface, but gravity almost immediately turns him towards the sun. Oren, however, does not have his face visor down like the others, and his eyes are instantly singed. By the time he closes his sun-blocking visor, it is too late: the exposure has rendered him blind (*Deep Impact* 00:49:26–54:20).

Blind, but not dead. The death in this scene belongs to the character of fellow astronaut Gus Partenza (played by Jon Favreau). With the comet's gas jets bursting from the surface as the sun quickly rises, enveloping the comet in dangerous sunlight, the astronauts return to the ship, hurrying along as best they can in lumbersome spacesuits. As a scientist on one of the newscasts covering the event indicates, remaining on the surface at this point "must be like trying to work in a minefield" (*Deep Impact* 00:50:25–27). Indeed, it is. When Gus unknowingly "steps" on one of the comet's exploding gas jets, he is instantly propelled into deep space and is gone forever (00:55:01–07).

Because he is so suddenly and tragically lost to space and time, it would be easy to peg Gus Partenza as the Poignant Character in *Deep Impact*. There is even a certain amount of the requisite narrative grief in the film immediately following Partenza's death, much of it conveyed via a business-like but respectful obituary heard over a sorrowful musical score and rendered by lead character, MSNBC reporter Jenny Lerner (Téa Leoni).

But despite the fact that Oren and his fellow astronauts on this mission will ultimately sacrifice themselves by piloting the ship into the core of the comet in order to explode it from the inside (the initial attempt having failed), the blinding of Oren Monash positions him as a particularly heartbreaking Poignant Character due chiefly to the enormously pulled heartstrings of the audience as a result of his accident. You see, the viewer has been informed in an earlier scene that Oren's wife, Mariette, is pregnant. Later on, towards the end of the movie, just before the astronauts undertake their suicide mission, all of them are granted the opportunity to bid farewell to their loved ones via satellite link-up. Mariette and her newborn baby, little Oren, so named after his father, appear on the ship's screen. In a scene milked for every ounce of sentiment it can get, big Oren is introduced to his newborn son, a son who he would never get to see were he to survive this mission but will now never get to see nor hold. Oren hears his son's voice, and he smiles with pride as his eyes well with tears, the hopes and dreams of a new father for his son all telegraphed at once in this instance. He reaches his hand to touch the screen as Mariette holds the young baby to the screen on her end. The two Monash men, father and son, share a connective subliminal moment that passes between the two of them before the connection is lost (*Deep Impact* 01:49:16–50:38). Eldard's skill as an actor allows him to truly sell this moment and no matter what you think of this movie (for the record, I do not care for *Deep Impact* at all—I find it manipulative and boring), there is little denying the fact that this is a touching scene. Only an audience member with a cold, black, breaking heart would be able to resist the sentiment of the moment. Despite Oren's eventual death along with those of his fellow astronauts, I would argue that due to the extraordinarily moving situation surrounding Oren's blindness and the fact that he will never meet his newborn son, along with the fact that all of the astronauts and many of the supporting characters in this film meet their fates as well, Oren Monash serves as the most qualified Poignant Character in this particular disaster film.

However, no matter the generic variation or convention mash-up, if there is one character that, more so than any other in the disaster film canon, personifies the concept of the Poignant Character, I think that everyone will agree that it is Shelley Winters as Mrs. Rosen in *The Poseidon Adventure.*

The Quintessential Poignant Character: Shelley Winters in The Poseidon Adventure

In this classic film, Mr. and Mrs. Rosen (Albertson and Winters) are a congenial and grandparently couple embarking on this romantic, luxury cruise as the first part of a larger voyage to Israel, where they will finally meet their two-year-old grandson.

The Rosens, as well as the rest of our core group of survivors, have entrusted their faith in the Reverend Scott to lead them to safety following the horrific capsizing of the S.S. *Poseidon* due to the massive tidal wave which, in turn, was caused by an underwater earthquake. At approximately one hour and twenty-five minutes into the film, the group, on its perilous journey from the ship's ballroom to its hull (or, from the "top" of the ship to the "bottom"), encounters an impasse: a corridor leading to the engine room, which the Reverend Scott had previously targeted as a passage to the hull, is now totally submerged. It seems that the only possible solution to this magnificent obstacle is for someone in the group to perform a dangerous underwater swim so a rope may be affixed to the bulkhead on the other side in order that the others can pull their way to safety one by one.

Having been a championship swimmer in her youth (she was, in fact, the Underwater Swimming Champ of New York), Mrs. Rosen sees this trial as her opportunity to repay the group in the only way she can for having been, she feels, a burden throughout the voyage. She is not a spry, agile young woman anymore and she feels a tremendous sense of guilt at, perhaps, slowing down the progress of the group due to her heft coupled with her age. Underwater breath control is a specific skill that she can confidently say she possesses more so than any other member of the group. This underwater swim is a specific exercise that she knows, in her gut, that she can handle (*The Poseidon Adventure* 1:25:53–26:54).

Shelley Winters's Golden Globe-winning and Oscar-nominated supporting turn as Mrs. Rosen is arguably the most famous example of a Poignant Character in a disaster film, and for good reason: the character ticks all of the check boxes we have discussed that pertain to this chapter's definition of the character trope. For this reason, it is easy to apprehend why Mrs. Rosen takes the crown for the quintessential Poignant Character in a disaster film.

Mrs. Rosen Had Prominence

For starters, it's as basic as the casting: Mrs. Rosen is played by Shelley Winters, a two-time Academy Award-winning actress.* But in 1972, Winters was in her 50s and was probably no longer in quite the same demand for the put-upon wives and jilted girlfriends she had portrayed in movies like *The Night of the Hunter* (Charles Laughton, 1955) and *A Place in the Sun* (George Stevens, 1951). Her casting in *The Poseidon Adventure* lent a certain cachet to the movie, while, simultaneously, offering younger, and definitely more commercially desirable, audiences an introduction to an esteemed character actress not regularly used in major popular entertainments such as *The Poseidon Adventure*.

Winters's Mrs. Rosen was by no means the lead role in *The Poseidon Adventure*; that honor went to Gene Hackman as the Reverend Scott. However, her screen prominence and outsized, blustery performance as Mrs. Rosen ensured that she was by far the most memorable character in the film. Significantly, this is the primary reason why the Reverend Scott cannot be designated as an appropriate Poignant Character, despite his self-sacrificial death in the film's final act. Hackman is the clear protagonist in the film and is played by a current (at the time) and very notable leading man. Hackman had won the Oscar for Best Actor in a Leading

---

*Best Actress in a Supporting Role—1960, *The Diary of Anne Frank* (George Stevens, 1959), and Best Actress in a Supporting Role—1966, *A Patch of Blue* (Guy Green, 1965) ("Shelley Winters").

Role for *The French Connection* the year prior to *The Poseidon Adventure*'s release ("Gene Hackman").

While the Reverend Scott's death during the finale of *The Poseidon Adventure* might lead one to ponder that he could make an appropriate Poignant Character, and indeed, his death includes many of the elements of the Poignant Character, the Reverend Scott's death must disqualify him as the Poignant Character for a few reasons. Firstly, Gene Hackman is the headliner in the film, plain and simple. His star status alone is enough to disqualify him as the Poignant Character. Secondly, it is true that the Reverend Scott does, indeed, commit the ultimate act of self-sacrifice by purposefully plunging into a fire in the engine room after closing a steam valve and encountering searing hot steam (*The Poseidon Adventure* 01:49:02), and his death does provide the final thrust for the core group of survivors, now minus Linda (Stella Stevens), to make it to the propeller shaft to anticipated safety. However, regardless of this selfless act of heroism, the Reverend Scott's death is less motivated by a call for sympathy from the group and more specifically and functionally orchestrated so that the hatch can open and allow the others to enter the propeller shaft. The movie ends quite soon thereafter with little explicit mourning of the Reverend Scott from the core group of survivors.

For these same reasons, Graff in *Earthquake* and Harry S. Stamper in *Armageddon* must also be disqualified as Poignant Characters.

Mrs. Rosen Elicited Audience Sympathy Due to Her Self-Sacrifice

Mrs. Rosen makes the ultimate sacrifice so that the other members of the core group of survivors have a better chance of making it through to the hull, and to the surface, alive.

At one point, it becomes clear that something has gone wrong with the Reverend Scott's first attempt to swim and secure the rope to the bulkhead. Mike Rogo, who is tethering the rope on the opposite end, can no longer detect any slack on the rope that the Reverend Scott has been pulling through the submerged corridor. Mrs. Rosen, admittedly a woman past her prime in terms of her athletic heyday, is convinced that, due to her past as a swimming champion, she alone possesses the necessary skill and training to endure such a taxing underwater swim. Despite her age and her diminished dexterity, yet comprehending the mortal urgency of the group's situation, Mrs. Rosen rises to call upon her sense-memory and her training in breath control, dive in, assess and remedy whatever issue is stalling the Reverend Scott, and successfully complete the task.

She does, indeed, rescue the Reverend Scott, who proceeds to tie off the rope to the bulkhead, but her now mature body simply cannot withstand the immediate aftermath of the rigorous swim. She dies a heroine, cradled in the Reverend Scott's arms (*The Poseidon Adventure* 01:28:23–32:23).

Throughout the film, the audience has grown to enjoy watching Mrs. Rosen make the journey to the top (bottom) of the overturned S.S. *Poseidon* and has been rooting for her success perhaps more so than any other member of the core group of survivors. Turning the archetype on its ear, Mrs. Rosen, a middle-aged grandmother, becomes an unlikely action heroine that conceivably reminds audience members of the almost unthinkably horrifying notion of their own beloved mothers or grandmothers undertaking the same journey. Consequently, Mrs. Rosen's death strikes a particularly melancholic note. Upon her death, the Reverend Scott cries out in anguish, "Not this woman!" (*The Poseidon Adventure* 01:32:30).

A short time after Mrs. Rosen's death, once the remaining members of the core group of survivors have successfully resurfaced in the engine room, the Reverend Scott reveals that he thinks he has found the group's means of escape: the propeller shaft. As he urges the others to follow him upwards, Rogo shouts at him in sheer exasperation. After all, Mrs. Rosen has just died. It is here that the Reverend Scott explains (as only someone with the authority of Gene Hackman can) that the group must stay strong and persevere, for it's what Mrs. Rosen would have wanted (*The Poseidon Adventure* 01:39:49–40:10). If the group only sits idle and wallows in its misfortune, her death will have been for naught. The assembly of the core group of survivors following Mrs. Rosen's death and the Reverend Scott's subsequent speech is the comedown that ultimately feeds into the surge of narrative energy that will propel the core group of survivors through the final hurdle to safety.

Mrs. Rosen's Death Scene Was a Stand-Alone Scene

No sooner has the Reverend Scott tied off the rope to the bulkhead than Mrs. Rosen begins to experience what appear to be agonizing abdominal pains. As sure as we know that when someone in a period drama so much as coughs, that person will die of consumption, we know Mrs. Rosen's pain will not be a run-of-the-mill cramp. She collapses into the water, whereupon the Reverend Scott immediately pulls her over to a steel beam upon which he rests her. Slowly, we watch as the heretofore formidable life force drains out of Mrs. Rosen. The scene lingers on Winters' face while Hackman watches helplessly as she draws her last breath, nestled in the comfort of his pious arms (*The Poseidon Adventure* 01:30:50–32:23). This is old-fashioned emotional histrionics at play.

This particular scene is layered with melodrama, designed to not leave a dry eye in the house. As the Reverend Scott cradles her head, Mrs.

Rosen pleads with him to allow her to die. "Let me go," she begs (*The Poseidon Adventure* 01:31:49). She asks that the Reverend Scott give her necklace to her husband, Manny, in order that he might bestow it on their grandson, the grandson she now realizes she will never get to meet (01:31:52–32:06). The inclusion of the necklace, which contains a charm consisting of the chai symbol, the Jewish letters (chet and yud) that together signify "To Life," is significant in underscoring the melodrama. Mrs. Rosen is passing on a charm symbolizing life, her life, to her young grandchild, via her still living husband to whom she will never have the chance to say goodbye. This sequence can be read as a sort of "circle of life" moment, but in the context of a disaster movie, it is more accurately understood as Mrs. Rosen literally sacrificing her life so that the others can live. She is bequeathing a shot at survival, a chance at life to the core group of survivors.

One by one, as each remaining member of the core group of survivors surfaces on the bulkhead and takes a breath, each of them reverently looks over at the dead body of Mrs. Rosen. Manny, the first of the remaining group to resurface, sobs as he lovingly clutches his deceased wife's head. Eventually, the entire remaining cast presents in the engine room and takes a moment before the surge to reflect upon Mrs. Rosen and the sacrifice she has made so that the rest of them have a likelier chance of survival (*The Poseidon Adventure* 01:38:00–39:48).

As I have indicated earlier in this chapter, of the three criteria that I have pointed to which should be met in order to qualify as an appropriate Poignant Character, it is the evocation of audience sympathy that can, perhaps, be construed to be the most defining factor. There are many people that are going to perish in a disaster movie; that's part of what makes said movie a "disaster" movie. But if there is no character in the narrative with which the audience can develop any sort of deep emotional resonance, then the net effect of the audience relationship to the characters in the story is that of just a bunch of nameless extras dying under horrible and unthinkable circumstances. Only the most sadistic personality would endeavor to watch that.

Meaningless and macabre deaths are the province of horror movies, like *The Texas Chainsaw Massacre* (Marcus Nispel, 2003), slasher movies like the *Friday the 13th* series, or the oeuvre of musician-turned-filmmaker, Rob Zombie, the writer-director behind 2003's *House of 1000 Corpses* and 2005's *The Devil's Rejects*. More recently, numerous ghastly (and, to give credit to the filmmakers where credit is due, creative) deaths have been the province of a relatively new subgenre of the horror film: so-called "torture porn" flicks, such as *Saw* (James Wan, 2004) or *Hostel* (Eli Roth, 2005), and their related sequels. The torture porn subgenre is a rather dubious cinematic subgenre to say the least. You see, these types of movies revel in and celebrate the gory and heinous, daring audiences to avert their eyes in disgust. I would hazard a guess that the audiences of the *Saw* movies, the *Hostel* movies, etc., are not necessarily seeking to sympathize with the characters in these movies, but rather they are expecting to elicit a perverse glee in watching them be systematically eviscerated. Much of the scenes depicting character deaths in movies of this type are over-the-top, outlandish, and almost comical in their effect. The game that is played by the audience in a torture porn movie is not so much of the "who will and who won't survive?" type that is enjoyed by the audience of a disaster movie (Keane 5), but a much darker and more morbid game of which character is going to receive the most painful, gruesome, and ugly disemboweling or dismemberment. The underlying amusement for an audience member might be similar in a disaster movie as in a torture porn movie, but the avenue and intention of that amusement's procurement is vastly different. While the staging of some death scenes in disaster movies may be harrowing—for instance, falling to one's death or being blown to pieces by an explosion—they will not be portrayed as overly graphic. You are more likely to see one character's horrific *reaction* to another character's death than the overt splat on the pavement or severed limbs you might see in a horror or torture porn movie. One might say that the disaster movie appeals to the average sportsman while torture porn appeals to the average sadist.

This is because disaster movies tend to be, more often than not, pieces of pop entertainment. They are released by major studios, or subsidiaries of major studios, whose sole objective (let's be honest) is to make money. A typical disaster movie rarely rises above a PG-13 rating (*Outbreak* is rated R, to name one anomalous example). Not that money can't be made from torture porn films, which are typically lower budgeted fare as far as major motion pictures go; Lionsgate clearly made a small mint from the *Saw* and *Hostel* franchises given the numerous sequels each movie had. But the big budgets and expensive stars normally procured for disaster movies mean that more is at stake for a studio to make money, or at least, make any sort of return on its investment. In order to do that, the movie produced must be exhibited as a wide release to thousands of theaters worldwide and appeal to much more generalized audiences than the niche audiences a movie like *Saw* or *Hostel* will appeal to. That's why the inclusion of characters in a disaster film such as Lisolette, Harry, or Stan are so crucial to the disaster film. In the course of the drama, the Poignant Character engages the audience's sympathy in a more melodramatic, more heart-tugging fashion than characters in a horror movie ever really could.

This is why, despite the fact that his death wasn't self-sacrificial in the way that Harry or Stan's was, Nick Cordero is a prime candidate for the Poignant Character in *The Sibylline Scourge*. His marriage to Amanda appeared, if her Instagram feed is anything to go by, idyllic. The two genuinely enjoyed one another, and their bond, their love for each other, seemed to be something that the average person would envy. They sang together, they danced together, they laughed together. The salad days for Nick and Amanda appeared as though they would be eternal. In an Instagram Live broadcast, Kloots said of her relationship with Nick, "We pushed each other's buttons in the best of ways" (Melas). These two clearly had what every true relationship should have: they brought out the best in each other.

Which is why it was especially devastating when Nick passed away on July 5, 2020, rendering Amanda Kloots a widow and leaving her to raise Elvis, left with only memories for him to know his father by. When considering a larger scale, Nick's illness and death resonated with the society at large in a big way. Covid-19's grip on Nick Cordero, a young and exuberant man, new father, and loving husband, was nothing short of a cruel dealing by the hands of fate. How malicious it was for this pathogen, this scourge on the face of the planet, to sink its evil into a man arguably in the prime of his life. The support Amanda received from Nick's colleagues in the theater community, as well as from strangers throughout the world, strengthened her spirits in what was, presumably, her darkest hour. People rallied in support of Nick's recovery and of Amanda, a woman who kept an incredibly positive attitude throughout her unthinkable ordeal. "It is honestly how I'm getting through this.... People I don't even know all over the world are joining me every day at 3 p.m. to sing his song so he can hear us," Kloots told TODAY (Stump).

So, Nick Cordero's death, in the context of *The Sibylline Scourge*, evokes widespread sympathy and grief from the society at large. The entire world seemingly mourned when Amanda announced Nick's death on her Instagram feed. The continuation of her July 5, 2020, Instagram post referenced at the beginning of this chapter follows:

> I am in disbelief and hurting everywhere. My heart is broken as I cannot imagine our lives without him. Nick was such a bright light. He was everyone's friend, loved to listen, help and especially talk. He was an incredible actor and musician. He loved his family and loved being a father and husband. Elvis and I will miss him in everything we do, everyday.
>
> To Nicks extraordinary doctor, Dr. David Ng, you were my positive doctor! There are not many doctors like you. Kind, smart, compassionate, assertive and always eager to listen to my crazy ideas or call yet another doctor for me for a second opinion. You're a diamond in the rough.
>
> I cannot begin to thank everyone enough for the outpour of love, support and help we've received these last 95 days. You have no idea how much you lifted my spirits at 3pm everyday as the world sang Nicks song, Live Your Life. We sang it to him today, holding his hands. As I sang the last line to him,

"they'll give you hell but don't you light [sic] them kill your light not without a fight. Live your life," I smiled because he definitely put up a fight. I will love you forever and always my sweet man [Kloots, "Nick Cordero"].

We have already discussed how the disaster film is particularly conducive to a hybridization of genres across the cinematic spectrum. In many respects, the Poignant Character is the melodramatic contribution to a disaster movie genre mash-up. The melodrama as a storytelling motif can be seen in various incarnations throughout history and European culture (Elsaesser 454). However, the melodrama, as we are currently and commonly familiar with the term, refers to a work that "is all but synonymous with a set of sub-genres that remain close to the hearth and emphasize a register of heightened emotionalism and sentimentality: the family melodrama, the maternal melodrama, the woman's film, the weepie, the soap opera, etc." (Singer 94).

However a filmmaker chooses to stage the death of the Poignant Character, the resultant effect on the audience must remain the same: to allow for a feeling and an instance of melancholy and melodrama; an instance of oversized emotion and introspection that occurs before, and perhaps explicitly instigates (as is the case in *The Poseidon Adventure*), the core group of survivors to muster strength and push through to the story's conclusion.

Nick Cordero's tragic death and the consequent outpouring of grief from individuals both inside and outside of the Broadway community, and really across the world, enforces further haste among the leaders of *The Sibylline Scourge* to rescue the survivors from the grip of this pandemic. The edicts have finally now been driven home that everyone must do their part, there is no room for interpretation: wear a mask, socially distance, avoid crowds, etc. No one, young or old, is immune. If Nick's death were to be construed as simply a footnote in the overall Covid-19 narrative with no import or sincerity attached (i.e., Amanda's gut-wrenching yet hopeful and paradoxically positive Instagram updates), this young father's death would hold no resonance. Instead, the core group of survivors, as well as the society at large, are bound to soldier on and to honor Nick's mighty and poignant consequence for the sake of *The Sibylline Scourge*.

CHAPTER 6

Proactive vs. Reactive

As the virus, having now been officially christened Covid-19, an acronym of "coronavirus disease 2019," so designated by the World Health Organization on February 11, 2020 (Centers for Disease Control and Prevention), further and further infiltrated the United States, our elected leaders sprang into action. (While the overall motives and the honorability of such leaders from jurisdictions across the country is not the focus of this book, this author certainly has his opinions!) School, restaurant, and venue closures, as well as public service shutdowns, social distancing, mask mandates, PPE—all were buzz terms heard and spoken at socially distant press conferences around the country during most of 2020. Some press conferences were occurring daily by governors, civic leaders, mayors, even the president of the United States, all in an ostensible effort to keep the public at large informed about this strange, novel coronavirus and what they could do to remain virus free. The daily press conferences of New York State Governor Andrew Cuomo, *The Sibylline Scourge*'s co-secondary lead, were must-see television during the first few months of the pandemic. Governor Cuomo's briefings became even more compelling once his kid brother, CNN journalist Chris Cuomo, began to interview the Governor regularly (the ethics of which would be called into question months later) on his popular CNN show, *Cuomo Prime Time*.

By this point in the narrative, an unmitigated atmosphere of chaos, coupled with uncertainty and confusion, covered New York City, as well as the nation, like a fine mist. The United States of America, heretofore a stalwart symbol of strength and fortitude, unbelievably began to shut down, something absolutely unthinkable just a few months earlier. The country was meekly conceding to the onslaught of a faceless invader that was very quickly overtaking our lives. Every cough and every sneeze was a cause for alarm. Just a normal wintry bout of feeling under the weather became a reason to panic and to get your affairs in order. The simple everyday act of washing one's hands assumed an entirely different type of urgency; not doing so could now very well mean the difference between life and death.

In early 2020, Governor Cuomo took the unprecedented and historic (there's that word again) step of "pausing" New York, a move which would thrust the state and, particularly, New York City into economic turmoil. On March 20, 2020, Cuomo signed an executive order authorizing the New York State on PAUSE (Policies that Assure Uniform Safety for Everyone) program. This program stipulated that, among other orders:

- "Effective at 8PM on Sunday, March 22, all non-essential businesses statewide will be closed."
- "Non-essential gatherings of individuals of any size for any reason (e.g., parties, celebrations or other social events) are canceled or postponed at this time."
- "Individuals should limit outdoor recreational activities to non-contact and avoid activities where they come in close contact with other people" ("Governor Cuomo Signs").

The New York State Governor also mandated specific guidelines for citizens over seventy years of age or who were otherwise thought to be vulnerable or at-risk, such as people who had weakened or compromised immune systems or carried underlying health conditions. Among the governor's orders to these most vulnerable constituents, which were, of course, seen as intended to ensure the safety of these at-risk members of the population, were to remain inside, not to use public transportation unless such a trip was deemed absolutely necessary, and to only venture outside for solitary exercise ("Governor Cuomo Signs"). Introverts everywhere had won.

Although these mandates were enacted solely for New York State, other states across the nation followed a similar suit. California, Connecticut, Maryland, even somewhat gonzo Florida, whose governor, Ron DeSantis, had previously been reluctant to place restrictions upon his constituents, all issued stay-at-home orders, albeit to varying degrees and lengths of time. Most states permitted residents to leave their homes for essential reasons, such as food shopping or to seek medical care or if their jobs were now classified as "essential" (Wu et al.). However, for the majority of Americans at this moment in time, the message was as clear as could be: don't go outside. If you do, you might catch a virus that could kill you. The situation in which the United States now found itself was nothing short of apocalyptic ... and terrifying.

The majority of the time during the cycle of disaster films in the 1970s, the undisputed heyday of the disaster subgenre, the Primary Disaster was a showstopping sight to behold (Shaer, "Canonical Films" 9). The sequence depicting the capsizing of the S.S. *Poseidon* surely must have been an awesome cinematic spectacle for audiences in 1972. Indeed, the visual effects in *The Poseidon Adventure* even won a Special Achievement Award at the 1973 Academy Awards ("The Poseidon Adventure"). Hell, even contemporary critics such as David Fear of *Rolling Stone* are wont to laud the technical achievement of the spectacle in *The Poseidon Adventure*: "The effects here run the gamut from grandiose to goofy, but watch the upside-down ballroom sequence again. It's a set piece of pure destructive bliss, set to a symphony of screaming and breaking glass. Awesome" (Fear). The initial explosion of *The Towering Inferno* and the bombastic eight-minute earthquake sequence in *Earthquake* definitely set the bar for disaster showstoppers as subsequent disaster movies across the board tried to keep pace.

Yet, interestingly, in the 1970s cycle, the Primary Disaster, following its initial appearance, tended to take a backseat to the drama between the characters in the film as they battled the odds of survival and each other. Conversely, during the 1990s cycle of disaster films, audiences were treated to a more inflated spectacle, and the visuals required more grandeur in order to heighten the thrill for audiences that had, in the ensuing years since the 1970s, grown ever more increasingly numb to the proliferation of bloated special effects (Shaer, "Canonical Films" 9).

While I was in the process of conducting my research into the disaster films of the 1970s, 1990s, and later, I began to notice an overarching pattern present within each cycle I explored. What I uncovered was that there were, essentially, two avenues of societal response that were discernable in disaster narratives. In one scenario, following the incidence of the Primary Disaster, the disaster in question retreated to a backdrop position to the drama between the characters. This tactic, I noticed, was employed in the majority of 1970s disasters films, such as *The Poseidon Adventure* and *The Andromeda Strain*. At the same time, however, I noticed that there were films in which, subsequent to the Primary Disaster, the disasters remained all but centrally situated within the drama, almost as much a character as the ones portrayed by actors. This tactic, on the other hand, I would argue was seen more often in the 1990s cycle, in movies like *Speed* and *Dante's Peak*. This observation is outlined in the table below.

Title	Narrative Trajectory
Airport	Backdrop/Proactive
The Andromeda Strain	Backdrop/Proactive
Skyjacked	Backdrop/Proactive
The Poseidon Adventure	Backdrop/Proactive
Airport 1975	Backdrop/Proactive
Earthquake	Central/Reactive

Title	Narrative Trajectory
The Towering Inferno	Backdrop/Proactive
Flood	Backdrop/Proactive
The Cassandra Crossing	Backdrop/Proactive
Airport '77	Backdrop/Proactive
Fire	Backdrop/Proactive
The Swarm	Central/Reactive
Avalanche	Backdrop/Proactive
The Concorde.... Airport '79	Backdrop/Proactive
City on Fire	Central/Reactive
Meteor	Backdrop/Proactive
Disaster on the Coastliner	Backdrop/Proactive
Cave-In!	Backdrop/Proactive
Speed	Central/Reactive
Outbreak	Backdrop/Proactive
Twister	Central/Reactive
Independence Day	Backdrop/Proactive
Daylight	Central/Reactive
Dante's Peak	Central/Reactive
Volcano	Central/Reactive
Titanic	Central/Reactive
Deep Impact	Backdrop/Proactive
Armageddon	Backdrop/Proactive
The Core	Backdrop/Proactive
The Day After Tomorrow	Backdrop/Proactive
Snakes on a Plane	Central/Reactive
2012	Central/Reactive
Contagion	Backdrop/Proactive
San Andreas	Central/Reactive
Geostorm	Central/Reactive
Greenland	Central/Reactive
The Sibylline Scourge	Backdrop/Proactive

Further to this concept, when we are at work deconstructing in depth the plots that flesh out the stories in a disaster film, it becomes evident that whatever disaster film we are watching will fall into one of two narrative trajectories: one that is proactive, or one that is more reactive. This designation is important because it refers primarily to how the core group of survivors (i.e., the assemblage of characters that the audience is meant to empathize with the most during the course of the narrative) takes action following the onset of said disaster. A proactive or reactive narrative trajectory will dictate how the core group of survivors will react to its newfound and critical circumstance(s). Will its resulting actions in the wake of the disaster constitute more of an elaborate "fleeing in terror" scenario? This scenario aligns with that which Susan Sontag refers to in her essay "The Imagination of Disaster," when, "Cities are destroyed and/or evacuated. There is an obligatory scene here of panicked crowds stampeding along a highway or a big bridge..." (Sontag, 234). Or rather, will the core group of survivors strategically formulate a plan of attack to confront the disaster head on in a metaphorical game of chicken in which the core group of survivors is pitted against, to name one common cause of disaster, Mother Nature? If so, what are the course or courses of action that will be taken by the inevitable leader of the group (i.e., the main protagonist) who emerges in the aftermath of the Primary Disaster in order to lead the core group of survivors to hopeful safety?

With the notion of a *backdrop/proactive* disaster film or a *central/reactive* disaster film being offered as a thesis, I don't mean to imply that in the 1970s the disaster or spectacle presented itself in a film and then simply disappeared from the movie altogether. Nor do I mean to imply that in the 1990s there was little or no dramatic element present in the story. Rather, it might be more accurate to pronounce that in some disaster films, the headlining catastrophe was initiated as more of a springboard to propel the drama between the characters to the fore (a backdrop narrative arc), whereas in others, the choice was made at the structural level that the drama should be of lesser narrative import than the inclusion of a galvanizing spectacle (a central narrative arc). Let's examine each of these narrative arcs.

Backdrop/Proactive

A disaster movie that has a **backdrop/proactive** narrative constitution is one in which the disaster transpires, and the drama subsequently plays out during the remaining course of the movie (Shaer, "Canonical Films" 9). As a matter of illustration, let's take a look at this theory in practice. At twenty-seven minutes into *The Poseidon Adventure*, the ship capsizes (9). As per the template (established, in part, by this very movie), a core group of survivors emerges after this catastrophic event, led by the

Reverend Scott. Scott and his group assess the seemingly hopeless situation they now found themselves in, and, not wanting to be lost to the sea forever, take a *proactive* approach to eventual escape and survival. Referencing the "Ship of Fools" type of disaster narrative that Yacowar discusses (335), Scott and the other members of the core group of survivors (as well as the larger society) have paid the price for having the gall to conquer the oceans and will now attempt a perilous voyage to the hull of the cruise liner which, due to the capsizing, is now the only portion of the S.S. *Poseidon* that rises above the water. Comparatively, the majority of the stranded passengers in the ballroom following the capsizing opted for a more passive, a more reactive, approach and thought it safer and more practical to sit and wait for assistance. This proved to be a calamitous choice which ultimately and quickly resulted in their doom as water soon engulfed the overturned ballroom where everyone just a short time before had been enjoying the New Year's festivities (*The Poseidon Adventure* 52:07–53:17). Once on its journey and owing to its ingenuity and instinct, the core group of survivors withstands what amounts to a massive obstacle course, traversing the inner bowels of the ship that most passengers are never privileged to see—boiler rooms, kitchens, etc.—in order to reach its goal: the hull of the ship and potential rescue (00:27:59–01:57:00).

If we consider another 1970s example, *The Towering Inferno*, we witness the same proactive approach in action. In this blockbuster, the spark from the circuit breaker in the eighty-first floor storage room that ignites the catastrophic conflagration occurs at roughly twelve minutes into the film's almost three-hour running time (Shaer, "Canonical Films" 9). Not long after and upon realizing the extent of the blaze and the certain and imminent danger the disaster poses to the guests of the Glass Tower's dedication party, Paul Newman's Doug Roberts and his staff diligently conspire to work out a plan that will hopefully ensure that all of the people gathered in the Promenade Room are kept in the path to safety. Naturally, Roberts calls in the fire department, led by Steve McQueen's Fire Chief O'Halloran, and together, the two men, the leaders who have emerged from the core group of survivors, unite in a proactive manner to devise an actionable plan with which to evacuate the guests and, at the same time, extinguish the fire.

To hammer home this theory, we can even point to another film in the 1970s disaster canon: *Airport 1975*, the sequel to 1970's soap opera in the skies, *Airport*, which is the film that arguably begat the modern disaster film genre. Now, if you have never seen *Airport 1975*, then you may not be aware that this is the movie from which the smash hit spoof *Airplane!* filches many of its most gut-busting jokes (Travelling nuns? Check. Sick little girl in need of a critical organ transplant? Check. Little old lady relaxing herself with vice? Check.). In this disaster film, civilian pilot Scott Freeman (Dana Andrews) suffers a fatal heart attack while at the controls of his self-piloted twin-engine Baron. His mid-flight death causes the small airplane to fly out of control, ultimately impacting the cockpit of Columbia Airlines Flight 409, a jumbo 747 aircraft en route to Los Angeles from Washington, D.C. (this is the Primary Disaster). The crash creates a gaping hole in the side of the aircraft and instantly kills co-pilot Urias (Roy Thinnes) and navigator Julio (the character played by Erik Estrada), and renders Captain Stacy (Efrem Zimbalist, Jr.) incapacitated. The airplane's and, by extension, the passengers', only shot for survival is for first stewardess Nancy Pryor (the character played by Karen Black) to proactively take charge, assume the role of captain, and pilot the aircraft herself until proper (i.e., male) help can reach the plane. Meanwhile, Alan Murdock (the character played by Charlton Heston), a pilot and Nancy's paramour, and Joe Patroni, now the Director of Operations at Columbia Airlines (George Kennedy was the only cast member to return from this movie's predecessor and the only original cast member to appear in all four films in the *Airport* series), are on their way to the Salt Lake City airport, where 409 had been re-rerouted prior to the disaster due to bad weather in Los Angeles. Alan is at the helm of the aircraft and, via radio connection, walks Nancy step-by-step through the motions of turning the airplane in order to gain altitude and keep the piece of steel steady. Joe then proposes an insanely (and insane) daredevil plan to rescue Nancy and the passengers at risk on Flight 409. Patroni's plan involves lowering a pilot from a helicopter via cable into the cockpit of the damaged 747, so that the pilot can relieve Nancy, assume the controls, and land the plane safely (*Airport 1975* 00:40:33–57:24). (I'm not sure if this stunt has ever been performed in actuality, but the absurdity of the notion leads me to believe that it has not. Someone, please prove me wrong.) In any case, it is evident that almost no person in this film is sitting idly by and waiting, hoping, and praying that the disaster goes away. Oh, there's some of that, especially in the form of the guitar-playing nun played by Helen Reddy or in the appearance of classic Hollywood star Gloria Swanson, both of whom do no more nuanced acting other than looking scared. But for the most part, Murdock, Patroni, ground control, Nancy, Mrs. Patroni (Susan Clark), who happens to be on the flight, natch, and the entire flight crew in the air, are thinking proactively about their ultimate mission: to land the plane quickly and safely, while ensuring their own safety as well as that of all of the passengers on board the doomed aircraft.

In all three of the above-mentioned movies, we are witnessing a proactive response to the disaster wherein the core group of survivors (in the case of *Airport 1975*, the entire group of passengers on the flight—the society—can be considered the core group of survivors due to the confined nature of the disaster) confronts a disaster and bands together with the express purpose of formulating a plan of action in the hope of making it to safety before said disaster claims lives. Additionally, the observant filmgoer will recognize that in each of these cases, the disaster in question is presented to the viewer *not* as an ongoing and mind-blowing spectacle or series of spectacles that dwarf the drama between the characters in favor of the spectacle, but as more of a backdrop against which the drama (or dramas, as in the case of *Airport 1975*, the overabundance of which no doubt contributed to that film's camp value) can play out. The actual and physical disaster is not necessarily the primary focal point of the film.

I would be willing to suggest that much of the reason that we predominantly see the backdrop/proactive approach in the 1970s and the disaster films of that era that harbor a focus on the drama rather than the visual spectacular might have its roots in the state of Hollywood moviemaking at that time. Any film scholar or enthusiast of the films of the 1970s will tell you that the 1970s were a particularly transformative period in Hollywood's twentieth-century history. As the New Hollywood became emblematic of the era, the 1970s movies were still very much centered around the drama and the characters. In his book *Hollywood's Last Golden Age: Politics, Society, and the Seventies Film in America*, which examines the socio-political context of the times in which these films were made and the impact such societal turbulence had on influencing the stories that were told, author Jonathan Kirshner concurs. He states, "Seventies films also tended to be character driven rather than plot driven" (21). Even when considering the purview of the disaster movie, a subgenre not typically noted for its frank examination of cultural or political biases, there is evidence of Kirshner's observation. One of the major themes explored in *The Poseidon Adventure*, for example, regards the concept of moral skepticism, of questioning one's faith, especially in the face of such overwhelming adversity. This thematic element is, of course, personified in the character of the Reverend Scott. At the conclusion of the film, Scott wonders aloud in frustration in an impassioned sermon about God's seeming ambivalence to his plight and the plight of his flock, the core group of survivors. Scott questions His testing of the endurance of the group. "What more do you want of us? We've come all this way no thanks to you," Scott laments. Where has God been during the tribulations of the group throughout its perilous journey? Why hasn't He stepped in to help the group, announced His existence to Scott, a servant of His on Earth? How much more faith is Scott able to expound in a God that doesn't justify his faith in Him? Scott asks, "How many more sacrifices? How much more blood?" (*The Poseidon Adventure* 01:47:13–38). The "crisis of faith" trope could be seen in several films of the 1970s, most notably in *The Exorcist* (William Friedkin, 1973), in the character of Father Karras (Jason Miller), and in *Carrie* (Brian De Palma, 1976), with the character of Carrie White (Sissy Spacek). As the nation emerged from the ravages of an unpopular war and contended with rampant political corruption and social alienation, movies that addressed themes of religiosity and man's place in the world were particularly apparent, especially in the characters that had to confront such moral and philosophical dilemmas.

The 1970s was also notable as a period during which Hollywood and the creative community ushered in a crop of new, hungry, and audacious directors such as Francis Ford Coppola, Martin Scorsese, Brian De Palma, Paul Mazursky, and Peter Bogdanovich, to name just a few. These were artists, reared on movies churned out during the heyday of the studio system; a generation heavily influenced by the enormous effect that the French New Wave, works by Godard and Truffaut, for example, had on the direction of American cinema. The artists coming of age artistically during this momentous decade leaned on their influences in the French New Wave, as well as on groundbreaking American artists such as John Cassavetes, to examine personal themes and ideas, many of which reflected the then current state of significant political and social upheaval (Kirshner 32). The tumultuous times in which these artists were producing their films fed the substance of not only their work, but of the entire scope of their lives. The Vietnam Conflict, Watergate, nuclear warfare, the space race, and civil disobedience were all prominent social and political topics of the age. These topics of the day, in turn, contributed to the proliferation of deeper social, political, and cultural themes which presented themselves in the narratives of the period's entertainment, including disaster films; themes such as an acute distrust of the government, suspicions surrounding corporate greed, environmental concerns, and man's relationship with technology. Directors, writers, and other artists were creating bodies of work that had the purpose of not only contributing to what was deemed mass entertainment, but of being controversial and relevant works that sought to challenge viewers in a manner that greatly altered the process in which they absorbed Hollywood filmmaking and mainstream dramatic storytelling. Audiences at this time were becoming invested in new and exciting ways with the stories they watched on the screen and in the characters that populated those stories. Even *The Exorcist*, one of the most successful films of the decade not to mention of all time, and a film heavily reliant on special and shocking effects, paid special attention to the dramatic motivations and concerns of its characters. Like the Reverend Scott in *The Poseidon Adventure*, *The Exorcist*'s Father Karras spends large portions of the film attempting to confront his own very personal crisis of faith and his profound guilt stemming from the death of his mother. Meanwhile, Karras finds himself faced with the additional circumstance of refereeing the personification of purity and goodness (personified by Regan, the young girl played by Linda Blair) embattled in a tug-of-war with manifest evil (represented by the demon Pazuzu). When viewed within the context of the time and the substance of the films that were produced by, among others, the New Hollywood, it makes sense that the disaster films of the 1970s cycle would lean on the development and nurturing of character ingenuity and intellect in order for the core group of survivors to confront the disaster at hand and place the emphasis on this over the enormous and constant visual and audial stimuli of the spectacle.

By the time the 1990s cycle of disaster films began its own run, Hollywood, and specifically, Hollywood storytelling, had inverted to an extent that the visual now oftentimes trumped the narrative. This methodology was not only seen in disaster movies, of course, but in many films of the 1980s and beyond, many of which could be described as favoring "style over substance." After all, MTV had been around for over ten years by the time the 1990s disaster cycle hit theaters, having premiered in 1981. In the years since its inception, MTV and music videos had made an indelible mark on cultural tastes that, in turn, had a profound stylistic effect on the movies. Filmmakers were now beginning to incorporate techniques such as quick-cut editing, ultra-slick imagery, and computer-generated imagery (CGI) into their films. The conflation of shifts in esthetics, advances in technology, and budgets growing ever more mammoth from picture to picture precipitated a need for the disaster film to keep pace. As a result, one can surmise that this resulted in movies of this type to be focused more on, well, the disaster, the actual spectacle. The disaster movie had evolved into a pure "cinema of attractions" (Gunning, "Cinema of Attractions").

Central/Reactive

As a result of this tendency to favor the style over the dramatic in many films of the 1990s disaster cycle and later genre cycles, we find that now, the disaster depicted in these movies tended to be less of a backdrop to or a springboard for the drama, but central to the drama and perceptively and continually weaved throughout the course of the narrative. Now, this is not to say that the spectacular element wasn't at all prominent in earlier disaster films, of course it was. As we have discussed prior, the spectacle doesn't get much more prominent than the overturning of the S.S. *Poseidon*. However, in the 1990s cycle, the spectacle of the disaster was positioned front and center in the narrative, very much an ever-present and menacing character in its own right. With the release of disaster films of this sort such as Jan de Bont's *Speed* and his follow-up, *Twister*, and Roger Donaldson's *Dante's Peak*, the spectacle had graduated to become an awe-inspiring mix of glorious catastrophe and end-of-the-world annihilation. Due to technological advances in computer generated imagery used in the movies that simply hadn't been available to filmmakers during the 1970s genre cycle, a greatly enhanced visual stimulus of the spectacle was now possible and exploited which, as a result, didn't leave too much room for nuanced character-centered drama in the two or so hours of a motion picture. In order to support the minimal plot in *Twister*, for example, there is a basic dramatic skeleton (Shaer, "Canonical Films" 10), which is necessary on an elemental level, for an audience to remain interested in watching and engaging with the movie. However, the veritable spectacles of this film were, undeniably, the stunning tornado sequences (10). The overall effects produced by the whipping, spiraling cyclones were synched beautifully with the spectacular and thunderous sound design to deliberately and powerfully astound the viewer and to provide the audience with a truly unforgettable and awesome experience. So impressive were the visual spectacles in *Twister* that the movie earned Academy Award nominations for both Best Sound and Best Effects, Visual Effects (though, tellingly, no nominations were received in any of the acting or script categories) ("Twister"). The movie was, in reality, less about the trials and intellectual pursuits of a group of storm chasers and more about how to stun the audience with wild and trembling special effects.

Similarly, the audience withstands the superficial drama between the characters in *Dante's Peak* (Shaer, "Canonical Films" 10) in order that it might experience the excitement and visual knockouts of the movie's spectacles. The centerpiece attraction, the Primary Disaster, appears at around fifty-seven minutes into the movie as the cataclysmic eruption of the titular peak. Following this inciting incident, the society in both *Twister* and *Dante's Peak* try their darndest to get the hell out of harm's way as quickly as possible in order to avoid further peril. Yet, one will notice that in both of these movies, there is no development or implementation of a plan of action to mitigate the disaster, such as that which we have seen in the majority of the films of the 1970s cycle. Even the storm chasers in *Twister* know when it's time to duck and run. A disaster film that is running on this sort of narrative arc, where the disaster is more centrally ingratiated into the film, can be seen as being more reactive, one in which the characters in the narrative withstand the disaster yet attempt to do nothing more than save their own asses (10). This is the **central/reactive** narrative constitution.

As will be the case with any form of art, commercial or otherwise, the rules are, naturally, not so hard and fast. There will, no doubt, be exceptions and there will exist creative adjustments that filmmakers will experiment with once the standard is, more or less, confirmed. In an attempt to examine the myriad of definitions and specific representations of genre across all forms of artistic endeavors, Steve Neale quotes Robert Warshow as he speaks of "aesthetic 'types'":

> For a type to be successful ... its conventions have imposed themselves upon the general consciousness and become the vehicle of a particular set of attitudes and a particular aesthetic effect. One goes to any individual example of the type with very definite expectations, and originality is to be welcomed only in the degree that it intensifies the expected experience without fundamentally altering it. (qtd. in Neale 26)

Ultimately, a cinematic genre cycle's forward trajectory is typically one of movie-modification after movie-modification until the battle for the audience's attention (and dollars) waged between studios, directors, and their peers, finally boils over into the products of the absurd, echoing Schatz's theory of "generic development" as quoted in *Genre and Hollywood* by Steve Neale (referenced in the Introduction to this book). "Finally, once 'the genre's straightforward message has "saturated" the audience ... a genre's classic conventions are refined and eventually parodied and subverted...'" (qtd. in Neale 211–12).

Let's now look at a few examples which will be able to more clearly articulate how some disaster movies might be seen as exceptions to the commonly accepted generic template. It has already been discussed that the majority of disaster films in the subgenre's most famous cycle—the 1970s—can be understood to be proactive in nature, the disaster serving as more of a backdrop for the drama as opposed to the central spectacle. However, it is one of the disaster movie canon's founding members, 1974's *Earthquake*, that diverges and adopts a more reactive approach generally more perceived in subsequent genre cycles. In this film, the eponymous earthquake that strikes Los Angeles is a gargantuan, all-encompassing, and mind-blowing spectacle specifically calculated to thrill audiences (it even works when viewed at home, trust me!). Buildings collapse into a heap of gravel, houses tumble from their precarious support beams, streets split wide open, and the citizens caught in the crosshairs run for cover. Director Mark Robson stages the earthquake sequence in *Earthquake* as a dazzling smorgasbord of destruction. And let us not forget, to drive home the experience of being there, trapped with the actors in this monster of a natural disaster, this whole thing was presented in Sensurround, which intended to heighten the thrill even more for audiences by mimicking the ordeal of enduring such a natural disaster.

But unlike in *The Towering Inferno*, where Newman, McQueen, et al. try to quash the raging conflagration while simultaneously evacuating the guests to safety, or *The Poseidon Adventure*, in which the Reverend Scott leads his core group of survivors through obstacle after obstacle to safety rather than, unwisely, waiting with the rest of the doomed passengers for help to arrive, the core group of survivors in *Earthquake* don't do much in the way of being proactive by, say, evacuating people from problem areas or preparing them for the inevitable aftershocks. The society sustains the disaster, and the core group of survivors moves to rescue its members and others. The formula for this picture is simply this: disaster, then run. In *Earthquake*, there is little to no proactive attempt to mitigate the disaster or quell the forces of nature before things potentially get any worse.

To be fair, though, I suppose that there really is no other approach with which to dramatize an earthquake than that of reactivity. Regardless of the ability to predict a natural disaster such as an earthquake, once it hits, one can only devolve into rescue mode. I know I would. Alternatively, in virus-borne disaster movies such as *The Cassandra Crossing*, *Outbreak*, *Contagion*, or even our own *The Sibylline Scourge*, an astute viewer will notice that the narrative choice will most always be proactive in nature, i.e., the film will be constructed as a race against time for the characters in the story to come up with a plan to stop the virus from spreading or metastasizing and claiming more lives. This plan of action in these cases generally involves or culminates in the discovery of an antidote or a vaccine.

It is worth pausing at this juncture and exploring what I see is a common misconception involving disaster movies or movies that purport to be disaster movies. This is sometimes a tricky distinction to make with these sorts of films, for sure, but there are certain concrete disparities which arise between a "disaster movie" and a movie "about a disaster" that will be evident, and which will allow one to determine an easy distinction.

The Disaster Movie vs. The Movie About a Disaster

The wonderful thing about a work of art, no matter how highbrow or kitschy, is that it is meant to be personalized and interpreted differently from person to person. Some individuals might perceive an angel in a painting, others might see a fish (that's an exaggerated example, but you get my point). The disaster movie, itself a subgenre of the action film, abides by certain well-established tropes that fundamentally differentiate the film from movies having more in common with another genre or subgenre. Numerous definitions of the term "genre" have been offered by scholars and critics over the years, from its origins in literature to the study of genre within the larger context of film criticism (Buscombe 33). Warshow's definition of a successful "aesthetic 'type'" (noted a few paragraphs above) provides a terrific high-level explanation of genre, even if he doesn't explicitly use the word. Another good, more accessible definition is that of film scholar Tom Ryall, who says, "Genres may be defined as patterns/forms/styles/structures which transcend individual films, and which supervise both their construction by the film maker, and their reading by an audience" (qtd. in Neale 12).

What is apparent is that any generic film is composed of a certain series of conventions that inform a viewer as to what he or she should reasonably expect from buying a ticket to said generic film. For example, if I am purchasing a ticket to a western, I would reasonably expect to encounter a palette of harsh sunlight and burnt sienna tones, guns, the scorched faces of cowboys, a landscape resembling the American southwest, Clint Eastwood, etc. Whereas if I buy a ticket to a film marketed as a romantic comedy, I might expect to encounter a bright, colorful palette, a (more often than not, let's be honest) female protagonist, a bouncy soundtrack, perhaps more modern settings, Julia Roberts, etc. Naturally, as we have already touched upon in this book, genre tropes within a particular film can and often do exhibit substantial overlap; just look at the disaster film and the action film as proof. As Neale states, "...many Hollywood films— and many Hollywood genres—are hybrid and multi-generic" (Neale 51).

But even within this flexible framework of intertwining genres, there tend to be specific markers that distinguish certain pieces of drama from others in the creation of a genre. In this way, the audience is guided to more clearly comprehend the piece of work for which they are spectators and are able to adjust their expectations, their enjoyment, or their dislike of it accordingly by the terms and conditions set in place by the genre. In the introduction to the Fourth Edition of his collection of essays regarding genre theory and criticism, Barry Keith Grant defines genre in simple terms: "Simply stated, genre movies are those commercial feature films that, through repetition and variation, tell familiar stories with familiar characters in familiar situations. They also encourage expectations and experiences similar to those of similar films we have already seen" (Grant 16). When we buy a ticket to a movie in what we generally understand to be of a specific genre (horror, western, science fiction, etc.), we reasonably expect that movie to play by certain rules. When it doesn't, disappointment and negative reception can result. This failure, whether through a dysfunction of filmmaking or marketing, of a film to abide by the conventions set forth by the genre to which it purportedly belongs, leads me to discuss the perceived difference between a "disaster movie" and a "movie about a disaster."

First and foremost, the main difference between a "disaster movie" and a "movie about a disaster" has to do with how we seek to define a disaster film. In this book, I have examined (at least, I've *tried* to examine) how in order for a work of motion picture drama to fall into the category (which we can loosely think of as "genre") of "disaster movie," a majority of certain generic benchmarks should ideally be present. Among others, there is the Primary Disaster, the Poignant Character, the Second Disaster, a core group of survivors, etc. Some films might exhibit one or two of these elements, but it wouldn't necessarily be fair or accurate to refer to them as "disaster movies" in the same way that we have referred to some of the films referenced thus far in this book, such as the *Airport* series or *The Day After Tomorrow*. Buscombe references René Wellek and Austin Warren's *Theory of Literature* on this point:

> To begin with, common sense suggests that it is possible to draw up a list of elements found in films that, for the purposes of the argument, are called westerns and to say that any film with one or more of these elements is thereby held to be a western, though not therefore necessarily identical to other examples of the form [Buscombe 35].

Buscombe continues his referral to Wellek and Warren when he discusses their concept of genre as being composed of an inner form and an outer form. Per Buscombe, Wellek and Warren (for the record, although Wellek and Warren are discussing literary genres, the concept remains the same) state a genre should be thought of as having both an outer form, a layer that consists of the tangible—the visual conventions, or, as Grant specifies, the "iconography" (Grant 19)—and an inner form, which consists of the intangible, such as themes, subject matter, and tones (Buscombe 35). One can't exist without the other in order to be deemed an effective generic work. Buscombe argues:

> This idea of both inner and outer form seems essential, for if we require only the former, in terms of subject matter, then our concept will be too loose to be of much value; and if only the latter, then the genre will be ultimately meaningless, since devoid of any content [35].

Which brings me to the concept of a "disaster movie" versus a "movie about a disaster." For example, let's look at the 2014 spectacle *Pompeii*. On the surface, a movie that purports to dramatize one of the greatest and most catastrophic disasters in our planet's history would seem to be a no-brainer to warrant treatment as a disaster film. In fact, that's the lens through which many critics saw the film. "Not for nothing is *Pompeii*'s genre widely known as disaster porn," observed *Time*'s Richard Corliss (Corliss). Peter Debruge of *Variety* called *Pompeii* "a campy, concept-driven disaster pic" (Debruge). "This is a surprisingly old-fashioned disaster movie," wrote Glenn Kenny of *RogerEbert.com* (Kenny).

But upon closer examination, this conception doesn't entirely hold water. Principally speaking, in Pompeii (the movie and the actual event), the vast majority (if not all) of the citizens of the Italian coastal city perished while attempting to flee the fire, heat, and blinding ash caused by the ferocious eruption of Mount Vesuvius. Therefore, we as the audience know the ending. However, this, in and of itself, isn't the problem. After all, James Cameron's *Titanic* is a terrific disaster movie, and we all know the ending there. While the screenwriters (three of them!) behind *Pompeii* might have indeed introduced a core group of characters in order to flesh out the thin scaffolding of a story (Milo, Cassia, Corvus, Atticus, etc.), history has informed us that there will likely be no core group of survivors. As such, we are denied not only one of the basic pleasures of the disaster movie—the guessing game concerning which characters will survive the disaster (Keane 5)—but a character for whom we can root for, whom we hope will make it out alive. Whether or not there actually were any survivors of the real Pompeii disaster is irrelevant. People who have even the most perfunctory knowledge of ancient history from high school social studies or whatever, have come to accept the common rendering that the cataclysmic eruption of Mount Vesuvius decimated the city of Pompeii, including its entire civilization. To be fair, I won't go so far as to pretend to presume that Anderson's movie was intended to be a historical record of the disaster, but rather an expensive excuse for an awe-inspiring third act when the volcano finally erupts. And, again to be fair, it is, without question, a jaw-dropping spectacle, albeit an impressive study in CGI. Fire (*lots* of fire), lava violently exploding forth from the mouth of the volcano, ash raining down on the terrified populace, crowds of people fleeing for their lives in horror, buildings effortlessly tumbling like blocks in a game of Jenga around them ... no wonder TriStar pictures released this thing in 3D (*Pompeii* 01:12:49–23:44)! It no doubt looked tremendous on the big screen. Yet, while there are some generic disaster elements in place in *Pompeii* (a Preamble sequence involving an ominously bubbling lake that foreshadows the catastrophic event to come, a Primary Disaster when the volcano erupts, the "panic in the streets" scenario), there is no true and involving drama, other than the rather bland romance between Milo and Cassia, for the viewer to hold onto. On a purely elemental level, there is no one or no romance to root for since there will be no survivors. Thus, if we refer back to Buscombe's interpretation of Wellek and Warren's concept of genre and the outer and inner form, it is clear that *Pompeii* is all outer form. Accordingly, this renders the film, in Buscombe's words, "ultimately meaningless, since devoid of any content" (35). This is an indefensible omission when attempting to classify *Pompeii* as a true disaster film: quite literally, everybody dies at the end. *Pompeii* exists entirely as an excuse to stage a disaster in all of its majesty that will fill up the latter portion of the film. The movie uses its characters as tangential constructs only to pad out and justify its feature length running time.

Pompeii barely works in terms of a central/reactive narrative arc. The progress of the narrative once the Primary Disaster occurs is all reactive, to be sure. But since the disaster occurs so late in the film, there is no time expended for it to be considered truly central to the narrative in the way that the disasters in, say, *Twister* or *Speed* are (i.e., the disaster occurs, and the core group of survivors spend the second and third acts of the film avoiding further peril). *Pompeii* is nothing but third act.

Compare, then, *Pompeii* with *Titanic*, one of the greatest true disaster movies (and some people, including me, would argue, one of the greatest all-around movies) of all time, and one can absolutely see some similarities. For example, both movies can be deemed to (in the case of *Pompeii*, barely) follow a central/reactive dramatic trajectory. But in both movies, there are also some stark differences. Much like the eruption of Mount Vesuvius in *Pompeii*, an actual event, the audience member purchases their ticket to *Titanic* with preconceived knowledge, even if it is only a modicum of preconceived knowledge, concerning the legendary maritime disaster and knowing, however high-level, how the disaster turned out. Decades of history, movies, books, television specials, documentaries, and research (some by director Cameron himself who is well known to have long been fascinated by the titular wreck) have elevated the tragedy of the Titanic into the realm of lore. There are some historical characters in Cameron's film whose fate the audience knows from the outset from such historical documentation: the "Unsinkable" Molly Brown (played in the film by Kathy Bates), for example, or Captain Smith (played in the film by Bernard Hill). But the main characters who form the backbone of the story—Jack (Leonardo DiCaprio), Rose (Kate Winslet), and Cal (Billy Zane)—are works of fiction. So, unlike *Pompeii*, in which we are certain of the fates befalling everyone in the film, including the main group of characters, we can't be absolutely sure in *Titanic* which characters will make it onto a lifeboat and which ones will not (unless some jerk spoils the movie for us). Since we are aware from history that, in fact, some people *did* survive the *Titanic* disaster, it isn't a preordained conclusion that everyone in the film will perish, including the characters that we have come to empathize with throughout the course of the movie. The "who will survive" guessing game, to a certain degree, remains intact.

We are also able to compare the two films on a structural level. Whereas the movie *Pompeii* exists solely and purely to depict the third act eruption of Mount Vesuvius, and its associated disasters, as an eye-popping 3D CGI extravaganza that occurs well over an hour's worth into the film's one hundred and five-minute running time, Cameron structures *Titanic* along a more traditional Act One (The Buildup); Act Two (Primary Disaster—All Hell Breaks Loose); Act Three (Second Disaster—Out of the Woods?) archetype seen in the majority of disaster films. The ocean liner impacts the iceberg (the Primary Disaster) in the north Atlantic Ocean at just about an hour and a half into the film's epic three hour and fourteen-minute runtime, approximately halfway through the film. All hell breaks loose as the ship brings on more and more water and proceeds to sink throughout the second act while, at the same time, the drama involving the Jack-Rose-Cal triangle plays out. Then, at around two hours and forty minutes, the ship dramatically splits in half (the Second Disaster), condemning, in all probability, those remaining passengers—men, women, and children alike—who did not make it into the too-few lifeboats provided by the ship to their icy graves. Later, and at long last, rescue boats appear in the night.

So, if we are able to understand the underlying differences between these two movies with these situations in mind, it is easy to make out how the movie *Pompeii* works *exclusively* as a movie designed to showcase the disaster, or as a "movie *about* a disaster," whereas *Titanic*, while the outcome of the catastrophe is a foregone conclusion, can better be deemed a "disaster movie."

Similarly to *Pompeii*, Robert Wise's 1975 wannabe epic, *The Hindenburg*, is another "movie about a disaster." I don't care how much anyone proffers to explain that this film is an attempt to imagine the circumstances that might have led to the dirigible's monumental explosion ("The Hindenburg [1975]"), it is a movie constructed with the sole purpose of reconstructing the fiery 1937 crash of the titular Zeppelin in Lakehurst, New Jersey. Wise even goes so far as to intersperse black-and-white archival newsreel footage of the actual disaster within his film's reenactment of the episode (*The Hindenburg* 01:50:41–02:02:02). This documentary exercise only serves to underscore the point that the only possible reason for this film to exist is so that the filmmakers can stage a massive spectacle at the conclusion and ride the disaster movie wave, engage in a lame attempt to cash in on a contemporaneous craze, and legitimize the product as a semi-historical account of an authentic catastrophe (clearly, I hated this movie). There is no backdrop or centrality to the disaster since the disaster occurs at the film's conclusion, at just over the one hour and fifty-minute mark(!) in a roughly two hour and five-minute movie. But indeed, the sequence concerning the explosion and crash landing of the *Hindenburg* is a massive spectacle because much of the sequence is the *actual* spectacle! Paul W.S. Anderson would probably have incorporated archival footage into *Pompeii* during his staging of the Mount Vesuvius eruption if any such footage had existed.

The Hindenburg is, nonetheless, generally lumped into the subgenre of disaster movie. I suspect, however, that this is due more to the timing of the film's production and release in the thick of the 1970s disaster movie fad, and not so much to the film's merits as a true disaster movie. *The Hindenburg*, like *Pompeii*, was a movie which involved a well-known, real-life catastrophe. Wise's movie was released on Christmas Day 1975 ("The Hindenburg [1975]—Overview"), smack in the middle of the popularity of the 1970s disaster film genre cycle. The marketing materials for *The Hindenburg* surely didn't do much to distance the film from its disaster movie cousins heating up the box office during the 1970s. The poster art for *The Hindenburg* looked very much like any other disaster film poster art of the time: the titular disaster front and center and thumbnail photos of the all-star cast situated along the right side of the poster. A moviegoer could be forgiven, given the historical notoriety of the subject matter and the marketing of *The Hindenburg*, for thinking that they were, in fact, buying a ticket to a disaster movie starring George C. Scott and directed by the man who helmed the terrific disaster movie *The Andromeda Strain* just a few years before, and that it would deliver the same sort of entertainment that recent titles like *Earthquake* or *Airport 1975* had provided. The same forgiveness might be given to moviegoers who purchased tickets to several other films released in the wake of the enormous successes of *Airport*, *The Poseidon Adventure*, *The Towering Inferno*, and *Earthquake*, that were marketed under the guise of the disaster film but were, in reality, more along the lines of a traditional action-thriller. A few of these films included the Richard Harris-Anthony Hopkins starrer *Juggernaut* (Richard Lester, 1974), the George Segal-Sensurround thriller *Rollercoaster* from 1977, and the Charlton Heston (was there a movie in the 1970s that this man was *not* in?) headliner *Gray Lady Down* (David Greene, 1978). None of these films were really disaster films, at least not in the sense that I attempt to define such films and understand them to be.

When we examine *Pompeii* and *The Hindenburg* side-by-side such commonly accepted disaster films as *The Towering Inferno* and *Volcano*, the differences between a "movie about a disaster" and a true "disaster movie" become even more pronounced. The primary differentiator is structural. We've already discussed how *Pompeii* and *The Hindenburg* exist *only* to showcase their respective spectacles come the denouement of each film, aborting any real opportunity for the film to present an Act Two. In a true disaster film, the Primary Disaster is generally observed much earlier in the film and will indicate the story transition into Act Two. In the case of *The Towering Inferno*, the Primary Disaster occurs at thirty-eight minutes and thirty-nine seconds, when the fire that has been building up in the storage room on the eighty-first floor of the Glass Tower bursts forth and threatens to engulf the rest of the building, jeopardizing the lives of everyone celebrating in the skyscraper's top floor Promenade Room. In *Volcano*, the Primary Disaster occurs at thirty-one minutes and seventeen seconds, with the first spectacular: the explosive eruption of the fiery geyser from underneath the streets of Los Angeles. Once the Primary Disaster occurs in a true disaster film, the balance of the film presents the response by the characters, whether proactive or reactive, to the disaster. This structural necessity is absent in both *Pompeii* and *The Hindenburg* because there is no Act Two in which the characters can dramatically respond to the disaster; the disaster happens *during* the latter portion, Act Three, of the film. There is no core group of survivors. The only response any of the characters in both *Pompeii* and *The Hindenburg* can possibly have once the disasters hit is to flee, and to try, mostly in vain, to escape an agonizing death.

While we are on the subject of the characters, it is clear that the character types we see represented in *Pompeii* and *The Hindenburg* don't align with the character types we normally see in true disaster films. Sure, while both films possess a male and a female leading character (Milo [Kit Harington], Cassia [Emily Browning], Colonel Ritter [George C. Scott], Countess von Reugen [Anne Bancroft], respectively), a major component of any tried-and-true disaster film is missing from each endeavor: the Poignant Character. In *Pompeii*, there are surely some significant character deaths during the course of the film: Felix, Severus, Aurelia, Ariadne, for example. Some character deaths even register a certain amount, however minuscule, of poignancy, such as that of Severus (Jared Harris) and his wife, Aurelia (Carrie-Anne Moss). However poignant these deaths might be in the moment, in *Pompeii* there can fundamentally be no Poignant Character since, well, this is Pompeii and we know that everyone is going to die at the end one way or another. It is therefore impossible to realistically include a Poignant Character (as we have defined the archetype in this book) in *Pompeii* as the movie is presented, no matter how melodramatically such character death may be telegraphed to the audience, for this very reason. The audience is denied any character to root for (i.e., any character that we hope will make it out of the disaster alive); therefore, no investment in a Poignant Character can possibly be made. We recognize a similar circumstance in *The Hindenburg*, although there is not a situation of total character annihilation at the end (some of the aircraft's passengers are known to have managed to flee from the burning wreckage). But there is, quite literally, no Poignant Character to be identified in the film.

Now, there are several disaster movies that, however unwisely in my opinion, omit the Poignant Character: *The Andromeda Strain* and *Disaster on the Coastliner* (Richard Sarafian, 1979) represent two. To go this route is to deny the audience a primal reason for the effectiveness of narrative drama, that is, the emotional connection. Part of the reason why certain pieces of drama succeed more than others is due to the fact that some characters, when they are properly drawn by screenwriters or authors, are intended to produce at least some basic element of sentiment that allows for an audience to empathize with them. Even cartoonish serial killer characters like Michael Myers or Jason Voorhees have some degree (admittedly, a minimal degree) of pathos that permits an audience to not be absolutely repelled by them. There should be some emotional payoff for an audience, even if it is tiny, when a character perishes. In the disaster movie, oftentimes there are hundreds of collateral deaths related to the occurrence of the disaster, deaths which are personified by countless extras, and in more modern movies, CGI extras. We see this in movies such as *Earthquake, San Andreas,* and *Independence Day.* But, like all disaster movies, these movies narrow their stories to a core group of survivors which serve as audience stand-ins for the purpose of focusing the narrative to a manageable and coherent whole. When a member of the core group of survivors dies or is gravely injured, such as in the case of Oren Monash in *Deep Impact,* there should ideally be a significant emotional wallop that is experienced among the audience that has come to identify somewhat with these characters over the course of the movie. This emotional wallop is principally embodied in the Poignant Character and is the reason why including such a character in the disaster movie is such an important trope to encompass. If the filmmakers behind a disaster movie consciously choose to omit this character for whatever reason (remember, such a character doesn't necessarily have to *die* in the film, such as with Monash), it short-changes the audience of the powerfully heartrending impact that should come as a result of the emotional connection, a connection that has, hopefully, been cultivated throughout the film. The Poignant Character, and the emotional payoff that such a character produces, is one of the many facets that makes the disaster subgenre such a hearty piece of hybridized drama.

CHAPTER 7

Supporting Characters
Will They or Won't They?

Throughout the course of this book, I have mentioned that one of the primary attractions of the disaster film is, inarguably, the guessing game that consists of who will make it out alive and who won't (Keane 5). With a typically large, oftentimes all-star cast on board to endure the disaster, a large part of the fun is laying down the odds on who will and who won't survive the disaster. I wonder if back in the 1970s when times were simpler in many ways, before the advent of the internet forever altered the media and information landscapes, and during a period when disaster movies were all the rage, Las Vegas oddsmakers were prone to taking bets on such a gamble when a big disaster pic event such as *Earthquake* or *The Towering Inferno* was released. Although this notion wouldn't exactly surprise me, I do tend to think that this is probably pushing it.

Since a significant part of the enjoyment of the disaster movie is attempting to forecast who will and who won't survive the disaster (Keane 5), then the odds would practically favor multiple character deaths over the course of the film. Again, it must be stated that every rule has an exception. The only character death, supporting or otherwise, in *Airport*, for instance, is that of D.O. Guerrero. Also, although Gwen is injured when Guerrero's bomb detonates onboard the Golden Argosy, her fate isn't one hundred percent assured. We know from Chapter 2, which discussed the leading character types in a disaster film, including *The Sibylline Scourge*, that these multiple character deaths must be in addition to our leading characters. It is reasonable to assume that in a film like *Earthquake* or *San Andreas*, scores of unnamed extras or implied off-screen deaths might occur just by virtue of what we know to be the usual mortality rate for a disaster on the scale of an earthquake of the sort depicted in those films and films like them. Those are not the additional character deaths I or watchers of disaster films are really paying attention to. When discussing additional character deaths, what I am really speaking of are those truly secondary or supporting characters in the story. Those characters whose deaths will be presented in a distinct and, perhaps, particularly dramatic fashion.

Let's take a look at some supporting characters from the movies we are discussing.

Title	Supporting Cast (minus leads and Poignant Character)
Airport	George Kennedy, Helen Hayes, Maureen Stapleton, Larry Gates
The Andromeda Strain	David Wayne, James Olson, Paula Kelly
Skyjacked	James Brolin, Susan Dey, Leslie Uggams, Roosevelt Grier, Claude Akins, Walter Pidgeon
The Poseidon Adventure	Ernest Borgnine, Stella Stevens, Carol Lynley, Roddy McDowall, Red Buttons, Jack Albertson, Leslie Nielsen
Airport 1975	George Kennedy, Efrem Zimbalist, Jr., Susan Clark, Helen Reddy, Linda Blair, Sid Caesar, Roy Thinnes, Gloria Swanson, Erik Estrada, Myrna Loy
Earthquake	George Kennedy, Ava Gardner, Marjoe Gortner, Victoria Principal, Richard Roundtree, Barry Sullivan
The Towering Inferno	William Holden, Fred Astaire, Susan Blakely, Richard Chamberlain, O.J. Simpson, Robert Vaughn, Robert Wagner, Susan Flannery
Flood	Cameron Mitchell, Ann Doran, Carol Lynley, Roddy McDowall, Leif Garrett
The Cassandra Crossing	Martin Sheen, O.J. Simpson, Lionel Stander, Ann Turkel, Ingrid Thulin, Ava Gardner, Burt Lancaster
Airport '77	Lee Grant, Joseph Cotten, Olivia de Havilland, Darren McGavin, Kathleen Quinlan, Gil Gerard, Robert Foxworth, Pamela Bellwood
Fire	Donna Mills, Lloyd Nolan, Erik Estrada
The Swarm	Olivia de Havilland, Ben Johnson, Fred MacMurray, Richard Chamberlain, Bradford Dillman, Richard Widmark

Title	Supporting Cast (minus leads and Poignant Character)
Avalanche	Barry Primus
The Concorde.... Airport '79	Eddie Albert, Bibi Andersson, John Davidson, Andrea Marcovicci, Martha Raye, Cicely Tyson, Avery Schreiber, Mercedes McCambridge
City on Fire	Shelley Winters, Leslie Nielsen, James Franciscus, Ava Gardner, Henry Fonda
Meteor	Karl Malden, Brian Keith, Joseph Campanella, Henry Fonda, Richard Dysart
Disaster on the Coastliner	Paul L. Smith, Raymond Burr, Pat Hingle, E.G. Marshall, Lane Smith
Cave-In!	Leslie Nielsen, James Olson, Julie Sommars, Sheila Larken, Lonny Chapman, Ray Milland
Speed	Dennis Hopper, Joe Morton, Alan Ruck, Glenn Plummer
Outbreak	Patrick Dempsey, Morgan Freeman, Donald Sutherland, Cuba Gooding, Jr.
Twister	Cary Elwes, Jami Gertz, Philip Seymour Hoffman, Alan Ruck
Independence Day	Mary McDonnell, Harvey Fierstein, Brent Spiner, Randy Quaid, Robert Loggia, Judd Hirsch, James Rebhorn
Daylight	Viggo Mortensen, Marcello Thedford, Claire Bloom, Dan Hedaya, Jay O. Sanders, Vanessa Bell Calloway
Dante's Peak	Charles Hallahan, Grant Heslov, Kirk Trutner, Arabella Field, Tzi Ma
Volcano	Don Cheadle, Gaby Hoffman, Jacqueline Kim, Keith David
Titanic	Billy Zane, Kathy Bates, Frances Fisher, Victor Garber, Gloria Stuart, Bill Paxton, Suzy Amis, Danny Nucci
Deep Impact	Vanessa Redgrave, Morgan Freeman, Maximilian Schell, Blair Underwood, Mary McCormack, Aleksandr Baluev, Jon Favreau, Elijah Wood, Leelee Sobieski

Title	Supporting Cast (minus leads and Poignant Character)
Armageddon	Billy Bob Thornton, Will Patton, Steve Buscemi, William Fichtner, Owen Wilson, Keith David, Michael Clarke Duncan, Peter Stormare, Jessica Steen
The Core	Bruce Greenwood, Tcheky Karyo, Stanley Tucci, Richard Jenkins
The Day After Tomorrow	Richard McMillan, Ian Holm, Adrian Lester, Perry King, Dash Mihok, Tamlyn Tomita
Snakes on a Plane	David Koechner, Nathan Phillips, Rachel Blanchard, Flex Alexander, Kenan Thompson, Bruce James, Sunny Mabrey
2012	Woody Harrelson, Thandiwe Newton, Chiwetel Ejiofor, Oliver Platt, Danny Glover, Tom McCarthy
Contagion	Gwyneth Paltrow, Laurence Fishburne, Elliott Gould, Marion Cotillard, Jude Law, Bryan Cranston, Enrico Colantoni
San Andreas	Alexandra Daddario, Paul Giamatti, Colton Haynes, Archie Panjabi, Ioan Gruffudd, Hugo Johnstone-Burt
Geostorm	Jim Sturgess, Abbie Cornish, Andy Garcia, Ed Harris, Richard Schiff
Greenland	Roger Dale Floyd, Andrew Byron Bachelor, Hope Davis, David Denman
The Sibylline Scourge	Governor Andrew Cuomo, President Donald Trump, Vice President Mike Pence, Speaker of the House, Congresswoman Nancy Pelosi, Dr. Li Wenliang, Lawrence Garbuz, Dr. Robert Redfield, Mayor Bill de Blasio

During the cycle of 1970s disaster movies, the guessing game of who will survive was much more of an explicit invitation on the part of the filmmakers and the producing studio to engage the viewer to participate in the film. After all, following a few disaster movies, this became part of the formula: the big casts of familiar names and subsequent wondering by the viewer of who will emerge victorious (i.e., alive) at the end. As Keane notes in *Disaster Movies: The Cinema of Catastrophe*, this is, in fact, one of the primary appeals of the disaster movie (Keane 5).

The invitation to the ticket buyer was clear and present in the marketing materials of the movies. If you look at the posters for *The Poseidon Adventure, The Towering Inferno, Earthquake, Airport 1975, Airport '77, The Swarm, The Cassandra Crossing*, even *The Hindenburg*, you will notice that thumbnail photos of the all-star casts of each film are laid out somewhere prominently on the graphic, in a straight line. This is meant to draw your focus to their pictures. In this way, the studio is directly asking the viewer, "Want to know which of your favorite stars will survive this catastrophe? Buy a ticket and find out!" Just look at the marketing poster for *The Poseidon Adventure*, which (grammatically *in*correctly) asked, "Who Will Survive—In One of the Greatest Escape Adventures Ever!" Audiences were up for the game in the 1970s, that's for sure, and in playing it, made the 1970s the undisputed golden age of the disaster film.

In later disaster film genre cycles, the taglines remained pithy as ever, of course. The brilliant tagline in 1972 for *The Poseidon Adventure* was "Hell, Upside Down." Later, in 1997, the tagline for *Volcano* was the similar "It's Hotter Than Hell." The tagline for *Snakes on a Plane* advised us to "Sit Back. Relax. Enjoy the Fright." Yuk, yuk. But subsequent to the 1970s cycle of disaster films, movie studio marketing departments opted not to handle the marketing of disaster movies in such an overtly gimmicky manner; gone were the thumbnail headshots of the all-star casts. Yet, even while the disaster movie convention of the large, all-star cast has never really gone away, more recent iterations of the disaster film tended to narrow their focus on one or two headlining, bankable stars. To make a comparison to the marketing used in the 1970s, take a look at the movie poster for *Speed*. While the names of stars Keanu Reeves, Dennis Hopper, and Sandra Bullock are printed at the top of the poster, only Reeves's visage is prominently featured in the poster along with what is, arguably, the film's real star— the speeding bus, pictured as a smaller thumbnail to the right of Reeves. Conversely, but similarly at the same time, the poster for *Armageddon* shows the faces of co-stars Ben Affleck and Liv Tyler flanked behind the front-and-center photo of headliner Bruce Willis. Furthermore, Willis's name is singularly indicated on the poster, though Affleck and Tyler were certainly recognizable and somewhat bankable names at the time of the film's 1998 release. The poster art for *Dante's Peak* featured the gorgeous mugs of stars Pierce Brosnan and Linda Hamilton above the strong, block lettering of the movie's title. Like *Speed*, the real star of the film was, arguably, the disaster—the titular volcano—which was represented as a threatening cloud of smoke in an image placed underneath the movie's title. It's a cool poster, but the stars are the headlining attraction on the poster with the movie's spectacle positioned as secondary.

The films of the 1990s genre cycle and those that came afterward, to a certain degree, eschewed the all-star convention. In the more contemporary disaster movie, the supporting cast tended to be fleshed out with recognizable character actors whose names may or may not have been recallable at the time, rather than outright all-stars. The disaster movie didn't necessarily resemble an extended episode of *Battle of the Network Stars* anymore. In much the same way that filmmakers behind the 1970s films oftentimes used respected, older actors (Olivia de Havilland, Helen Hayes, Fred MacMurray, Fred Astaire, etc.) who may have been looking to cut loose in a big budget action-y movie, and who would, perhaps, add a touch of class to the proceedings, later disaster films were likely to employ the names of more contemporarily esteemed actors for similar reasons. Names of talented character actors such as Alan Ruck (*Speed*), Viggo Mortensen (*Daylight*), James Cromwell (*Deep Impact*), Paul Giamatti (*San Andreas*), and Andy Garcia (*Geostorm*), among others, showed up in disaster films during the last decade of the twentieth century and into the twenty-first. And as we discussed in the chapter on proactive versus reactive disaster films, the narrative scopes (not the disaster spectacles) in the films of later disaster cycles were generally not as expansive as in the cycle of 1970s movies. Now, the focus was more on the headlining spectacle rather than the drama. To that end, there may not have been as much of a demand for a sentimental investment or attractive novelty on the part of the viewer in revisiting with their favorite stars of decades past.

Yet, the disaster subgenre, as we have discussed, has a specific template that is, more or less, to be followed. Since these character actors, esteemed as they may be, are still portraying supporting characters in a disaster movie, the generic formula states that some of them, unfortunately, must die, or at least incur enough mortal danger to the point where an audience member might assume that the character will succumb, even if they ultimately survive (that's part of the game). This is the circumstance that befalls Meg (Lois Smith) in *Twister*, for example.

By definition, a supporting character, sometimes called the secondary character, will never be the leading role. This character or group of characters serves as "support" to the protagonist in the narrative and is fully formed. "The secondary character is more than just a minor character. He or she is necessary to the story because this character reveals key details, motivates the protagonist, foils the protagonist, or helps define the story's setting" (NY Book Editors). Renowned author Margaret Atwood goes into more detail in her definition:

> A supporting character is a person who plays a role in the life of a story's protagonist. Novelists and screenwriters don't anchor a story around supporting characters, but they use them in the process of worldbuilding to create a compelling backdrop to the main character's story arc.

A well-written supporting character will have a character arc, a strong point of view, and clear personality traits. In many cases they will be the types of characters a reader might recognize from their own life and—like main characters—they will grow and change over the course of the storyline [Master-Class Staff].

The supporting character can often be found playing the part of the best friend, the boss, the spouse, the co-worker, or even the president, among other roles. In a disaster film, the Poignant Character, which we discussed in Chapter 5, will always be a supporting character, albeit one with a very specific purpose, as will the villain of the piece (or any dramatic piece, really). Richard Chamberlain in *The Towering Inferno* and Viggo Mortensen in *Daylight* are two disaster villains that deserve an honorable mention. Supporting characters may encompass characters that are colorful, quirky, or downright weird. Russel Casse and Charlie Frost (the nutjobs played by Randy Quaid in *Independence Day* and Woody Harrelson's in *2012*, respectively) are supporting characters. Lee Grant's fabulously vain and blowsy Karen Wallace in *Airport '77*, Helen Hayes's little old stowaway in *Airport*, Steve Buscemi's comic astronaut in *Armageddon*, Martin Sheen's criminal boy toy in *The Cassandra Crossing* ... all supporting characters. These characters round out the typically large disaster movie casts and inform the scenario of the diegesis.

In *The Sibylline Scourge*, we have identified our male lead (Dr. Anthony Fauci), our female lead (Dr. Deborah Birx), our secondary leads (Governor Andrew Cuomo and President Donald Trump), and our Poignant Character (Nick Cordero). Because of the global nature of the Covid-19 pandemic through which we all persevered over the past few years, we are able to draw from a wealth of supporting characters in this real-life disaster movie to populate the supporting cast of *The Sibylline Scourge*. In keeping with the disaster tropes and the general character archetypes that we have discussed, there are a few notable individuals that a spectator might slot into the supporting character roles, as defined above, of this disaster scenario. It is primarily through the cast of supporting characters that the disaster movie game of who will and who won't survive is played.

Supporting Character: Dr. Li Wenliang

I would be inclined to argue that the most prominent and featured character within the context of *The Sibylline Scourge* is Dr. Li Wenliang. Dr. Wenliang was a 34-year-old ophthalmologist who was working as usual at Wuhan Central Hospital in China when he became aware of a group of patients that had contracted a virus that, he thought, bore a remarkable resemblance to the deadly SARS virus that had attacked the world in 2003. Concerned and cautious, Dr. Wenliang alerted his fellow physicians of this anomaly. But Dr. Wenliang was summarily and suspiciously silenced by Chinese authorities who turned around and accused Dr. Wenliang of "spreading rumors" and "disturb[ing] the social order." That was in late December 2019. In early January of 2020, Dr. Wenliang came down with a cough, then a fever. Soon afterward he was hospitalized with the novel coronavirus, the same coronavirus that he had, just a short time earlier, tried to warn the Chinese medical establishment about. Then, in the early morning hours of Friday, February 7, 2020, Dr. Wenliang succumbed to the virus (BBC News). Upon his death, Dr. Li Wenliang became a symbol of the need for immediacy of action in the face of a looming and potentially global biological crisis.

Dr. Wenliang's death is a critical moment insofar as the tragic timeline of the Covid-19 disaster is concerned. Here was a high-profile person (perhaps not so much in America, but certainly in his native China), ensconced in the medical establishment, who keenly sensed that a pathogen with the potential to be catastrophic on a global scale was encroaching on the horizon. He had sought to get the word out about it but encountered resistance from the Chinese government that had nefariously attempted to silence him (this sounds like the premise of any number of whistleblower movies). Now, depending upon how the director(s) and screenwriter(s) of *The Sibylline Scourge* ultimately choose to depict the events surrounding Dr. Wenliang's death within the structure of the narrative and how they elect to focus the disaster, Dr. Wenliang's story may easily be positioned within the Preamble. Though, I suspect that Dr. Wenliang's death, unquestionably necessary from a dramatic standpoint, would be more appropriately inserted into the story somewhere in Act One. After all, his death occurred on February 7, 2020, situated squarely within the narrative confines of Act One, assuming our story is focused on the toll Covid took in the United States, localized for the purposes of the narrative in New York City (similar to the manner in which *Contagion* concentrated that story in the city of Minneapolis). Moreover, Wenliang's death contributed significantly to the sense of mounting dread, to the portentous snowball effect which, as we have already determined, is crucial for the purposes of building the dramatic element of the story, the buildup. In placing Dr. Wenliang's death neatly in Act One, one of the confounding questions *The Sibylline Scourge* could ask would be, "If a doctor, a man of medicine who was studying this strange virus, became infected and couldn't survive it, would the lay population that constitutes the rest of the unassuming world have a chance?"

Supporting Character: Lawrence Garbuz

Also included on the roster of supporting characters in *The Sibylline Scourge* might be Lawrence Garbuz, New York City's Patient Zero. Garbuz, an attorney at his eponymous law firm specializing in estates, trusts, and elder law, contracted the virus (though he didn't know it at the time) in early February 2020. It started with a cough. Then again, who isn't coughing or sneezing or somehow aching in New York City in February? It's the height of flu season, for Pete's sake! But while the cough was initially not a cause for undue concern, a fever quickly followed. Then a doctor's visit. Then the hospital. Then the intensive care unit. Then a ventilator. Then, it was official: Garbuz tested positive for the novel coronavirus on March 2, 2020. The upstate city of New Rochelle, about a half-hour north of Manhattan, was essentially cordoned off, a veritable citywide biohazard containment zone (Nolan). I can recall thinking to myself at the time from the safety of my studio on West Ninety-Second Street, "Woah … this is some surreal shit!" Garbuz was New York City's first confirmed case of coronavirus. In a city like New York, germs, like words, spread fast. The storm had made landfall.

But even if the inclusion of Garbuz within the narrative amounts to little more than his character showing up for an extended one-or-two scene cameo, his presence is significant for the establishment of a jumping-off point for the narrative proper. In the interest of focusing our story in the New York City area, Garbuz's confirmed case of the coronavirus can be considered our Primary Disaster. With the confirmation that Garbuz had contracted Covid-19, the bug had, from an official standpoint, infiltrated New York City, a city commonly thought to house approximately eight million people. Sure, the outbreak was first localized in New Rochelle, a northern suburb of New York City. But like any invisible invader, its reach would most definitely and quickly begin to spread. There was little doubt that the dreaded virus would disperse its tentacles fast, far, and wide. Indeed, not long after Garbuz was hospitalized in late February 2020, cases of Covid infection in those individuals who had experienced a direct connection to the Westchester lawyer began to emerge and grew to number at least thirty-seven by March 6, 2020, roughly a week following his hospitalization (Hogan, Marsh, et al.). On March 10, in a move that foreshadowed the dystopian lockdowns that would soon dam the country, Governor Cuomo called in the freakin' National Guard to enforce a mile-radius "containment zone" centered around the Young Israel of New Rochelle synagogue, Garbuz's house of worship (Hogan, Roberts, et al.).

Thankfully, Garbuz recovered from his illness. But I am of the opinion that in a virally-centric, biological disaster film, a Patient Zero character is critical. This is the character that establishes a mortal beginning for the dramatic arc of the story, a tangible moment which the viewer and/or the main protagonist can refer back to at the conclusion of the story. For reference, see Paltrow's character in *Contagion* or Patrick Dempsey's character in *Outbreak*. The Patient Zero character in *The Sibylline Scourge* would take on the unfortunate role of joining their tragic company.

Let me be clear: we are discussing Dr. Wenliang's and Mr. Garbuz's places within the *drama* of *The Sibylline Scourge*. I do not want any mention of the roles they play within our narrative to be misconstrued as any kind of a slight on their lives or accomplishments. With that said, it might be tempting, and certainly understandable, for one to want to make the argument that Dr. Wenliang should occupy the Poignant Character space in the narrative. However, I would challenge Dr. Wenliang's assumption of the role of the Poignant Character for a few reasons. Most importantly and obviously, Dr. Wenliang's death occurs much too close to the beginning of the narrative, which makes it far too unlikely that the audience would have developed the requisite sympathy for the doctor, sympathy that is essential for Dr. Wenliang to be designated as an appropriate Poignant Character. The first case to hit American shores was reported on January 21, 2020 (Taylor); Dr. Wenliang passed away on February 7, 2020, just over two weeks later (Taylor). The first reported American death from Covid-19—the man from Washington State—occurred roughly three weeks after that, on February 29, 2020 (Taylor). At that point in the Covid timeline, the fear and the paranoia that eventually would become widespread in the pandemic had only barely begun to register. Moreover, a national emergency wasn't issued by President Donald Trump until March 13, 2020, and a recommendation for the wide and abundant use of masks wasn't issued until April 3, 2020 (Al Jazeera). Remember what we have indicated from the chapter concerning the Poignant Character should be the desired resultant effect of such a character, "to allow for a feeling and an instance of melancholy and melodrama; an instance of oversized emotion and introspection that occurs before, and perhaps explicitly instigates (as in the case in *The Poseidon Adventure*), the core group of survivors to muster strength and push through to the story's conclusion." As tragic as Dr. Wenliang's death (or any death for any reason, for that matter) was, his position within the narrative, combined with the overwhelmingly American focus of our story, makes him an inadequate Poignant Character. Dr. Wenliang's death would be more reasonably situated as part of the buildup and more appropriately used as a harbinger of the tragedy to follow.

Dr. Wenliang is, unquestionably, an admirable figure in the Covid-19 narrative, as any perceived whistleblower might be in their own narrative. In terms of his character's significance within the narrative, however, the consequence of Dr. Wenliang's death might be likened more to the death of Dr. Erin Mears in *Contagion*. Dr. Mears is a scientist from the CDC who travels to Minneapolis to conduct her research on the ongoing viral outbreak raging throughout the area. At some point, she begins to show symptoms of the illness and eventually succumbs to it, mirroring the fate of Dr. Wenliang. Dr. Mears passes away from the very illness she had been dispatched by the CDC to research.

Even though Dr. Wenliang has been disqualified from any contention to assume the role of the Poignant Character, he nonetheless remains an important and valuable character within our story. Therefore, his death must be treated as a vital supporting character death in *The Sibylline Scourge*. As the coronavirus took hold in the United States and the world throughout the winter and spring of 2020, and people from all walks of life and all standings of health became ill by the thousands, the mortality rate of this insidious disease shot up. In the process, and in addition to Dr. Wenliang, there existed several high profile and notable people and celebrities whose deaths could be attributed, at least in part, to Covid-19. While the dramatic scope of *The Sibylline Scourge* may not be large enough in a feature length format to flesh out and support all of these notables as true supporting characters in our narrative, we might want to consider referring to them under the category of supporting character deaths for the purposes of reinforcing the disaster scenario of *The Sibylline Scourge*. These celebrities would include actor Mark Blum; musician and lead singer of rock group Fountains of Wayne, Adam Schlesinger; magician and iconic Las Vegas entertainer Roy Horn; and legendary playwright Terrence McNally.

It is an interesting paradox, however, to recognize that although the "game" of the standard disaster film is comprised of trying to speculate who will and who won't survive the disaster, many films of the disaster subgenre, including many of those discussed in this book, don't, in fact, depict many, if any, supporting character deaths, name actor or not. I would even include *The Sibylline Scourge* within this strange paradox. Other than Dr. Wenliang and Nick Cordero, our Poignant Character, the other true supporting character deaths aren't as apparent. *The Sibylline Scourge* is not unlike disaster movies such as *Earthquake*, *Avalanche*, *San Andreas*, or *Greenland*, in the sense that there are countless extra-type characters who perish, but not so many of the featured characters. In order that we may break this trope down to specifics, let's examine some of the character death statistics in some of the disaster films we are referencing in this book. Note that these numbers *do not* include the Poignant Character, the countless extras who are often collateral damage that results from the disaster, the male or female lead (if he or she happens to expire in the film), or any prominent kids who don't survive (very rare, even in the most cartoonishly catastrophic of disaster movies, but it happens).

Movie (year)	Character Deaths	Character (actor)
Airport (1970)	0	
The Poseidon Adventure (1972)	2	Acres (Roddy McDowall), Linda Rogo (Stella Stevens)
The Towering Inferno (1974)	3	Dan Bigelow (Robert Wagner), Lorrie (Susan Flannery), Simmons (Richard Chamberlain)
Earthquake (1974)	1	Jody (Marjoe Gortner)
Airport 1975 (1974)	0	
The Swarm (1978)	6	Maureen Schuester (Olivia de Havilland), Felix (Ben Johnson), Mayor Clarence (Fred MacMurray), Dr. Hubbard (Richard Chamberlain), Major Baker (Bradford Dillman), General Slater (Richard Widmark)
Speed (1994)	1	Howard Payne (Dennis Hopper)
Independence Day (1996)	4	Marilyn Whitmore (Mary McDonnell), Marty Gilbert (Harvey Fierstein), Dr. Brakish Okun (Brent Spiner), Russell Casse (Randy Quaid)
Deep Impact (1998)	0	(essentially, they all die)
Armageddon (1998)	2	Oscar (Owen Wilson), Gruber (Grayson McCouch)

Movie (year)	Character Deaths	Character (actor)
Dante's Peak (1997)	1	Paul (Charles Hallahan)
Volcano (1997)	1	Rachel (Laurie Lathem)
Outbreak (1995)	1	Jimbo Scott (Patrick Dempsey)
Daylight (1996)	3	Roy Nord (Viggo Mortensen), Kadeem (Marcello Thedford), Eleanor Trilling (Claire Bloom)
San Andreas (2015)	1	Daniel Riddick (Ioan Gruffudd)
Geostorm (2017)	4	Makmoud Habib (Richard Regan Paul), Duncan Taylor (Robert Sheehan), Rico (David S. Lee), Karl (I think, Billy Slaughter)
Greenland (2020)	3	Colin (Andrew Byron Bachelor), Twin Otter Pilot (Holt McCallany), Twin Otter Co-Pilot (Adam Cronan)

You will notice that *The Swarm* has the highest supporting character death count of the 1970s cycle, while *Independence Day* takes the lead for the 1990s genre cycle, and *Geostorm* holds the title, so far, in the 2000s. While *The Poseidon Adventure*, *The Towering Inferno*, and *Earthquake* were certainly epic pictures produced on a pre–CGI massive scale in their day, those films essentially established the disaster movie template. *The Towering Inferno* even represented the first instance in which two major Hollywood studios, Warner Bros. and Twentieth Century–Fox, joined forces to co-finance and co-produce a film ("The Towering Inferno [1974]"). As any film aficionado who has ever witnessed a genre cycle can attest, once the cycle has been established, not only do the cheap imitators emerge, but each subsequent film is produced in an attempt to outdo the previous entry in the cycle. On this point, we can once again refer to theorist Steve Neale's indication of the final stage of Thomas Schatz's theory of genre development: "Finally, once 'the genre's straightforward message has "saturated" the audience ... the genre evolves into what [art historian Henri] Focillon terms the age of refinement. As a genre's classic conventions are refined and eventually parodied and subverted, its transparency gradually gives way to *opacity*: we no longer look *through* the form ... rather we look *at* the *form itself* to examine and appreciate its structure and its cultural appeal'" (qtd. in Neale 211–12; emphasis in original). Perhaps, then, it might be a fair statement to say that the bigger the bloat of the movie in question, the bigger the body count. In other words, the more extravagant a movie, such as an *Independence Day* or *Geostorm*, the more characters in secondary roles will perish by film's end. This may not, in reality, be a function that is serving the narrative so much as a function of a "more to work with" scenario. More money equals more people, which equals more time to stage supporting character death scenes.

Still, sometimes a move in the supporting character guessing game amounts to a great, big, fake-out. A supporting (sometimes leading) character that has been shot/maimed/infected and whom we are certain is going to be on the "won't survive" list, ends up miraculously pulling through and making it to the end of the picture, surviving the disaster, although maybe not entirely in one piece. For example, Jacqueline Bisset's stewardess Gwen in *Airport* is severely injured as a result of the mid-flight explosion from the suitcase bomb, smuggled aboard the Golden Argosy by D.O. Guerrero (the character played by Van Heflin). The explosion blasts Gwen to the other side of the galley and will elicit an especially dramatic and jaw-dropping "Oh no!" moment from the audience, which I'm sure was director George Seaton's intention. Now, Gwen is a character whom the audience has developed quite a sympathetic relationship with over the course of the movie. She's a young, independent, and at the time (1960s), modern woman, in love with a womanizer (Capt. Demarest) who is, of course, married. But he is affable, charming, and he loves her. Furthering the audience's emotional jolt when Gwen is injured, we know from an earlier scene in which Gwen and Demarest have a heart-to-heart prior to the flight even departing Lincoln International Airport, that Gwen is carrying Demarest's child. The audience is endeared to Gwen and secure in the fact that we know she is not some calculating succubus out to trap a man for financial gain. She makes it clear to Demarest that she has no expectation of significant support from him. She is wholly aware that he is a married man, and she has no intention of assuming the role of a homewrecker and inserting herself between him and his wife. Gwen is a woman in charge of her career and in control of her life (her emotions are another story). So, the audience would be put in a position of extreme grief and sadness should Gwen, an extremely likeable character, succumb to the injuries she suffers as a result of the explosion. Will she make it or won't she?

But alas, Gwen does not perish, and she is subsequently wheeled out on a stretcher back at Lincoln International Airport once the aircraft arrives. In fact, Demarest is so focused on Gwen, and walking right alongside the stretcher as it is wheeled into the arrivals area, that he doesn't even realize that his wife is waiting anxiously at the gate to welcome him. That tells us all we need to know about how the relationship between Gwen and Demarest will transpire following the events of the movie. Even though by this time, however, Demarest has finally and tearfully confessed to Gwen that he loves her, so their romantic subplot has come full circle. Gwen survives, but according to the rules I've defined herein, is still denied the position of a suitable Poignant Character since she is the female (co-) lead in the film. Thus, *Airport*, a founding member of the disaster subgenre and a wildly successful award-winning movie, becomes an example of a disaster film that lacks an obvious Poignant Character. Unless one can see fit, as I have, to assign that role to the only supporting character death in *Airport*, the ostensible villain of the piece, D.O. Guerrero. This is primarily due to the pitiable circumstance of his financial desperation that anyone can potentially relate to, and which prompts him to smuggle a bomb on board the aircraft, as well as the overwhelming grief and regret expressed by his suffering wife, played by Maureen Stapleton, in a wonderful performance that earned her an Academy Award nomination for Best Actress in a Supporting Role for the 1971 Awards ceremony ("Airport—Awards").

While *Outbreak* in 1995 isn't a movie that can be accused of lacking an appropriate Poignant Character (Kevin Spacey's Casey fits that bill), Rene Russo's Dr. Robby Keough serves in a similar "will she or won't she survive the disaster" capacity as Bisset's Gwen. As Casey lies in his hospital bed, violently convulsing and on the verge of death with a 106-degree fever(!), Sam, Robby, and other medical staff work feverishly to cool his body temperature down using ice bags. The medical team, working in hazmat suits, is desperately striving to keep Casey alive and lucid. As Dr. Keough is drawing blood from Casey's arm, however, the disintegrating man experiences a particularly violent convulsion, and this results in Dr. Keough accidentally pricking her finger with the contaminated needle. Although she tells Sam at the time that the needle prick didn't, in fact, puncture the outer layer of her hazmat suit, she knows that it did (*Outbreak* 1:17:00–18). Presented here is another "Oh no!" moment that prompts the audience to collectively gasp at this unexpected episode. The emotional intensity of the moment is even more heightened because the audience has spent a significant amount of time with the characters of Sam and Dr. Keough (her needle prick occurs at seventy-seven minutes into the one hundred twenty-eight-minute movie). We know that they are an estranged couple who nonetheless share a deep love and respect for one another. Both of them are likeable characters in their individual ways, and the scenario regarding them is constructed in such a manner that the audience is led to presume, to hope, that the ordeal they endure in the film will bring the two closer together and that they will reunite as a couple by film's end. The relationship between Sam and Robby is the sort of romantic subplot we see evidenced in the majority of disaster films.*

Dr. Keough, of course, becomes sick with the illness (the movie would be cheating if she didn't) and ends up in much the same dire condition as Jimbo (the character played by Patrick Dempsey) and Casey. The disaster film survival game swings into action once again as the audience isn't entirely sure whether the screenplay will allow Dr. Keough to survive the disaster or whether she will end up a victim of the story. In the end, she is afforded the same narrative fate as Gwen. Dr. Keough lives and, presumptively, ends up with her man, Sam. If Dr. Keough had perished, she, like Gwen in *Airport*, still wouldn't have made a suitable Poignant Character because she is the female lead. However, unlike *Airport, Outbreak* possesses a well-defined Poignant Character in Casey, and thereby more closely abides by all of the designed properties of the subgenre.

One of the salient parallels between the disaster movie as it exists in fiction form and the disaster movie in real life, i.e., *The Sibylline Scourge*, is the roster of plentiful supporting characters that populate the story. Of course, since *The Sibylline Scourge* is, or will be, based on a true story, and certain characters will be, by necessity, dramatizations of their real-life counterparts, only those who survive in truth will be able to survive the disaster in the story. Likewise, for those who will, unfortunately, pass away. So, for example, as tempting as it might be to dispatch a particularly loathed character in *The Sibylline Scourge*, there will not be a whole lot of room to allow for creative license in this regard within the confines of a true story.

At the same time, it is critical to recognize that as we shape our movie version of *The Sibylline Scourge,* some of the real people and the real situations we know them to have encountered throughout the Covid-19

---

*After Robby pricks her finger, she immediately runs over to a room adjacent to the operating room, rinses it with water, and washes the wound with iodine. Sam follows her into the adjacent room and directs her to do what she has already done: wash it out, clean it, etc. Robby, understandably on edge at this particular moment, becomes agitated and angrily brushes him off. She is beside herself, admonishing herself for not taking more care in handling a needle while drawing blood from the severely ill Casey. Sam tries to calm her, but she is much too upset to be soothed by him. He takes her by the shoulders and basically shakes her to attention. He barks at her, "Listen to me!" She angrily responds, "There's nothing to say, Sam!" Sam looks deep into Robby's eyes, gently caresses her face through her hazmat face shield, and affectionately responds, "there is." The implication in Sam's words being that he wants to say (or does, once the scene ends), "I love you." (*Outbreak* 1:17:21–1:18:20).

pandemic may, driven by dramatic and structural constraints, take on a less prominent or important role than they might have during the actual crisis. Many of these people occupy roles that, in the film, would be classified as supporting or tertiary. In our current disaster film, examples of characters that might occupy these roles might include the following:

- **Speaker of the House, Congresswoman Nancy Pelosi**
  ◊ Pelosi was an outspoken critic of President Donald Trump, practically since the beginning of his term in office. Who can forget the ballsy and spiteful moment in which House Speaker Pelosi tore up President Trump's remarks after he had just completed a State of the Union address? A very public and borderline disrespectful motion that didn't do much to bridge the chasm of partisan politics.
- **Vice President, Mike Pence**
  ◊ Despite Trump charging his second-in-command with spearheading the White House Coronavirus Task Force (of which leading man, Dr. Anthony Fauci, and leading lady, Dr. Deborah Birx, were members), Pence was, for the most part, a silent character in this unfolding real-life drama. Sure, he was present and was visible when he needed to be, but his efficacy was never really lauded by a public demanding clarity of information.
- **New York City Mayor Bill de Blasio**
  ◊ The widely reviled New York City mayor, like it or not, was large and in charge during the course of the pandemic. His famous sparring matches with Governor Cuomo were legendary in the early days of the crisis and an unequivocal contributing factor to the City's state of confusion and frustration. I mean, our elected leaders were, if I may be crude for a moment, engaged in a gigantic dick-swinging contest for the public's affections. What these two men failed to adequately realize was that we didn't care who was the loudest or most forceful. We wanted accurate and consistent information from our elected state and city leaders, and we did not receive it. Furthermore, de Blasio's signature folly was, perhaps, the well-intentioned but disastrous redirection of thousands of the city's mentally ill residents from area shelters to boutique hotels located in residential neighborhoods, ostensibly to ease crowding and virus transmission in area shelters. The hotels used for this misguided mission were located primarily on the Upper West Side of Manhattan. For the better part of 2020, the posh and relatively

peaceful neighborhood became a mosh pit of drug use and criminality, as residents struggled to conduct their lives among a population of the mentally ill and homeless who were largely given free rein to do drugs and harass passersby in the area.

- **Dr. Robert Redfield**
  - ◊ From 2018–2021, Dr. Redfield was the Director of the Centers for Disease Control and Prevention ("Past CDC Directors"). Due to his organization's prominence in the disaster, Redfield would be a good supporting character to have in our story. If there was technical or administrative exposition that needed to be conveyed somehow, for example, Redfield might be a good character from which to espouse it. Don't forget, Dr. Ellis Cheever (the character played by Laurence Fishburne in *Contagion*) was the director of the CDC, so there is precedent.
- **Patient Zero**
  - ◊ We are not talking about New York City's Patient Zero here (Lawrence Garbuz), but rather the unidentified 35-year-old man in Washington State who is widely believed to be the vessel for the first confirmed coronavirus case in the United States. This character, should the scenarists choose to include him in the dramatization at all, would almost certainly be a tertiary character. At the risk of sounding flippant, though that is obviously not my intention, Patient Zero's only engagement with *The Sibylline Scourge* was that he *was* Patient Zero. He didn't pioneer any of the vaccines or contribute to the research surrounding the bug in any scientific or noteworthy way. In fact, for his own protection, his identity remained (and still remains, to my knowledge) anonymous throughout the course of the pandemic. While Patient Zero is an important character to note within the story, an extended cameo (such as that of Patrick Dempsey as Jimbo in *Outbreak*) or explicit reference to his character in the screenplay would suffice.
  - ◊ And then, of course, there are the **high-profile celebrities** that have withstood their own personal battles with Covid-19, including Tom Hanks and Rita Wilson, and Alyssa Milano. The famed playwright Terrence McNally ultimately passed away from complications due to Covid.
  - ◊ It would hardly be reasonable to assume that these celebrities would want to play themselves in the story. For what? Again, at the risk of sounding unintentionally flippant, the only significance of these characters in the narrative is that they are high-profile personalities who contracted the virus.

In addition to those potential characters mentioned above, we must still travel further down the roster of supporting players in *The Sibylline Scourge* in order to round out our cast and begin to fill in the true supporting and tertiary characters. In the average disaster film, examples of characters occupying these roles might be Dan Bigelow (Robert Wagner) in *The Towering Inferno*, Capt. Stacy (Efrem Zimbalist, Jr.) in *Airport 1975*, Grace Calloway (the character played by Vanessa Bell Calloway) in *Daylight*, or Dennis French (Enrico Colantoni) in *Contagion*. These roles do not have the same impact on the crux of the narrative as the leads and secondary leads do, and they are generally not responsible for decisions within the narrative that need to be made. These characters do not demand the same amount of audience attention. In *The Sibylline Scourge*, the characters of Dr. Fauci, Dr. Birx, Governor Cuomo, President Trump, and possibly New York City Mayor Bill de Blasio will be the characters that will garner the most screen time by virtue of their prominence in the real-life disaster. Don't let any potentially distracting casting fool you, however. The prominence of some of these supporting or tertiary characters in the narrative notwithstanding, they may nonetheless be portrayed by particularly notable celebrities, such as the character of Beth Emhoff, played by Gwyneth Paltrow, in *Contagion*.

There are many instances, especially in films that are based on true stories, when you might encounter (whether you know it or not) what is referred to as a "composite character." This is a character that is invented by the scenarists for the express purpose of combining several real-life persons in a story. Think about it. If a scenarist were to include in the narrative every single person connected to a story, it would almost certainly serve to clutter the narrative. Furthermore, some people, even though they may figure somehow in the course of the story, might not warrant the need for an individual, genuinely fleshed-out character. A filmmaker or screenwriter might choose to incorporate a composite character into the story in order to streamline or focus the narrative and to allow for the screenplay to progress with more ease of rhythm, creating more accessibility and engagement for an audience. Insisting that an audience keep track of too many characters, especially tangential or narratively unimportant characters, will only cause confusion in an otherwise compelling story.

In the case of *The Sibylline Scourge*, it might be worth it for a writer, in attempting to expound some of the inherent humanity in the story, to search for select individuals or families, whose personal, not necessarily public, stories hold some resonance and sentimentality. The screenwriter, rather than bogging down his or her screenplay with too many of these stories related to the effects that the pandemic had on ordinary citizens, may choose to combine several of these stories into one. In this way, the screenwriter will be able to target the story of a specific fictional character, while at the same time paying homage to all of the individual stories that the time and narrative constraints of a feature film would not accommodate. Or perhaps a screenwriter might find himself or herself littering the story by referencing too many medical or administrative characters. In this case, he or she might elect to simply funnel several of these characters, who would probably end up as tangential characters, into one who holds more prominence.

All of these characters, whether real or composite, supporting or tertiary, and the actors who will eventually portray them, furnish the disaster movie with the aforementioned audience guessing game of "will they or won't they survive the disaster." But as we have discussed, not every supporting character perishes because of the disaster. Sometimes, very few supporting characters will, in fact, die over the course of the movie. So, rather than attempting to deduce which characters will and which characters won't survive the disaster, perhaps a more fitting disaster movie guessing game might be "which characters will, and which characters won't encounter grave circumstances which may, *somehow*, result in his or her death during the course of the disaster." In fact, I would agree with film critic Mark Kermode who made a positively astute observation in a discussion on his podcast, *Kermode on Film*, when he postulated that one of the major attractions of disaster films is that they are "oddly life-affirming" (33:01–33:07). Disaster movies, as a general rule, provoke in the viewer the sense of a close call. A viewer might witness a character or characters scrambling to escape a destructive avalanche, the creeping lava of a volcano, or the terrifying prospect of a plane crash and think, "Phew! Thank goodness I'm not in that situation!" Indeed, Kermode speaks to the mindset of disaster film spectators as "thanking your lucky stars that you're not involved in whatever this situation is" (32:12–22).

In this way, disaster films work the same way as some contemporary (and some might argue, egregiously exploitative and, well, idiotic) reality television. I can recall one New Year's Eve several years ago when I was at home, by myself. It was a typically frigid December in New York City. There was no party to attend, there were no friends available for whatever reason, there was no one to ring in the New Year with other than myself. On a night when the entire world is in a celebratory mood and heeding the annual call for festivity, dancing, drinking, making resolutions for the new year, and wishing farewell to the past year as it fades into nothing more than a memory, I sat in my apartment, alone, watching TV. It might appear trifling, perhaps, but in my pitiable state of mind at the time, I thought that sitting alone in a tiny New York City apartment on New Year's Eve was as depressing as it got. I was probably picking my nose or doing something else gross and primal that people do when no one else is around, but I remember flipping through the channels on TV and eventually settling on an episode of the A&E reality show *Intervention*. This program, for the uninitiated, chronicles various individuals who are caught up in the agonizing throes of addiction. In a last-ditch effort to save their lives, addicts are confronted by their family and friends in an extremely emotional, staged intervention that is orchestrated to convince the addict to consent to enter a rehab facility. Now, sometimes they do, sometimes they don't, and sometimes they do and don't complete the program. Exploiting pain and suffering for ratings.

The show is, in a *very* broad sense, reminiscent of my solo New Year's Eve pity party that night in my apartment all those years ago: on the whole, a rather morose affair. But there is a glimmer of a silver lining in the show. The theme of hope and resilience, coupled with the, more often than not, successful outcomes from the interventions, drapes the program in an aura of redemption and triumph, much like the disaster film (Kermode 27:11–19). Yet, as I sat on my couch, feeling sorry for myself on that lonely New Year's Eve so long ago I can't even recall the specific year, I couldn't help but think, "Well, it could be a lot worse. At least I'm not the subject of an episode of *Intervention*."

ACT THREE

Out of the Woods?

CHAPTER 8

The Second Disaster

The Covid-19 pandemic chartered its insidious course through major cities in the United States ever since it bored its roots into the world in late January 2020. Yet, no American city endured the sort of crippling devastation as did New York City. According to the CDC, the 7-Day Moving Average of Covid deaths in New York City was reported as six on March 21. Only one week later, that number would jump to eighty-nine. A week after that, the number would climb to two hundred and twenty-six. By the third week of April, the 7-Day Moving Average of Covid deaths in New York City had hit an apex of one thousand, one hundred and ninety-three ("Trends"). With the death toll continuing to rise to unimaginable heights coupled with food and grocery shortages, shuttered storefronts, and deserted streets, the American landscape had come to resemble something on the level of a biblical apocalypse (Shaer, "Canonical Films" 9).

Even as the death toll in New York City looked undeniably staggering, New York State was, around this time, actually experiencing the first signs of a decline in the number of deaths related to Covid-19. As a matter of fact, Governor Cuomo delivered some oddly ironical good news on April 18 that the death toll in New York State was "past the plateau and starting to descend" (Cramer et al.). The curve had been flattened and was now, mercifully, on the decline. By May 2, the 7-Day Moving Average of Covid deaths in New York City had fallen to two hundred and eighty-seven ("Trends"). As spring started to spring, homebound New Yorkers, who had been harboring uncharacteristic cabin fever in their (most likely, this being New York City) tiny apartments for the previous two months, began to cautiously open their apartment doors and peek through the musty cracks like mice inching bravely into a living room. The call of the outdoors was intoxicating in a way it had never been before. Local watering holes offered communally starved urbanites a much-needed measure of social interaction with the introduction of "to go" cups (open containers had never been a thing in New York City). A large number of city restaurants would soon begin to erect auxiliary dining rooms on the streets outside of their establishments as part of New York City's Open Restaurants Program. The mayor's office, in an all-too-rare positive development for the city, decreed that certain streets throughout the city be shut to thru traffic during the daytime so that pedestrians and fresh air-starved New Yorkers could enjoy some valuable outdoor leisure space. The storm, seemingly, had passed and New York City could once again, exhale (Shaer, "Canonical Films" 9).

While this collective relief was not exactly what one would refer to as a cause for celebration, the residents of New York City were, nonetheless, once step closer to possibly regaining a semblance of the city they loved.

But then, as if on a cunning cue, *The Sibylline Scourge* presented an event that jolted the story out from a momentary lull in the narrative prior to the engagement of the third and final act. This event can be classified as *The Sibylline Scourge*'s Second Disaster: the May 25, 2020, killing of a forty-six-year-old man by the name of George Floyd by Minneapolis police officers. These officers, four in total, had purportedly apprehended Floyd for attempting to pass a counterfeit twenty-dollar bill at a local market. Hardly a cause, it would seem, for a violent arrest, but that's exactly what transpired. Images were seen around the country, and the world, showing an arresting officer (identified as a man named Derek Chauvin), kneeling on Floyd's neck as the unarmed would-be perp lay face down on the side of the street. Troubling, terrifying. Public outcry was immediate, deafening, and impactful. Such an instantaneous uprising had arguably not been seen since the Los Angeles Riots of 1992, precipitated by the vicious beating of Rodney King by members of the Los Angeles Police Department. In the viral aftermath of George Floyd's death, the already alarming words "I can't breathe" assumed a much more dire and burning immediacy due to the manner in which Floyd died: suffocating to death as the arresting officer had him pinned to the ground with his knee pressing on the back of the dying man's neck (Deliso).

Massive protests—masks be damned—sprung up in cities nationwide. Black Lives Matter, a movement created in 2013 in response to the murder of Trayvon Martin by George Zimmerman and which focuses on social and political empowerment for all members of the Black communities ("Herstory"), quickly conflated into even more of a cultural force for social and racial justice (Shaer, "Canonical Films" 10). "I Can't Breathe" was emblazoned on T-shirts and intoned by incensed protestors marching in revolt. Even with Covid-19 still very much a pressing concern and even as officials warned of a future second wave of the disease that was sure to come later in the year, civic tension was on the rise and people were taking to the streets. The skylines of major cities across America were foregrounded against the orange glow of fire and the persistent drones of protest.

As a result of violent clashes between protestors and the police stemming from wild and frequent marches and widespread looting, urban areas across the country authorized authoritarian curfews in a desperate endeavor to maintain public safety (Shaer, "Canonical Films" 10). The breakdown of society concept, a foundational element in any disaster narrative, was in full force. As they continued to work through the emotional trauma following several months of enforced confinement, fear, and doomsday dread, citizens were given a shot of fuel with which to further conflagrate the civil unrest.

In the wake of these protests, calls arose in cities across the country for the defunding of police departments. The chants of protestors calling on local governments to "defund the police" were heard in many urban areas. This call to action grew out of a mass demand for the cessation of what much of the general public perceived as police violence disproportionately directed towards people of color. In some United States cities, such as Minneapolis, police departments were, in fact, defunded (to an extent). In other locales, such as New York City, police budgets were severely slashed by those in power in the heavily democratic administration (led by Mayor Bill de Blasio) and funds reallocated to social initiatives. In an unbelievable paradox, policemen and women were now placed in the role of villains, enemies to be confronted and vanquished. Understandably frustrated by an ever-increasing critical scrutiny surrounding them, many dispirited members of the force chose to take early retirement. Some of their brothers and sisters in blue were simply too scared to uphold their professional ideals and actually carry out police work out of a debilitating fear of legal or even physical reprisal. Everyone from the highest tiers of city and state government to the laypeople of the general masses and even to police officers caught in between were out-and-out terrified. Lawlessness, it seemed, was now the norm, at least it was in New York City (Shaer, "Canonical Films" 10).

As Act Two draws to a close, the Primary Disaster is now clearly established and has been underway. If the movie is of the type that is on a *proactive* narrative arc, a plan of action has by now been put in motion for reining in the disaster and for mitigating further destruction and death. If the movie is of the sort which is on a *reactive* narrative arc, the society established in the film has been fleeing to safety for some time now. By this point, the core group of survivors on which the narrative is centering has aggregated and is well into enduring the disaster. Some members of the core group of survivors have survived the ordeal up to this point, and some, unfortunately, have not. The proper authorities may have even been called and armed forces have perhaps been deployed into action. The requisite leaders have emerged who, along with whatever plan of action has been put into motion, if applicable, will guide the core group of survivors to, we hope, safety. The airplane in *Airport '77*, for example, has been underwater without rescue for quite a while and time is running out. Jack Lemmon's pilot, Don Gallagher, has stepped up and assumed leadership control of the situation as best as can be expected under the circumstances, relying on support from his first stewardess, Brenda Vaccaro's Eve. (Sidebar: I know Jack Lemmon didn't reflect fondly upon this film, but he is really quite good in it. He makes for a perfectly adequate, albeit unlikely given his onscreen persona as a comic actor, action hero.) A plan of action has been suggested to try and get a radio-equipped life raft to the surface of the water and, in doing so, notify whatever authorities are searching for the sunken plane. Some of the core group of survivors (in this case, as is the case in all of the movies in the *Airport* series, the core group of survivors and the society are basically same thing due to the confined nature of the settings) have been lost, such as piano player Steve (Tom Sullivan) and Poignant Character Martin Wallace (Christopher Lee). More lives will unquestionably be lost before the group is lifted to safety. In *Armageddon*, to cite another film, the president of the United States has been notified of the massive asteroid heading towards Earth, a collision which would be, as Billy Bob Thornton's Dan Truman puts it, "the end of mankind" (*Armageddon* 00:11:30). A plan of action is initiated to enlist the services of Bruce Willis's Harry S. Stamper and a motley crew of astronauts to blast into space, drill a hole in the asteroid, and explode it to kingdom come. Some of the core group of survivors (in the case of *Armageddon*, this only includes the astronauts on board both the *Freedom* and the *Independence*) have been lost, including Oscar (the character played by Owen Wilson) and most of the astronauts on board the Independence. Like *Airport '77*, more members of the core group of survivors will perish before film's end.

If we refer back to the analogy of the roller coaster, this period in the film corresponds to the episode after the coaster train has reached the peak of the ride and descended down the other side of its hill. The excited screams of the passengers have been subdued for the moment, and arms which had been waving in the thrust of the wind during the descent have returned to their natural positions by their sides. The initially exhilarating rush of adrenaline that was felt when conquering the first terrifying hill or loop of the roller coaster has been fully experienced, resulting in a sense of accomplishment mixed with bravado among the ride passengers. All aboard can take a minute to breathe, to exhale, following what should have been a heart-pounding exhibition of the spectacle.

Hopefully, that same sense of pride in accomplishment, that same heightened thrill incurred by the passengers on the roller coaster after descending the first hill will hold not only for the survivors (so far) of the catastrophe in the disaster film, but for the audience watching it. No matter how the specific narrative elements of Act Two of the disaster film might be written on the page, whether the narrative trajectory is proactive or reactive, there will, in all probability, be a Second Disaster after the Primary Disaster. This Second Disaster will be the unofficial event in the disaster film that will signify the entrance into the third and final act. The Second Disaster constitutes the second hill, the second loop of the roller coaster, the final exhilarating thrill for the audience. I refer to this as The Law of the Second Disaster (Shaer, "Canonical Films" 8).

The Law of the Second Disaster makes the case that before an audience can settle too comfortably into a state of stasis following the initial rush and heightened stimulation brought about by the Primary Disaster and its subsequent deceleration, another major disaster will present itself and jumpstart the senses, reenergize the audience's stimuli before the film ends and they are sent off back into the ho-hummery of the real world. This Second Disaster may take a less severe form than the Primary Disaster, or even be the centerpiece spectacle of the film (the Primary Disaster having served basically as an elaborate tease when viewed in retrospect). To illustrate, witness as the Titanic is sinking and the terrified passengers are frantically seeking any means of safe escape (Shaer, "Canonical Films" 8–9). Scores of men, women, and children are hurled screaming about the sinking ship, their survival instincts in full effect as they desperately try to cling to any rod or beam for security, mostly to no avail. A perilous mosh pit forms as passengers flock to obtain a seat on one of the too few lifeboats that are being lowered from the ship. The situation couldn't be more dire, and the passengers know beyond a doubt that they are in mortal danger. It is inconceivable to imagine that things could get any worse.

Then the Law of the Second Disaster kicks in, and the ship dramatically (seriously, this is a particularly stupendous sequence in a movie full of them) splits in half, accelerating the doomed ship to take its final resting place on the floor of the frigid Northern Atlantic. All remaining passengers are now essentially condemned to what will likely be an icy, watery grave (*Titanic* 02:30:34–44:46; Shaer, "Canonical Films" 9).

To further comprehend the Law of the Second Disaster, we may also look at the events following the volcanic eruption, the Primary Disaster, that sends the residents of Dante's Peak scurrying in terror in an attempt to escape assured catastrophic destruction. Our core group of survivors, including Dr. Harry Dalton, Mayor Rachel Wando, and the Wando children, understands that getting out of the path of the fiery explosions and flowing lava enveloping the no longer idyllic mountain town, while treacherous, will put the group on the road to safety. Then, in the Law of the Second Disaster, a ferocious pyroclastic cloud uniformly and swiftly envelops the once sleepy village in a terrifying and powerful progression through the town's center and collars our heroes as they attempt to evade certain death (*Dante's Peak* 01:27:49–29:15; Shaer, "Canonical Films" 9).

As was briefly mentioned when discussing the Primary Disaster, in the Irwin Allen-produced TV movie *Fire,* Mrs. Malone (the character played by Donna Mills) senses danger when she notices, to her horror, smoke rising up from the nearby woods during her scan of the area for her lost student, Judy. This was the Primary Disaster, the disaster that instigated the narrative thrust of the movie (i.e., to extinguish the flames of the out-of-control forest fire). The Second Disaster, I would argue, was a bit subtler but nonetheless contained just as much of a sense of urgency. After Dr. Wilcox (Alex Cord) rescues little Judy from the woodsy brush where she has passed out, potentially sentencing herself to a fiery fate, Wilcox, Judy, and Sam Brisbane (Ernest Borgnine) hightail it out of the area. Seconds later, Dr. Wilcox and Sam observe the wind and smoke billowing off of the forest fire. Dr. Wilcox remarks that the winds must have shifted (*Fire* 00:54:56–56:56). This plot pivot now imperils the rest of the core group of survivors hunkered down at Wagner Lodge, waiting expectantly for Dr. Wilcox, Judy, and Sam to return. These members of the core group of survivors patiently sit in wait, per Sam's instructions, in what is supposedly out of harm's way, unaware that they are now in even more danger than they thought they might have been in previously. Sam's mission has now become one that is concentrated on evacuating everyone at Wagner Lodge, including his romantic interest, Martha (Vera Miles), before the dangerous winds reach them.

This film follows the true disaster movie timeline, in which a concrete plan of action has been implemented to address the fire. Authorities, rescue personnel, and firefighters are all working tirelessly to smother the raging wildfire (*proactive* arc), employing every means at their disposal, including water drops, smothering, aerial fire retardant, etc. So, with the Primary Disaster having occurred, been acknowledged, and been so far attended to, the Second Disaster, in the form of the shifted winds headed to Wagner Lodge, arises. But it does not take the form of an explosion or secondary and far more dangerous burst of flames. Rather, it is Sam and Dr. Wilcox's *observation* that the winds have shifted, threatening the core group of survivors. Dr. Wilcox and Sam have identified another major dire situation that will most definitely and expeditiously escalate into a bona fide disaster. The men must now take a proactive approach in their attempt to rescue those holed up at Wagner Lodge that will lead us into the third act of the story.

As we have already discussed with regard to creative adjustments, each movie may project a unique or innovative method or combination of methods with which to present their disasters/spectacles. The Primary Disaster, for instance, might indeed be a visually impressive sensory spectacular, whether fire, flood, earthquake, what have you. However, the Second Disaster in the film may take a verbal, more oratory form in which a character grimly explains a horrific scenario that is destined to ensue, such as in the previous example from *Fire*. Of course, depending upon the specific structure and subject matter of the disaster film in question, there is no reason why the reverse couldn't certainly be true as well. Such is the case with de Bont's high-octane hit, *Speed*.

In this movie, the Primary Disaster is marked when Jack (the character played by Keanu Reeves) is notified by the madman, Payne (the character played by Dennis Hopper), that there is a bomb on board the city bus. As if this wasn't bad enough, this bomb has been rigged to detonate should the bus's speed fall below fifty miles per hour (*Speed* 00:29:51–30:01). From this point on, the second act action transpires and delivers all of the story's dramatic elements aboard the bus (among the passengers, between Jack and Annie [the character played by Sandra Bullock], between Jack and headquarters, etc.) as well as the police team activity back at headquarters, spearheaded by Harry (the character played by Jeff Daniels). Eventually, the bomb-on-bus plot is thwarted and the core group of survivors (the passengers on the bus) is rendered safe. At this juncture, however, the Second Disaster occurs, when Payne hijacks a subway car speeding on its track below Los Angeles. Once again, as if this wasn't bad enough, Payne is holding Annie hostage in anticipation of a final confrontation with Jack (01:39:44). In contrast with the Primary Disaster notification of the bomb on board the bus, the Second Disaster aboard the speeding subway car is more along the lines of a traditional spectacle. Jack and Payne duke it out in this truly action-packed, body-slamming, loud, masterfully choreographed and filmed, turbulent sequence of a ride (as subway rides, in my experience, usually are). Once Payne is killed, Jack and Annie embrace and, in the final moments of the scene, unbelievably confront what could very well be their violent, messy deaths, as the subway car barrels through the uncompleted tunnel (01:47:52–49:16).

Whether a movie is of the type that focuses more on the expository (such as *Fire*) or a movie that leans more toward a spectacularly driven show (such as *Speed*), several types of disaster entertainments utilize a verbal notification or actual realization moment of the Second Disaster mechanism. In addition to the films we have referenced above, *Airport 1975*, another undisputed canonical member of the disaster film subgenre, manifests the Second Disaster in the form of Nancy's realization that radio communication with the Salt Lake City air traffic control tower has been lost. This unfortunate development forces upon Nancy the terrifying prospect of having to land the plane safely, without any guidance or assistance from the ground. We also see this method used in *The Cassandra Crossing* wherein Dr. Jonathan Chamberlain (the character played by Richard Harris) relays to Col. Mackenzie (the character played by Burt Lancaster) that the eponymous railway crossing over a deep gorge is unsafe to travel across (*The Cassandra Crossing* 01:29:59). This notification and realization instance forecasts the third act spectacle of the collapse of The Cassandra Crossing and the train crumbling into pieces as it plummets into the gorge.

In *Deep Impact,* a staunchly non-spectacular-focused movie (with the exception, of course, of the final act of destruction when the comets finally impact the earth in a dazzling special effects sequence), both the Primary and the Second Disaster might arguably be seen as occurring in the vocalization or realization vein. The Primary Disaster in *Deep Impact* can be understood to be the announcement by President Beck (Morgan Freeman) that there is a comet heading directly towards the earth. This doomsday proclamation by President Beck sends the world into a frenzied state of uncertainty and fear, much like New York City immediately following the arrival of Covid-19 onto its storied streets. The Second Disaster, occurring later in the story, can be construed to be the subsequent pronouncement by President Beck that the comet has now split into *two* parts, greatly amplifying the scope of the impact and which impact will certainly cause devastating destruction to Earth. Beck's second announcement compels all of the characters, as well as the society at large, to race to come to terms with their impending mortalities. Even though the final destruction sequence in *Deep Impact* is quite the cinematic disaster to behold (the only real reason to see the movie, if you ask me), the comet's impact to Earth can more accurately be understood as a *consequence* of the disaster, much in the same way that the deaths in *Outbreak* are consequences of the virus. When viewed through the cinematic mechanism of *The Sibylline Scourge*, the illness and death that resulted from the novel coronavirus was a direct effect of the virus's escape from Wuhan. Furthermore, the terrifying violence, impassioned protests, and general civil unrest, all of which occurred across the country and even in some parts of Europe and Africa (Reuters Staff) in mid–2020, were direct consequences of the death of George Floyd and the historical and systemic racism present in the United States that Floyd's death brought to the fore. In all of these cases, you see, it isn't the actual death or violence or destruction that is the true disaster, but rather the *vocalization* or the inciting incident that is the real disaster, which then precipitates the more spectacular episodes of violence and death that follow. The vocalization of the disaster method works because it ushers in the utter panic that occurs in Act Two.

Of course, there are still many disaster movies that are perfectly happy to adhere to the traditional visual spectacle method of presenting the disaster. Truth be told, that's fine with me. There is nothing like a true blue, major special effects extravaganza of light, image, and sound to remind one why some movies are much better experienced on the big screen. Being a filmmaker is not a profession for the heedless, and audiences are not stupid. A disaster movie director would be wise to be keenly aware of the millions of dollars that have been invested in their picture, ostensibly to provide audiences with a big-budget, special effects marvel to "wow" them. Indeed, if I, as a ticket buyer, am going to fork over my hard-earned cash for ever-inflating movie ticket prices to watch a film that centers around an erupting volcano, earth-shattering earthquake, crashing tidal wave, whatever, whether in the movie theater or via a streaming platform, which has become a more and more common mode of cinematic distribution and exhibition since the onset of the pandemic, you better believe that I would expect to get my money's worth in spectacle and entertainment.

In a true disaster movie, a Second Disaster will always occur, no matter the shape it takes. Witness the instances of the Second Disaster in the following table.

Title	Second Disaster
Airport	bomb explodes midflight
The Andromeda Strain	realization that Andromeda functions like an atomic reactor
Skyjacked	re-routing of plane to Moscow
The Poseidon Adventure	explosion in the ballroom
Airport 1975	loss of radio contact with Salt Lake City tower
Earthquake	aftershock
The Towering Inferno	blowing the water tanks
Flood	bridge blocking water run-off; needs to be exploded

Title	Second Disaster
The Cassandra Crossing	Chamberlain notifies Mackenzie that Cassandra Crossing is unsafe to cross
Airport '77	discovery of water leaking into fuselage
Fire	realization that winds have shifted
The Swarm	destruction of Houston via flamethrowers
Avalanche	n/a
The Concorde.... Airport '79	cargo doors explode open, decompressing plane
City on Fire	fire erupts inside the hospital
Meteor	water breaks through the tunnel as survivors try to escape
Disaster on the Coastliner	attempt to try to disconnect the engineer's car from the rest of the train with the passengers
Cave-In!	a major cave-in traps all the stars; bigger disaster than the first
Speed	Payne hijacks the subway car
Outbreak	notification that virus is airborne
Twister	F5 tornado
Independence Day	the final battle
Daylight	mid-river collapse
Dante's Peak	pyroclastic cloud

Title	Second Disaster
Volcano	second eruption
Titanic	ship splits in half and sinks
Deep Impact	announcement of comet breaking into two parts
Armageddon	secondary government protocol/system override
The Core	realization that the core's material is too thin to withstand the nuclear explosives
The Day After Tomorrow	notification that the storms are growing and that one of them will hit NYC very soon ("inside an hour")
Snakes on a Plane	air conditioning fails
2012	notification that the earth's crust has begun to shift—tsunamis will soon follow
Contagion	virus mutates
San Andreas	earthquake in SF
Geostorm	Geostorm alert
Greenland	notification of largest fragment of Clarke to cause global extinction
The Sibylline Scourge	the national riots and civil unrest instigated by the murder of George Floyd

The One-Two Visual Spectacle Approach: Dante's Peak

Dante's Peak is a perfect exemplar for the one-two visual spectacle approach to disaster representation. In this film, the Primary Disaster that depicts the awesome eruption of the titular volcano is a good, old fashioned, sensational movie spectacular rife with pandemonium and destruction. The effects of the erupting volcano—the seismic vibrations, the projectile fire, etc.—cause buildings to topple over, the earth to tremble, and the society of the film (the townspeople of Dante's Peak) to run for their lives in terror through the streets of the small mountain town, their cars and trucks bottlenecking the roads in a futile attempt to escape (*Dante's Peak* 00:56:20–1:01:43). Although Susan Sontag is discussing science-fiction films specifically in her essay, this is the moment that she refers to in "The Imagination of Disaster," when, "Cities are destroyed and/ or evacuated. There is an obligatory scene here of panicked crowds stampeding along a highway or a big bridge ..." (Sontag, 234). It is immediately subsequent to this monumental occurrence in the disaster film when "All Hell Breaks Loose."

As they watch with incredulity as their small mountain village crumbles like falling Legos around them, Dr. Harry Dalton and Mayor Rachel Wando try feverishly to maneuver their SUV through the crowds of panicked and fleeing townspeople in an attempt to get to Rachel's house to retrieve her children, Lauren and Graham. The kids aren't immediately responsive when Rachel calls for them, but eventually, Lauren and Graham are located having, unbelievably (and if you ask me, absolutely ridiculously), commandeered Rachel's truck in a foolhardy mission to rescue their grandmother from her mountainside cabin. The kids have travelled *up* the mountainside through scant visibility and blinding ash that continues to spew forth from the erupting volcano as though they were perfect stunt drivers. Totally plausible. In any case, having rescued grandma and been reunited with Harry and Rachel, now the priority for the assembled core group of survivors is to get the hell out of town. At this point, there is the expected brief comedown period (the descent of the roller coaster) during which the family works its way down the mountain. In the process, however, it loses Grandma Ruth (the character played by Elizabeth Hoffman), who will hold the title of Poignant Character in *Dante's Peak*. Having lost the use of its previous vehicle, the group spots and appropriates a vacant truck, steals it, and continue its trek. Meanwhile, emergency and military services are deployed to aid in the evacuation. Harry, Rachel, Lauren, Graham, and Roughie come upon and meander through the now deserted and disintegrated town, staring out at their once picturesque village with reflective sorrow (*Dante's Peak* 00:58:41–01:27:00). Roughie, by the way, is the family dog. Oh yeah, they rescued the dog. Beloved pets, usually dogs, rarely, if ever, perish in disaster movies. No mainstream director of a big-budget, Hollywood studio, PG-13-rated movie would ever kill the family dog. I mean, come on!

Then, right on cue, the Second Disaster explodes onto the scene in the form of a massive explosion from the mouth of the volcano that produces a gigantic pyroclastic cloud. The smoke from the cloud determinedly sweeps through and engulfs the decimated town with uncompromisingly brutal force, annihilating everything remaining in its path (*Dante's Peak* 01:27:48–29:18).

There are times when, unlike in *Dante's Peak*, the Second Disaster won't be an actual *visual* spectacle that will viscerally charge the audience in the run-up to the story's conclusion. We have briefly addressed in the chapter concerning the Primary Disaster, how some films utilize a *vocalization* or a *realization* of a Primary Disaster. The same can be said for the telegraphing of the Second Disaster. In other words, in some disaster films, what qualifies as the Second Disaster will be the realization that something terrifying is imminent, that the filmic disaster, which was previously thought to have been thwarted or at least temporarily avoided, is not finished with our core group of survivors just yet.

* * *

The One-Two Vocalization or Realization Approach: Outbreak

Once again, it is in biological disaster movies that we tend to witness the vocalization or realization tactic of telegraphing the catastrophes. We, once more, refer to our previous example from the chapter on the Primary Disaster, Wolfgang Petersen's *Outbreak*. As we have previously discussed, Col. Sam Daniels is notified by way of a telephone call (vocalization) from General Ford that a Level 4 biohazard has possibly been identified in Zaire (*Outbreak* 00:07:05–59). Regardless that the viewer is hit with this Primary Disaster right off the bat at seven minutes and forty-five seconds into the film, we are thrust into the thick of the plot at this moment as the characters mobilize into action.

The vocalization or realization method of presenting the Second Disaster is identified later in the film when a doctor at a makeshift hospital in Cedar Creek asks Sam to take a look at a patient who has become ill. This patient has fallen sick even though he has been admitted to the small-town hospital for a purpose entirely unrelated to the outbreak of the virus and has not had any contact with any isolated, infected patients with the mysterious illness. Sam, the fear visibly registering on Hoffman's face, slowly turns and looks up at an air vent. Ballhaus' camera then tracks briefly through an air duct and settles back on Sam's terrified face in another area of the room. Sam looks at the doctor and gravely informs him, "It's airborne" (*Outbreak* 00:50:58–51:37) This is the evidence of the adherence to the Law of the Second Disaster, occurring at fifty-one minutes and thirty-seven seconds into *Outbreak*'s one hundred twenty-seven-minute runtime.

We have discussed how it is that the vocalization or realization method of delivery for the Primary or the Second Disaster can be just as profound as the grand, visual spectacle sort in which the viewer would experience an explosion or show-stopping CGI catastrophe. Some film buffs might argue that the realization that disaster is looming can be even *more* frightening than the onset of the actual disaster itself. This anticipation works on a psychological level in much the same way as it might in horror movies, when what is *not* seen on screen can oftentimes be even more terrifying than copious amounts of gore and graphic displays of ghastly death. But, we have previously also mentioned that there are examples of movies that may use a combination of the two methods, a vocalization or otherwise realization of a disaster followed by a more grand, visual spectacle, or vice versa. Such is the case in *Greenland*, for example.

* * *

The Combination Spectacle Approach: Greenland

In this 2020 flick, a fragment from the comet Clarke touches down on Earth outside of Tampa and completely vaporizes the Florida city. John Garrity (the character played by Gerard Butler) and his family, along with some of their neighbors, are gathered in the Garrity's family room, intently watching a televised newscast as the destruction in Tampa is reported on by the news anchors. Suddenly, the group hears a thunderous rumble outside. When John steps outside to take a look, he is quickly blown off of his feet when the path of the comet careens right past him in a quick, but terrifyingly earth-shattering sequence of image and sound (*Greenland* 00:14:13–16:18). This incident sends the whole neighborhood into panic and confusion (beginning to sense the genre tropes here?), and while not the mind-blowing special effects spectacle like in *Twister* or *Dante's Peak*, the comet's brief but consequential impact can be considered *Greenland*'s

Primary Disaster, and it occurs at approximately sixteen minutes and eighteen seconds into the movie. This instance is the inciting incident that moves the story into Act Two, in which the bulk of the plot plays out. The Second Disaster comes later in the film, as it naturally would, and is conveyed via the news report indicating that the largest fragment of the comet is on course to make impact with Earth, which will cause a global "extinction level event" (we heard this same term used in *Deep Impact* ... very disaster-y). This notification occurs at roughly the eighty-minute mark of *Greenland*'s one hundred and nineteen-minute running time, and, like any self-respecting Second Disaster should, sets in motion the events of the final third of the film, in which the Garrity family makes haste to catch a flight to Greenland, to the classified bunkers that will shield them from the impending apocalypse.

I would present the argument that in *The Sibylline Scourge*, the world bore witness to the combination spectacle approach discussed above. In our story, there are two major, spectacular disasters that follow traditional disaster film beats. The Primary Disaster, as discussed, occurred with the notification that the novel coronavirus had finally and inevitably broken through to New York City with the confirmed case of the attorney Lawrence Garbuz. The Primary Disaster in our narrative, having taken place in the most populous and densely packed city in the United States, created true and pressing panic. It is no wonder, then, when one considers the compacted volume as well as the international composition of a city like New York that this city soon became the epicenter of the Covid-19 pandemic throughout most of 2020. As news and cases of the pandemic spread throughout the world and the nation's population became glued to their televisions, computers, and smartphones anxiously trying to sort through the bewildering amount of information, sometimes accurate, sometimes not, people scattered in terror to anywhere where there was more of a guarantee, however precarious, that they wouldn't necessarily be confronted with large crowds of people: country houses, second homes, suburbs. Worldwide panic and pandemonium caused by the most acute prospect of death that many had ever experienced in their lives was exacerbated by creepy mask mandates, strict and ever-changing travel restrictions, seemingly draconian stay-at-home orders, food shortages, uncertainty, disorder, the list goes on. Even though the Primary Disaster as it related to our narrative was centralized in New York City, as a countrywide populace, we were now at the apex of the roller coaster.

Then, pursuant to the laws of gravity as well as the Law of the Second Disaster, the roller coaster began its descent. Recall Governor Cuomo's April 18 statement that the death toll in New York State was "past the plateau and starting to descend" (Cramer et al.). The "curve" began to flatten and the number of confirmed Covid-19 infections and hospitalizations, thankfully, was beginning to experience a downturn (Berke). After an outraged and petrified public demanded more testing venues from governmental agencies, testing for the potentially deadly pathogen *finally* became more widely distributed and available. People formed lines of the sorts usually seen outside a big box store on the morning of Black Friday or around the blocks of urgent care centers, waiting patiently yet nervously to get their noses stabbed … I mean, swabbed. The fear, while unquestionably remaining as a major cloud hovering over everyone's head, at last started to dissipate and take a relative backseat to the need for fresh air and social interaction, however minimal. While Cuomo nevertheless reminded his constituents that this was "not a time to get complacent" (Berke), the light at the end of the tunnel was slowly beginning to come into focus.

Almost as if real life was taking its cue from the timeline created by decades of disaster movies past, the second half of the combination spectacle of *The Sibylline Scourge* appeared on May 25, 2020, with the murder of the unarmed George Floyd by Minneapolis police officers. This inciting event set the United States—the extended society in our narrative—on the second incline of the roller coaster as social, political, and racial tensions exploded onto the national stage in a cacophony of violence and civil unrest. Now we can observe in retrospect that whereas the Primary Disaster of our narrative was of a *vocalizing* nature (word and abject fear spread concerning the dangerous outbreak of a novel coronavirus in New York City after Garbuz's diagnosis caused the society to panic), the spectacle of the Second Disaster was clearly of a more *visceral* nature. Images flashed across millions of television sets and laptops of violent protests in the streets, police cars that were set on fire by angry mobs. On their screens, the public saw Molotov cocktails, widespread looting and lawlessness, antagonized police officers throwing riled up protestors forcibly to the ground and placing them under arrest, retail stores up and down formerly tourist-heavy streets such as Fifth Avenue in New York City with boards in their shop windows as though out of business but, in reality, assembled in a protective measure meant to prevent destruction to their storefronts and looting of their merchandise. Residents of affluent neighborhoods armed themselves with ammunition in anticipation of attacks in their backyards, such as in the story of the St. Louis couple whose armed defense of their home as a Black Lives Matter protest wound its way through their neighborhood went viral. On the streets of major cities throughout America, it looked as though, if decades of post-apocalyptic images from movies and television shows were to be viewed as any sort of reference point, Armageddon was upon us, certainly more so than it had ever seemed to be before.

However prominent the Primary or Second Disaster may be in the course of the story, it is more often the case that disaster movies tend to include several smaller or mini disasters in addition to the centerpiece Primary and Second Disasters. We can't have the audience losing interest, can we? That's a cardinal sin of motion picture entertainment. Yet, when it comes to identifying the official Second Disaster, and there always will be one in a true disaster movie, the process can get a little tricky if there are several disasters in a film. We see this practice in action in *Meteor*, for example. We can identify the Primary Disaster as the notification by Sherwood that a major piece of the asteroid Orpheus is hurtling towards the earth (*Meteor* 00:11:33). We can also identify the Second Disaster as the moment when water breaks through the subway tunnel as the core group of survivors is attempting its shot at escaping to safety (01:29:46). But there also exist several other smaller, mini disasters that take place in between the two that, while not major or focal disasters, are still disasters in and of themselves. There is, for example, the instance wherein a fragment of the meteor strikes a peak near a ski village in the Swiss Alps, triggering a catastrophic avalanche (00:57:02); or when a tidal wave, caused by another impact of a fragment of the meteor, practically wipes out Hong Kong (01:08:51); or yet again, when another fragment of the meteor collides with New York City, decimating the metropolis (01:17:31).

We are even able to see this practice come about in real life during the course of *The Sibylline Scourge*. An example of a mini disaster in our own narrative might be Governor Cuomo's disastrous March 25, 2020, directive that required New York State nursing homes to admit patients discharged from hospitals regardless of if they had Covid-19 or had been infected with the illness. This instruction, many argue, resulted in the deaths of more than six thousand four hundred nursing home patients (Villeneuve and Peltz). As one might correctly presume, residents of nursing homes, the elderly, were a demographic particularly vulnerable to Covid, but also, in reality, vulnerable to any fast-moving, wide-spreading illness. While not observed as a major storyline in our narrative, this episode involving Cuomo's widely maligned order could serve as a separate plot strand constituting a tragic mini disaster all its own.

Disaster movie behemoths such as *2012*, *Armageddon*, and *The Day After Tomorrow* go even further and seem to practically construct their stories entirely around several small disasters. Nevertheless, there will always be a Primary and a Second Disaster. The Primary Disaster is typically easy to identify—it's the reason why we bought a ticket to the damn disaster movie in the first place! We bought a ticket to *Dante's Peak* expecting to see a movie about an exploding volcano, so it figures that the first explosion sequence should be and would be a showstopping Primary

Disaster. Likewise for a movie such as *Earthquake*, with its impressive eight-minute quake sequence. Even if the disaster takes the form of a dire notification or of a vocalization, the moment of realization regarding the impending catastrophe is almost always easy to pinpoint; it's the notification of the disaster that sets the action of Act Two into motion. For example, just look at *The Cassandra Crossing* when Mackenzie notifies Chamberlain that there is a deadly virus on board the train he is travelling on (*The Cassandra Crossing* 00:41:24). Or you could reference Bay's *Armageddon* (a very apropos title for a disaster movie if there ever was one), when word comes down that there is an asteroid barreling towards Earth and that humankind has only eighteen days to destroy it (*Armageddon* 00:10:51–11:52).

As a general rule, however, I like to think that the disaster that causes the most interference, the most concrete upsurge in panic following the occurrence of the Primary Disaster, is the one that can be construed to be the Second Disaster. Again, one must keep in mind that this Second Disaster may not take the form of a massive explosion or a torrential deluge or some other type of destructive scenario. Instead, the Second Disaster may be something as simple as a character uttering a particularly ominous sentence that forecasts certain doom. Or a character expounding some unexpected yet devastating turn of events for the core group of survivors. Look at *The Cassandra Crossing* again, at the moment when Chamberlain explicitly states to Mackenzie that The Cassandra Crossing is unsafe to cross, portending undeniable death for the passengers on board the train who are still in the midst of a deadly virus outbreak (*The Cassandra Crossing* 01:29:59). Or refer to the point in *The Core* (Jon Amiel, 2003), when Zimsky (Stanley Tucci) realizes that the material in the earth's core is too thin to withstand the massive amounts of nuclear energy that the *Virgil* crew had intended to use to jumpstart it into spinning again. As a result, the crew of the *Virgil* must implement the covert and dreaded Project Destini (*The Core* 01:24:31–25:09).

But no matter how the filmmakers or scenarists choose to stage the final act of their stories, ninety-nine percent of the time such conclusive act will always begin with the occasion of the Second Disaster. To return once again to our roller coaster analogy, it is safe to assume that adventure seekers on the amusement ride wouldn't speak very highly of the ride or, indeed, get their token's worth, if the ride only ascended and descended one hill. Now, it is also fair for one to assume that in the early days of cinema, a solitary disaster would have been enough to thrill an audience; the medium of cinema was in its infancy and the masses were not privy to the advanced workings of photography and surely did not conceive of what to expect from this new medium. Stories have circulated in film history circles since the advent of the medium, however mythic they most assuredly are, of audiences fleeing the theater in terror at the image of an arriving train in Louis Lumière's early cinematic short film *Arrival of a Train at the Station* (Gunning, "Aesthetic"). But as we barrel forward in time and approach the quarter mark of the twenty-first century, expectations as well as technology have matured to the point that both are being challenged on an almost daily basis, in our entertainment and in our real lives. The spectacles, therefore, must keep pace so that audiences return time and time again for bigger and better thrills. The poster for *Airport '77* explicitly promised a film that was "All New—bigger, more exciting than 'Airport 1975.'" Not sure I agree, but I appreciate the effort.

CHAPTER 9

Things Settle Down

As the cruel spring of 2020 mercifully came to a turbulent end, the summer and autumn seasons appeared on the horizon like a lighthouse finally glimpsed through a foggy mist after a perilous sea voyage. Testing for Covid-19, only weeks before having represented the great divide between the haves and the have-nots, became more and more accessible to the masses. Facial masks, articles that just a year prior had been cause for snickering at by much more stylish passersby on the streets, now became as much a part of the daily wardrobe as socks and underwear. As businesses and cities slowly initiated the process of coming back to life, retailers such as The Gap picked up on this novel clothing trend and designed and offered their own on-brand facial masks in their physical and online outlets. The promise of fresh air, warm sun, and freeing oneself from the harsh captivity experienced by most people over the dark months of the previous winter was nothing short of exhilarating. Some summer camps even accepted their adolescent charges, if only for half of the season and with stricter health protocols roundly in place. City and state officials commenced discussions surrounding the reopening of schools for virtual and/or in-person classes for the fall of 2020. Local bars across New York City, desperate for any means of staying afloat in this dicey economic climate and unable to welcome customers inside, offered to-go cups and, if establishments had the capacity to, constructed outdoor spaces in which to allow patrons seeking not only an adult beverage, but human (albeit socially distant) interaction, the chance to finally mingle with one another.

On June 22, 2020, New York City officially commenced its Open Restaurants program. This measure offered a much-needed lifeline to restaurants whose bottom lines were crippled by the lockdowns of the previous months and whose businesses, as a result, were now, literally, on life support. The program allowed for desperate restaurants and pubs to widen their dining rooms a regulated distance into city sidewalks and streets (Warerkar). Restaurants taking advantage of the Open Restaurants program used this opportunity extended to them to get creative with their al fresco dining rooms as they explored various interesting methods in which to welcome long-lost diners back into their folds. Some establishments erected dining pods or handsomely and lavishly decorated their extensions, for example. The outdoor dining spaces constructed at some restaurants even seemed to rival their indoor dining rooms as some establishments enthusiastically embraced outdoor dining altogether. A local Italian/Greek restaurant near my apartment on the Upper West Side of Manhattan transformed itself into a de facto community gathering place for the locals. Live music was performed while customers gathered for good food, social interaction, and information exchange. It was a lively and welcoming place in which to reinvigorate one's sanity in a city just beginning to recover from a crushing disaster.

But while cities across America carefully and cautiously crawled out from beneath the gloom and despondency of the previous months and experimented with regaining some of their pre-pandemic culture, there were still scrapes and bruises that hadn't quite healed on the weathered body of American society. Urban policing, and public attitudes towards law enforcement in general, had been irrevocably altered forever. In response to the popular outcry denouncing law and order that grew out of Floyd's murder and the emergence of the Black Lives Matter movement, some school curriculums controversially addressed the current wokeness pervasive throughout the nation. The school of thought known as "critical race theory" was addressed in some pools of academia and in the wider media landscape. Private and public companies both large and small, international as well as local, hired DEI (Diversity, Equity, and Inclusion) personnel and thoroughly reevaluated their best practices surrounding DEI in an effort to provide a more culturally and socially comfortable and inclusive workplace for their employees.

In the aftermath of both the outbreak of Covid-19, the disease caused by the novel coronavirus that left a global community wounded with nothing but a trail of death and devastation in its wake, as well as the widespread civil and political unrest that transpired all over the country and much of the world sparked by the tragic death of George Floyd (as well as several other high-profile, racially-charged incidents, such as the death of Breonna Taylor and the shooting of Jacob Blake), the United States was flung into a metamorphosizing period of swift and dramatic social changes which many would argue were long overdue. Terms like "new normal," "social distancing," and "systemic racism" were now firmly ensconced in the popular vernacular. Cities and municipalities across the fifty states worked overtime to respond and adapt to the new safety recommendations put forth by both local and federal government bodies. At the same time, governments and employers throughout the nation moved to correct what many viewed as historical racism, established and enabled by the predominantly White patriarchy for far too long.

Despite all of the changes to policy and inclinations that started to work their way through the cultural fabric of the country, the reality was that there were, and always would be, social and political issues that needed to be confronted. In addition, there would remain no shortage of those activists eager to take up the cause of justice for the democracy. Governments have been, and forever would be, we hope, learning from the people to whom they are charged to represent.

It remains our responsibility as a constituency to elect the proper candidates to office and to maintain a diligent system of checks and balances on our governments, whether local or federal. There is little question that infractions are and will continue to be made as American society adjusts to this post-pandemic "new normal." One thing we can all agree on is that the trials, challenges, and heartbreaks that we collectively endured as a nation and as a global community in the years 2020 and 2021 are some that we hope and pray we will never, ever, have the occasion to experience again in our lifetimes.

Subsequent to the Second Disaster, most disaster movies will come to a quick close. The train of the roller coaster slows and carefully eases into the passenger loading dock as the frazzled but exhilarated passengers exhale and reflect upon their ride. At this point in the disaster narrative, there really isn't much more of the story left to tell. The Preamble, if present, has foretold of the threat of danger that is yet to come; the audience has become acquainted with the society of the filmic world; the viewer has been introduced to the notable cast of characters, most of whom will compose the core group of survivors, including our male and female leads, and mapped out their relationships to one another; romantic conflicts have been proposed and resolved; disasters (both Primary and Second) have been initiated, endured, and overcome; the core group of survivors has made it through the ordeal with their lives and limbs intact (or, at least, most of them have), while a few have unfortunately met their fates along the way; and the filmic society depicted onscreen collapses in exhaustion after having withstood such trying circumstances. The world created by the narrative of the disaster movie in question moves forward, perhaps a little weather-beaten or with a few less buildings, but nonetheless changed forever, and maybe a little more steadfast owing to its resilience.

By the time a disaster movie, such as the many that we have explored in great detail throughout this book, comes to a conclusion, all of the generic hallmarks that we have mentioned herein should have been addressed. These include the identification of a distinct, non-politician male lead, identification of the female lead, identification of the Poignant

Character, onset of the Primary Disaster, and, following later in the film, the Second Disaster (whether these disasters are visual spectacles, vocalization or realization spectacles, or a combination of the two), the determination of whether the story represents a proactive or a reactive story trajectory, etc. Of course, with cinema being an art form, and therefore subject to interpretation, and in consideration of whoever the director(s) or screenwriter(s) of our feature film turns out to be, we must allow for space to embrace some editorial and directorial license. *The Sibylline Scourge*, lest we forget, is based on a true story, so while editorial and directorial license will naturally be incorporated into the development of the film, there will be restrictions on how far the creative personnel will be able to go in stretching this license in the final product. Nevertheless, all of the aforementioned generic elements should be squarely in place for a movie to be accurately distinguished as a true disaster flick. As I have tried to make the case for in this book, the salient generic elements that I have identified in these pages were certainly and uncannily accounted for in the contemporaneous narrative that was the outbreak of the Covid-19 pandemic, a once-in-a-lifetime episode in history that I have dubbed for the purposes of this book, *The Sibylline Scourge*.

The "Things Settle Down" portion of a disaster movie is the section that immediately precedes the final fade out. It is the intended purpose of this final scene or couple of scenes to return the audience to a state of relative stasis following the adrenaline rush that the previous two hours have, hopefully, provided. The sendoff from a disaster movie can be, in many ways, likened to a large exhale, a huge sigh of relief. This contrasts with, say, a thriller film wherein there is often a twist ending that sends the audience off into the night, gleefully attempting to piece together the events of the previous two hours. Or that of a horror film, in which, more often than not, the story culminates in a last-minute jump scare or a sudden shocker with which to jolt the audience one final time before the credits start to roll. But in a disaster film, the audience has withstood two hours of catastrophe, mayhem, and death accompanying the society and, more specifically, the core group of survivors as it races against both time and the elements to make it to safety. No matter the type of disaster, a good disaster movie will, by design, be something of a thrill ride for an audience, and an effective disaster movie allows for audience members to, however reluctantly, project themselves onto the characters and their circumstances, if only to say, "Thank God that's not me!" or "I don't know what I'd do in such-and-such a situation." Like film critic and historian Mark Kermode observes in the disaster movie episode of his podcast when quoting the legendary Master of Disaster, producer Irwin Allen, "Irwin Allen always said that the key thing about disaster movies is it puts you in the center of the disaster, from a safe distance, 'cause you're watching from the sidelines, and it makes you think, what would I do?" (25:05–25:14). Indeed.

As the end of a disaster movie reflects the roller coaster ride coming to an end as the passengers breathe a sigh of relief in gratitude for having survived the ride unbroken, some disaster movies literalize this sensation in their final frames. Let's look at *The Towering Inferno*, as a matter of example.

Things Settle Down: The Towering Inferno

In the commission of the Second Disaster, the building's water tanks have been purposefully blown open, mercifully drenching the Glass Tower in much-needed water. The conflagration that has consumed the awesome edifice on the night of its gala dedication finally begins to subside. The bruised and battered men and women who have, against the odds, survived the blaze assist one another on their way out from inside the wreckage. Meanwhile, police and fire personnel on the scene assess the extensive damage and try to treat the injured and the scarred who are, at the same time, trying to locate their loved ones lost amongst the chaos. Duncan has learned his lesson to no longer value a fabricated position as Lord of the Skies, placing his own wealth and prosperity over the lives of others. He vows to never allow a situation of the type that gave rise to the towering inferno from ever occurring under his watch in the future. "All I can do now is pray to God that I can stop this from ever happening again," Duncan intones as he comforts his daughter in the outside safety of the building's plaza (*The Towering Inferno* 02:38:59–02:39:06). Duncan's punishment falls in line with one of the film's major themes concerning the evils of personal and corporate greed, but also clearly aligns with Yacowar's more theologically thematic analysis of The City Fails, one of his eight types of disaster movie and the type to which *The Towering Inferno* conforms. "Here people are most dramatically punished for placing their faith in their own works and losing sight of their maker. So their edifices must crumble about them" (Yacowar 336). In the final shots of the film, O'Halloran emerges weary and soot-stained from the destroyed building and briefly stops to chat with Doug about the hazards of "firetraps" like the Glass Tower. A bird's-eye camera zooms up and out as O'Halloran drives away into the night, leaving Doug and Susan sitting on the steps outside the smoldering building, looking exhausted and charred (*The Towering Inferno* 02:39:10–41:23). Fade out.

We can also point to another more recent example of this type of exhale conclusion following the heart-pounding finale sequence in *Volcano*.

Things Settle Down: Volcano

A building in downtown Los Angeles is seconds away from being exploded in the hopes of redirecting the flow of lava dangerously winding its way through the city. Mike Roark (the character played by Tommy Lee Jones) has, to his horror, spied his daughter, Kelly (Gaby Hoffman), in the immediate path of the soon-to-be-demolished building. The explosives are detonated. Then, like a parent instinctually rushing to the aid of their child who is caught underneath an automobile, Roark breathlessly races across San Vicente Boulevard in a heroic effort to rescue his daughter, and the young boy she is looking after, from being crushed to death by the collapsing building. Soon, the final remnants of the building fall to the ground in a billow of rock and glass, and the dust from the demolished building eventually settles. Dr. Barnes (the character played by Anne Heche) searches with decreasing optimism for Roark through the fog created by the rock and the soot, hoping he'll somehow emerge from the rubble. Since the detonation of the building seems to have succeeded in damming and diverting the lava from flowing straight through the City of Los Angeles, the society at large rejoices in having thwarted the disaster. But Roark, his daughter, and the young boy remain unaccounted for among the survivors of the eruption. Finally (though unsurprisingly, since there are two children involved and we are talking about a mainstream, PG-13 rated, multi-million-dollar Hollywood movie), the three emerge from a pile of rubble, ashen-faced, confused, but otherwise intact.

The audience is then treated to a wide shot of the smoldering metropolis. A local newscaster broadcasts to the residents of LA (and to the audience) that they can now breathe a sigh of relief: "And it is good news at last. Satellite pictures show the volcano is shutting down, the lava is subsiding" (*Volcano* 1:34:49–57). Phew!! The train of the roller coaster is successfully pulling into the station. We see images of survivors wading through the rubble and looking out over their devastated city, now able to fully process the destruction that this unlikely volcanic eruption hath wreaked. Faces covered with ash create a visual uniformity amongst the citizenry, a treacly, Emmerichian bit of social commentary espoused by a little boy attempting to identify his mother from out of all the people who now look remarkably similar. As the skies clear and a refreshing and welcoming rainfall descends upon the city (the society), Roark, Kelly, and Dr. Barnes sit and reflect upon the events of the day. After a brief reunion with his second-in-command, Emmit (Don Cheadle), Roark and Kelly hitch a ride with Dr. Barnes and depart the scene of the massive cleanup that is now underway. The camera tracks high above Los Angeles as Randy Newman's evergreen anthem to the city, "I Love LA," plays over the soundtrack (*Volcano* 01:30:38–38:23). Cut to black.

Then there are other times, perhaps in disaster movies that display a more patriotically or civically minded sensibility, such as *Deep Impact* or *The Day After Tomorrow*, when there will be some sort of an address made to the people, usually given by the president (or equivalent) character in the film. This typically uplifting message is intended to send the audience into the night with their heads held high as well as induce them into conducting a little moralistic soul-searching. Such a final address will normally encompass themes of hope and perseverance, which are standard themes to be found even minimally in any disaster movie, and might serve as an occasion to reflect upon lessons learned from past mistakes that may have led to the preceding disaster in the first place.

Things Settle Down: Deep Impact *and* The Day After Tomorrow

In the third act of 1998's *Deep Impact*, a massive tidal wave decimates the entire eastern seaboard (a breathtaking visual effect in an otherwise dull as dishwater movie), killing thousands (including female lead Téa Leoni) and sending countless others scurrying about in search of higher ground (*Deep Impact* 01:44:55–46:03). The astronauts charged with saving the world, now on a suicide mission to blast the comet speeding towards Earth from the inside, make tearful (and woefully overdramatic) goodbyes to their loved ones via satellite link-up (01:47:08–50:38). Near a Virginia highway that is hopelessly clogged with a mass of cars belonging to citizens trying desperately to flee to safety, Leo (Elijah Wood) and Sarah (Leelee Sobieski), with Sarah's infant brother in tow, manage to climb to a safe height on a hillside (01:51:26). Soon afterward, when all is said and done and the tidal wave sequence is over, President Beck delivers his address to a wounded and dispirited nation. [As a side note, it must be noted that the best move this otherwise glaringly cloying movie makes is in the casting of Morgan Freeman as President Beck. No other actor working today can elicit such a calming, yet at the same time rousing, address quite like Morgan Freeman.] President Beck rallies the nation with inspiring movie prose such as, "Cities fall, but they are rebuilt. Heroes die, but they are remembered." Upon uttering the film's final words, "So now, let us begin," the film cuts to a wide shot of a massive crowd of spectators who have gathered to hear President Beck's words in front of a severely damaged Capitol. Cut to black (1:51:44–1:53:22).

While President Beck's final speech in *Deep Impact* might be seen as really more of a rare example of a disaster movie epilogue, the presidential address method utilized in Act Three in 2004's *The Day After Tomorrow* operates rather as more of a simple coda (more on epilogues and codas in a little bit). Vice President Becker (Kenneth Walsh) has ascended to the role of president following his predecessor, President Blake's (Perry King), death. He addresses the nation with a speech that isn't necessarily contextualized to appear so much as rousing, but rather cautionary, a stern warning to the masses about the delicacy of the atmosphere which the earth's population has for years taken for granted and neglected to care for properly. Becker, in a not-so-subtle allusion to a global unification (the expected heavy-handed social and environmental sentiment in a Roland Emmerich film), offers thanks to the countries that have come to the aid of the millions of people around the globe who have now become displaced due to the film's disaster(s). Once Becker informs the nation that survivors of the dawning of the new Ice Age have been located in New York City, the film cuts to several helicopters as they fly high above the once formidable and now much snowier than usual metropolis. One of the choppers locates Jack Hall (Dennis Quaid) and company and lands on the icy ground to rescue them. As their chopper whirs away, the rescued occupants gaze through the helicopter windows and watch as hundreds of other survivors beckon for rescue upon the rooftops of the city's skyscrapers, helicopters pulling up to them like taxis during rush hour, to shuttle them off to safety. A brief final scene involves two astronauts looking out of the windows of their spaceship onto a newly designed and fantastically clear Earth. The camera zooms out on the planet and the picture fades out (*The Day After Tomorrow* 01:51:41–55:32).

However, it is most often the case that a disaster movie comes to a close with little to no further explanation of the events surrounding the preceding story. The narrative is unceremoniously concluded with nothing more to say. As soon as the disaster has been thwarted, loose ends have been tied up, and there is no remaining story left to tell, there is simply a fade out or a zoom out as the final credits start to roll. We can look at *Airport 1975* as a case for illustration. In this disaster sequel, Murdock has assumed the helm of the aircraft from Nancy (sexism be damned!) and brings the plane safely in for a landing, the plane's inflatable emergency slides are deployed, and the passengers chaotically scramble to jump upon them and slide down to beautiful ground. Young Janice (the character played by Linda Blair, in her questionable follow up to *The Exorcist* as well as the controversial TV movie, *Born Innocent*), once off the slide, is quickly positioned on a stretcher and shuttled into a waiting ambulance so that she may be whisked away to the hospital to receive her critically needed kidney transplant. After the last of the passengers have deplaned the banged-up aircraft, Murdock and Nancy, their love having been rekindled as a consequence of their perceived mortality in the disaster, emerge framed in the plane's doorway. Arm-in-arm, the couple descends the stairs to the safety of the tarmac as the camera zooms out and the credits roll (*Airport 1975* 01:42:16–44:40).

To perceive how this common attribute of the conclusion to a disaster has remained relatively unchanged over time, one can take a look at the terminating scene in 1996's *Daylight*, a movie that, in this author's opinion, is the best all-around example of a disaster film emanating from the 1990s disaster movie cycle. Kit and Madelyn (the characters played by Sylvester Stallone and Amy Brenneman, respectively) are violently propelled upwards to the surface of the Hudson River after the fuse that Kit had planted in the bombed-out Holland Tunnel's mud wall detonates. The two are rescued quickly thereafter by the U.S. Coast Guard and ferried to land to receive medical attention. Kit is placed on a stretcher while Madelyn prefers to walk on her own. Surrounded by rescue personnel, Kit and Madelyn are both led away to waiting ambulances. Following a brief and melodramatic moment in which Kit bestows the bracelet to Grace that Poignant Character George had intended on giving to her himself and one final quip from Kit about taking the bridge (it makes sense if you see the movie), the camera pans up and the picture fades to black (*Daylight* 01:45:07–48:42). Short and sweet.

Even the mother of all disaster movies, and still the current standard by which most disaster movies are, to this day, judged, 1972's *The Poseidon Adventure*, concludes in this quick-to-fade-out fashion. In this film, following the self-sacrificial and fiery death of the Reverend Scott, the remaining core group of survivors (which now include the characters played by Ernest Borgnine, Carol Lynley, Red Buttons, Jack Albertson, Pamela Sue Martin, and Eric Shea) soldiers on to the engine room. Once inside, the group hears banging noises coming from the other side of the hull, now, of course, the only portion of the ship above water. In short order, those doing the banging on the other side of the hull (which, it turns out, is the French Navy) burn a manhole through the metal and proceed to lift the members of the group one by one to the surface and lead them quickly into a waiting helicopter that flies everyone away to safety. Fade to black. Movie over (*The Poseidon Adventure* 01:50:10–55:12).

* * *

Epilogue/Coda

As briefly mentioned above, rarely will a disaster movie include an epilogue or a coda following the dissolution of the narrative proper. This is understandable since this particular narrative device, quite frankly, doesn't seem to fit very snuggly into the scaffolding of a disaster movie. At the end of a disaster movie, the disaster is over. I would imagine that those characters that have survived the tribulations staged in the film just want to go home and have a nice, hot shower and a good night's sleep. But sometimes, particularly in the more seriously minded disaster movies (which, in my humble opinion, aren't nearly as much fun as those that embrace the subgenre's penchant for silliness and do not take themselves so very seriously, like the above-mentioned *Deep Impact* seems to), the epilogue or coda will contain the only real possibility that can theoretically find a home in a disaster movie: some sort of hopeful optimism for the future, for harmony in the changed world or society in the aftermath of the disaster. In a way, *Deep Impact* manages to combine both the presidential address conclusion technique with an epilogue/coda. In this instance, though we are not informed as to how much, some time has presumably passed since the disastrous events of the film have taken place prior to President Beck making his address to the nation. His actual address, meanwhile, speaks of perseverance, of patience, and of the promise for a new future. Indeed, the movie's penultimate shot is of Freeman's calming, comforting visage (*Deep Impact* 01:53:14).

A more traditional example of an epilogue can be found in Roland Emmerich's *2012*. Here, it is following universal cheering and backslapping after Jackson (the character played by John Cusack) saves the day for everyone on the ark by unclogging the hydraulics, that the movie fades to black. After a few moments, a title card appears on the screen that reads, "Day 27 Month 01 Year 0001" (*2012*, 2:27:13). The text of the title card used here, and indeed, similar text in any movie regardless of the genre, is indicative of an epilogue. It is the equivalent of seeing a title card text that reads, "Three Months Later…" or something along those lines.

In the epilogue portion of *2012*, Dr. Adrian Helmsley and Dr. Laura Wilson (the characters played by Chiwetel Ejiofor and Thandiwe Newton, respectively) are now a romantic item, passing time on the ark like everyone else on board. Suddenly, while the two are in the middle of an embrace and about to share a passionate snog, Adrian is summoned to the ark's bridge. Regardless of their interruption, they kiss, and an announcement comes over the ship's loudspeaker: Captain Michaels (Stephen McHattie) informs the survivors (the multitudes of survivors, inclusive of the core group consisting of Jackson, Kate, etc.) that he is about to "unseal the decks." This means that for the first time in a long time, the passengers will be able to breathe some fresh air and look out onto clear skies. With soft, almost inspirational music accompanying the scene on the soundtrack, the deck doors are slowly and dramatically raised, and the orange-yellow glow of the horizon bathes the faces of the awestruck passengers while a slight breeze washes over them. Eagerly, yet cautiously, the passengers (the surviving society) on the ark emerge onto the deck to take in the scene. The camera flies over the arks (there are three of them), as the door decks are opened on all of the ships, signifying the dawning of a new day and a step forward into the future.

Meanwhile, on the bridge, Adrian is informed of some good news: the waters are receding. Furthermore, he is told that due to the flooding that took place in much of the world over the course of the film, the continent of Africa has physically risen. In a bit of stereotypical Emmerich heavy-handedness, the arks have set a course for the Cape of Good Hope (eye roll!). Meanwhile, while the passengers absorb the view on the deck, Jackson's daughter asks her dad when they will return home. Jackson responds that they will find a new home somewhere over the horizon. Cut to an overhead shot of the three arks on course to the future as the inspirational music swells. We zoom out through the soft clouds as the newly formed Earth comes into focus over Africa. Fade out (*2012* 2:27:13–2:32:25).

The epilogue portion of *2012* is much more of a self-contained chapter following the section in which Things Settle Down, similar to the manner in which *Deep Impact* concludes. It can be seen as more of a full circle wrap-up to the story. In contrast, 1978's *Avalanche* likens more to *The Day After Tomorrow*, concluding as a mere coda. Though, to be fair, both *2012* and *Avalanche* could not be more different, both in content and in quality. For one thing, *2012*, while far from a perfect movie, at least *looks* like the filmmakers spent the several millions of dollars I would imagine that it cost to make. Indeed, according to Box Office Mojo, the movie had a budget of $200 million dollars, and it looks beautiful ("2012"). *Avalanche*, on the other hand, appears as though it cost a buck and a quarter to produce, telegraphing every bit the disaster knock-off it presumably was. In fact, according to its IMDb page, *Avalanche* carried an estimated budget of $6.5 million in 1978 ("Avalanche [1978]"), which would roughly equal $21.4 million in 2009 dollars, the year in which *2012* was released ("Inflation Calculator").

In the coda portion of *Avalanche*, the search continues for survivors of the disaster while the wounded are transported away to the hospital in ambulances. Catherine (Mia Farrow) is on her way out of town when she stops by the ski resort (where the bulk of action in the film is located) to bid goodbye to her estranged husband, David Shelby (the character played by Rock Hudson), whose dream and vision of a world-class ski resort has just been buried under the weight of the titular disaster. On her way into the lodge, Catherine discovers a bottle of champagne rooted outside in a snowbank (nice touch). Inside, she and David share a glass in bittersweet farewell, both for their relationship and any hope of reconciliation. David owns up to his responsibility for the disaster and for neglecting the topographic risks inherent in building a mountain resort, especially building one in a location where there is a susceptibility to avalanches. Catherine and David exchange goodbyes and Catherine is driven away. The camera zooms out on David as he surveys the substantial damage and the ruins of his passion. Credits roll (*Avalanche* 01:27:00–30:52).

Now, according to the rules of the disaster genre as outlined and defined as I have attempted to interpret them in this book, there are two ways in which *The Sibylline Scourge* could conceivably conclude: the method utilized in the example of *Avalanche*, that of a brief coda, or the more formal method of a more involved and inspirational epilogue, such as that seen in *2012*. When I initially set out on the journey of writing this book, my intention at that point was simply to articulate how the Covid-19 pandemic drew parallels to your standard disaster movie; how the disaster of the pandemic corresponded beat by beat to the popular generic disaster movie. However, as I became more entrenched in the process of writing and began to further research in minute detail the movies I would be referencing in the book, I found myself leaning more toward a different approach, one in which I was asking myself and, by extension, the reader, "If we were writing the Covid-19 pandemic as a contemporary disaster movie, what would that look like? And while similar in many ways, it would not, and could not, be a duplicate of the fictional *Contagion*."

CHAPTER 10

The Coda

At the time I began the formal process of writing this book (early 2021), the subject of vaccines was only in the beta phase among the scientific and regulatory powers in the halls of government: the CDC, the FDA (Food & Drug Administration), etc. As a point we have underscored on several occasions throughout this book, information in the initial days of the pandemic and even in the early weeks of 2021 was rather difficult to keep up with. This was also true once the vaccine studies began in late 2020, primarily due to the necessarily strict trials and approval processes needed by the pharmaceutical companies in order to get their drugs on the market. These pharmaceutical companies, including Moderna, Pfizer, Johnson & Johnson, among others, were moving at an unprecedented and lightning-fast pace to release their vaccines, a process that under normal circumstances would take, at the very least, months to get through. In the real-life Covid-19 pandemic, as well as in *The Sibylline Scourge*, we learned, as is the case in the disaster movie, that we did not have that kind of time. These hindrances, coupled with individual state mandates, protocols, local governments, and state-sanctioned and directed vaccine rollouts structured by age, immunocompromised status, even socio-economic class (if we are being honest) cluttering an already obfuscated process, made clarity of information, no matter what category you fit into, near but impossible.

So, as I had now come to envision the culmination of *The Sibylline Scourge*, I thought that there, indeed, should be an epilogue or a coda. However, it seems that for the narrative to flow the smoothest and for it to make the most sense, this concluding section would, I think, be most appropriately authored in the vein of *Avalanche*, a brief scene and then to black. It also might be interesting and, considering the based-on-fact nature of the story, informative for the viewer to, perhaps, include a short update on the main characters or events subsequent to the events in the narrative proper. This update could take the form of a text crawl over the final live shots of the film, or even a conveyance via a couple of title cards immediately prior to the closing credits. Included within this proposed text would be: pertinent information indicating any advancement on the vaccine front (for example, a bullet point informing the viewer of the fact that the vaccines developed by Moderna, Pfizer, and Johnson & Johnson were approved for use in the United States, but the vaccine developed by AstraZeneca was not); updated illness, death, or hospitalization statistics (perhaps a mention of the emergence of the highly-contagious Delta variant as well as the discovery of breakthrough cases which, although rare, resulted in infection of fully-vaccinated individuals); and projections for how the global human population might adapt to their "new normal" (how parents are adapting to school regulations regarding the mandating of masks for their school-aged children versus viewing it as more of an issue of parental supervision and choice, for instance).

As I mentioned in the above paragraph, it would be prudent to include in a closing coda text crawl any noteworthy updates concerning our main characters: Dr. Fauci, Dr. Birx, (at this point, former) President Trump, (at this point, former) New York State Governor Andrew Cuomo, (at this point, former) Vice President Mike Pence, as well as any other characters, whether real or fabricated for the purposes of the story (recall the discussion of the composite character), that the audience has spent time with during the course of *The Sibylline Scourge*. For example, plain text on a black screen in a concluding coda might look something like this:

> Following a particularly contentious election period in late-2020, which, in addition to the usual partisan muckraking included allegations of massive voter fraud resulting from a widespread mail-in ballot system implemented to accommodate the Covid-19 pandemic, former vice president under Barack Obama, Senator Joe Biden, was ultimately elected the 46th President of the United States. Donald J. Trump reluctantly vacated the White House and retreated in defeat to his beloved Palm Beach estate, Mar-a-Lago. He is presently considering a presidential run in 2024.

Instead of some simple text over a black screen as a means of rolling out the coda, the filmmakers behind *The Sibylline Scourge* might opt to present the text superimposed over individual slow-motion vignettes showcasing each character in their present situation or predicament, dramatized against some mood-appropriate music on the soundtrack. The filmmakers might want to display seemingly innocuous scenarios, scenes that might, in essence, contradict the text that the viewer reads over the images of the subject. An image of Dr. Fauci in his lab coat as he goes about his daily work at the NIAID might carry with it accompanying text that refers to the public backlash over Dr. Fauci's apparent unassailability and his crude penchant for the spotlight (Podhoretz). The viewer could watch a heartwarming visual of Dr. Birx at home in Washington, D.C., preparing for another twenty-four-hour Christmas Eve buffet. With it, scrolling (or stationary) text may include details involving Dr. Birx's sudden retirement following the revelation that she had ignored her own guidelines around limiting contact to one's immediate family in the days prior to the 2020 Thanksgiving holiday, when she was found to have enjoyed the holiday with an extended family gathering at her property in Delaware (Bowden). Perhaps there would be a quick vignette of now-former President Donald Trump ignominiously leaving office, kicking and screaming like a petulant toddler. Or even one in which now-former New York State Governor Andrew Cuomo sits at his office desk in Albany with his head between his hands, contemplating his future, a future that has now become mired in scandal and shame, as his family's political dynasty crumbles around him.

In contrast, however, the filmmakers might also want to include in the coda quick scenes that telegraph more of a note of optimism, of the strength and resilience of the human spirit, themes so prevalent in disaster movies of all genre cycles. Perhaps the filmmakers would choose to include, however briefly, those characters that have more graciously endured the Covid-19 pandemic disaster. Individuals such as Amanda Kloots, the widow of our Poignant Character, Nick Cordero. There might be one or two short shots of Kloots as she adjusts to her new and unexpected life as a widowed, single mother, raising young Elvis with the same love and impossible fortitude with which she confronted Nick's plight, trying however she can to keep the memory of her deceased and beloved husband alive in herself and in their son. The creative decision might be made to showcase any reformed anti-vaxxers that we might have spotlighted in our story. The filmmakers might see it as fruitful to take a socially conscious page from Roland Emmerich's playbook and document a method in which these people are utilizing their newly converted stances on vaccinations in order to educate their former peers who might still be skeptical about getting jabbed with the vaccine.

Of course, in every story where there is a protagonist, there must be an antagonist, and there are some participants in this story, villains, if you will, on whom, some would say, justice was not adequately served (if it had been served at all). Villains who escaped relatively unscathed. Prime possible candidates for these ignominious roles might include Jared Kushner and Ivanka Trump, for example. The Stepford couple followed their father-in-law and father, respectively, to the Sunshine State by purchasing and moving into a sprawling, multi-million-dollar mansion in Miami, fleeing in shame from their formerly plush confines outside of Washington, D.C. Furthermore, our director(s) and/or screenwriter(s) might choose to briefly mention the fates of some of the other supporting or peripheral characters that have made a noteworthy appearance in our story: (at this point, former) First Lady Melania Trump, House Speaker Nancy Pelosi, Laurence Garbuz, Robert Redfield, and Patient Zero, to name a few.

The filmmakers and scenarists will need to decide in the initial stages of development of *The Sibylline Scourge* if they want to embark on a project that will present a strictly historical account of the Covid-19 pandemic, or present more of a dramatization of a real-life episode in time. Nevertheless, there are events indirectly related to our main cast of characters that a filmmaker or screenwriter might deem appropriate to include in the coda segment of the film. These episodes might serve to provide context to the time period immediately following the formal events of the film. For example, images included for this function might include news or archival footage from the Capitol Riots of January 6, 2021, in which the nation's seat of government was stormed and overrun by right-wing fanatics (a group of people that Hillary Clinton once referred to as "deplorables" but who Donald Trump, conversely, referred to as "patriots"), incensed over what they perceived as the bullshit presidential election victory of Joe Biden. Or perhaps, the scenarists might want to include images of the fall of the Afghan capital city of Kabul to the Taliban, which occurred in August of 2021. Instantly disseminated around the world were the unsettling images of Afghani citizens clinging to airplanes as the planes taxied and prepared to lift off and evacuate people out of the now-terrorist-run country, as well as heart-wrenching pictures of desperate parents trying to, unconscionably, hand their children over to British military personnel on the other side of barbed wire at Kabul's international airport. All of these images as well as updates from around the globe could be drawn upon in order to illustrate that no matter how far we've come in the fight against Covid-19, no matter how much of a grayish presence it continues to occupy in our daily lives, no matter how many people have been vaccinated or how close to herd immunity (whatever that actual percentage is) we become, the world pushes forward. Unfortunately, sometimes it pushes forward in what can paradoxically seem like a backwards momentum. New conflicts and disasters arise and will arise; that's life. In one form or another, though, the world will go on. In an odd way (and considering how much I've trashed this movie in the pages of this book, I can't believe I'm referencing it here), this could be viewed as a morbid thematic corollary to President Beck's final speech in *Deep Impact* concerning the eventuality of the subsiding waters. As Beck intones as only the great Morgan Freeman can, "Cities fall, but they are rebuilt. Heroes die, but they are remembered.... So now, let us begin" (*Deep Impact* 01:52:33–53:12).

There could even conceivably be room in the coda segment that finishes *The Sibylline Scourge* to counterpoint all of the gloominess inherent in the fabric of the story to showcase a few positive moments that may have occurred just outside and after the narrative proper. I mean, on a fundamentally Hollywood level, inserting a few images of this type would allow the disaster movie to fade to black on a tone of hopefulness and inspiration. Perhaps there could be a couple of images taken from the postponed 2020 Olympic Games, which finally took place in the summer of 2021 in Tokyo. Watching Olympic athletes go for the gold, stick that perfect landing, or cross that finish line with their arms raised and smiles wide in glorious victory always leaves a viewer with a heartwarming and uplifting tingle. There could be imagery included that consists of moving moments from populations around the globe, masked up but bravely and fearlessly forging ahead to resume a semblance of, now retro, normal human daily life and interaction. Filmmakers might see fit to insert warm pictures of smiling grandparents lifting up infant grandchildren for the first time in, at the very least, several months, at a family reunion. At long last, mothers hugging sons, fathers hugging daughters, children raising their hands at in-session classes, restaurant owners once again warmly and gleefully welcoming beloved regulars back to the indoors of their eateries as well as to their new outdoor spaces. We might watch city and suburban parks bubble with both masked and unmasked activity, street musicians providing a heavenly soundtrack once again for the urban masses, the heretofore insufferable, but now strangely welcoming, roar of car horns, the static hum created by the voices of everyday citizens trafficking along city streets, among other scenes and sounds of life's renewal. This would, no question, be a soul-stirring conclusion to the story of *The Sibylline Scourge*, as it should be. If Roland Emmerich were directing, the final shot might be in similar fashion to *2012* or *The Day After Tomorrow*: a fade out on a radically and eternally altered Earth.

Yes, as the writing process of this book has continued over the course of the year 2021, the lightning-fast clip of vaccine production and distribution, not to mention the introduction of virus mutations such as the Delta variant, has provided the necessity for a coda to be augmented rather than a simple and uninvolving farewell. Frankly, I tend to think that this book would be considered, at best, incomplete and, at worst, wholly inaccurate and out-of-date by the time it's published (it still may be so given how quickly circumstances are evolving) to not include how mankind has adapted to its new normal given all of the developments subsequent to *The Sibylline Scourge*. The world is far from perfect, as if it ever was. In the ensuing months, a new presidential administration has taken office, our leading man, Dr. Anthony Fauci, has faced his own scandal and blowback, the immigration crisis, particularly at the southern border of the United States, has exploded, and states are still divided as to how to negotiate their individual Covid-19 protocols. It would be abjectly irresponsible not to include information, however it ends up being presented, on state reopenings and social justice developments and progress in those areas made or not made since the resolution of the Second Disaster and the deceleration of the roller coaster.

But no matter how our filmmaker(s) or screenwriter(s) chooses to end our story, one fact remains crystal clear: *The Sibylline Scourge* is based on a true story, and respect must be paid to the real-life events that have provided the framework of our story. There is nothing worse or more deleterious than when a filmmaker trivializes a film that is based on fact, however tangentially, for shameless entertainment value. Depicting a story in this fashion is nothing short of exploitative and insults those whose lives have been in any way impacted by the events of the story in question. I would never want to see that happen to a story based on, or even used as a backdrop to, the Covid-19 pandemic. Too many lives have been lost, the constitutions of too many families and individuals have been changed, perhaps irreparably, forever. The price the world has paid for this pandemic has been too great to not treat the subject matter with the reverence it deserves.

If there is one absolute takeaway that can be gleaned from the story of the Covid-19 pandemic, it is that no matter where or how the story proper concludes, it is not over. There is no cure for the novel coronavirus, only vaccines that minimize its effects. Variants related to different virus strains arise all the time, much as they do with any viral contagion (like the flu, for instance). That's basic epidemiology. People are still dying, hospitals are still operating at maximum capacities (and sometimes *over* maximum capacities), mask mandates continue to be implemented in some states but are loosely regulated as mere advisements in others. The science is constantly developing, and an understanding of this new pathogen continues on a daily, even hourly, basis (as of this writing, a third "booster" vaccine shot is being rolled out to American citizens).

Maybe a coda isn't enough to contain the ongoing story of *The Sibylline Scourge*. Box office willing, maybe someone needs to greenlight a sequel.

FADE TO BLACK.

Filmography

Airport. 1969. Directed by George Seaton, Ultimate Disaster Pack, Universal Studios, 1997.

Airport 1975. 1974. Directed by Jack Smight, The Complete Collection, Universal Studios, 2002.

Airport '77. 1977. Directed by Jerry Jameson, The Complete Collection, Universal Studios, 2005.

The Andromeda Strain. 1971. Directed by Robert Wise, widescreen, Universal Studios, 2003.

Armageddon. Directed by Michael Bay, Disney, 1998. Amazon Prime Video.

Avalanche. Directed by Corey Allen, New World Pictures / Avalanche Productions, 1978.

The Cassandra Crossing. Directed by George Pan Cosmatos, Shout! Factory, 1977. Amazon Prime Video.

Cave-In! Directed by Georg Fenady, archive collection, Warner Bros. Pictures, 1979.

City on Fire. Directed by Alvin Rakoff, Astral Bellevue Pathe / TVA Films, 1979. Amazon Prime Video.

The Concorde: Airport '79. 1979. Directed by David Lowell Rich, The Complete Collection, Universal Studios, 1997.

Contagion. Directed by Steven Soderbergh, Warner Bros., 2011. Amazon Prime Video.

The Core. Directed by Jon Amiel, Paramount Pictures, 2003. Amazon Prime Video.

Dante's Peak. 1997. Directed by Roger Donaldson, collector's edition, Universal Studios, 2002.

The Day After Tomorrow. Directed by Roland Emmerich, Fox/Buena Vista, 2004. Amazon Prime Video.

Daylight. 1996. Directed by Rob Cohen, collector's edition, Universal Studios, 2002.

Deep Impact. Directed by Mimi Leder, Paramount Pictures,1998. Amazon Prime Video.

Deluge. 1933. Directed by Felix E. Feist, Radio Pictures / Kino Lorber, Inc., 2017.

Disaster on the Coastliner. Directed by Richard Sarafian, Metro-Goldwyn-Mayer/Orion Pictures, 1979. Amazon Prime Video.

Earthquake. 1974. Directed by Mark Robson, Ultimate Disaster Pack, Universal City Studios LLLP., 2002.

Fire. Directed by Earl Bellamy, archive collection, Warner Bros. Pictures, 1977.

Flood. 1976. Directed by Earl Bellamy, archive collection, Warner Bros. Pictures, 2004.

Geostorm. Directed by Dean Devlin, Warner Home Video, 2017. Amazon Prime Video.

Greenland. Directed by Ric Roman Waugh, STX Films, 2020. Amazon Prime Video.

The Hindenburg. 1976. Directed by Robert Wise, Ultimate Disaster Pack, Universal City Studios LLLP., 2003.

In Old Chicago. 1938. Directed by Henry King, Twentieth Century Fox Home Entertainment, LLC., 2005.

Independence Day. 1996. Directed by Roland Emmerich, 20th Anniversary Edition, Twentieth Century Fox Home Entertainment, LLC., 2016.

Meteor. 1979. Directed by Ronald Neame, American International/Twentieth Century Fox Home Entertainment, LLC., 2014.

Outbreak. Directed by Wolfgang Petersen, Warner Bros., 1995. Amazon Prime Video.

Pompeii. Directed by Paul W.S. Anderson, TriStar Pictures, 2014. Amazon Prime Video.

The Poseidon Adventure. 1972. Directed by Ronald Neame, digitally mastered, Twentieth Century Fox Home Entertainment, Inc., 1998.

San Andreas. Directed by Brad Peyton, New Line, 2015. Amazon Prime Video.

San Francisco. Directed by W.S. Van Dyke, Metro-Goldwyn-Mayer, 1936. Amazon Prime Video.

76 Days. Directed by Hao Wu, Weixi Chen, Anonymous, MTV Films, 2020. Amazon Prime Video.

Skyjacked. Directed by John Guillermin, Metro-Goldwyn-Mayer, 1972. Amazon Prime Video.

Snakes on a Plane. Directed by David R. Ellis, New Line Platinum Series, New Line Home Entertainment, 2006.

Speed. Directed by Jan de Bont, Twentieth Century Fox Film Corporation, 1994.

The Swarm. Directed by Irwin Allen, archive collection, Warner Bros. Pictures, 1978.

Titanic. Directed by James Cameron, widescreen collection, Paramount Pictures and Twentieth Century Fox, 1997.

The Towering Inferno. Directed by John Guillermin, Twentieth Century Fox, 1974. Amazon Prime Video.

Twister. Directed by Jan de Bont, Warner Bros. Entertainment, Inc. and Universal City Studios, Inc., 1996.

2012. Directed by Roland Emmerich, Columbia Pictures, Industries, Inc., 2009.

Volcano. Directed by Mick Jackson, Twentieth Century Fox, 1997. Amazon Prime Video.

Works Cited

Adcroft, Patrick, and Faraz Toor. "Timeline: How COVID-19 Changed NYC." *Spectrum News NY1*, Charter Communications, 11 Mar. 2021. www.ny1.com/nyc/all-boroughs/news/2021/03/10/timeline—how-covid-19-changed-nyc.

"Airport—Awards." *IMDb*. www.imdb.com/title/tt0065377/awards/?ref_=tt_awd. Accessed 26 Nov. 2021.

"Airport—Cast | IMDbPro." *IMDbPro*. pro.imdb.com/title/tt0065377/boxoffice. Accessed 28 Aug. 2021.

Al Jazeera. "A Timeline of the Trump Administration's Coronavirus Actions." *Coronavirus Pandemic News | Al Jazeera*, Al Jazeera Media Network, 23 Apr. 2020. www.aljazeera.com/news/2020/4/23/a-timeline-of-the-trump-administrations-coronavirus-actions.

Altman, Lawrence. "Rare Cancer Seen In 41 Homosexuals." *https://www.nytimes.com/#publisher*, 3 July 1981. www.nytimes.com/1981/07/03/us/rare-cancer-seen-in-41-homosexuals.html.

Andrzejewski, Adam. "Dr. Anthony Fauci: The Highest Paid Employee In The Entire U.S. Federal Government." *Forbes*, 25 Jan. 2021. www.forbes.com/sites/adamandrzejewski/2021/01/25/dr-anthony-fauci-the-highest-paid-employee-in-the-entire-us-federal-governm ent/?sh=4b6a8138386f.

"Anthony Fauci | Hilleman Film." *Hilleman: A Perilous Quest to Save the World's Children*, The Children's Hospital of Philadelphia. www.hillemanfilm.com/anthony-fauci. Accessed 22 Jan. 2021.

"Avalanche (1978)." *IMDb*. www.imdb.com/title/tt0077189/?ref_=fn_al_tt_1. Accessed 22 Jan. 2021.

Bass, Emily. "Can Deborah Birx Save Us from the Coronavirus?" *Washington Post*, 26 Mar. 2020. www.washingtonpost.com/magazine/2020/03/26/can-deborah-birx-save-us-coronavirus/?arc404=true.

BBC News. "Li Wenliang: Coronavirus Kills Chinese Whistleblower Doctor." *BBC News*, 7 Feb. 2020. www.bbc.com/news/world-asia-china-51403795.

Berke, Jeremy. "'We Are Flattening the Curve': Cuomo Says Shutdowns Are Working to Curb the Spread of the Coronavirus, But It's 'Not a Time to Get Complacent.'" *Business Insider*, Insider Inc., 8 Apr. 2020. www.businessinsider.com/coronavirus-cuomo-says-new-york-flattening-the-curve-2020-4?international=true&r=US&IR=T.

Blakemore, Erin. "This Was the First Major News Article on HIV/AIDS." *Smithsonian Magazine*, 3 July 2017. www.smithsonianmag.com/smart-news/was-first-major-news-article-hivaids-180963913.

Bordwell, David, et al. *Film Art: An Introduction*. 11th ed., New York, NY, McGraw-Hill Education, 2017.

Bowden, Ebony. "Dr. Birx Says She Will Retire After 'Overwhelming' Holiday Travel Scandal." *New York Post*, NYP Holdings, Inc., 22 Dec. 2020. www.nypost.com/2020/12/22/dr-deborah-birx-to-retire-after-holiday-travel-scandal.

Buscombe, Edward. "The Idea of Genre in the American Cinema." *Film Genre Reader IV*, edited by Barry Keith Grant, 4th ed., e-book, University of Texas Press, 2012, pp. 33–38.

Centers for Disease Control and Prevention. "Basics of COVID-19." *Centers for Disease Control and Prevention,* U.S. Department of Health & Human Services, 4 Nov. 2021. www.cdc.gov/coronavirus/2019-ncov/your-health/about-covid-19/basics-covid-19. html.

"Chinese Wet Market Tour and Important Warning." *YouTube,* uploaded by laowhy86, 26 Feb. 2020. www.youtube.com/watch?v=6P-P4vrY1Oc.

Collins, Kaitlan, and Kevin Liptak. "For Donald Trump, It's Business as Usual as Coronavirus Gains a Foothold in the Nation—CNNPolitics." *CNN,* 9 Mar. 2020. www.edition. cnn.com/2020/03/09/politics/coronavirus-reaction-donald-trump/index.html.

"Contagion (2011)." *IMDb.* www.imdb.com/title/tt1598778/trivia?item=tr5599416. Accessed 3 Aug. 2021.

Cooper, Helene, and Thomas Gibbons-Neff. "USNS Comfort Hospital Ship Reaches New York. It's Not Made to Contain Coronavirus." *The New York Times,* 30 Mar. 2020. www. nytimes.com/2020/03/30/us/politics/coronavirus-comfort-hospital-ship-new-york.html.

Corliss, Richard. "'Pompeii': Vesuvius Erupts, Magma Cum Loudly." *Time,* Time USA, LLC., 21 Feb. 2014. time.com/9028/www.pompeii-movie-review.

Cramer, Maria, et al. "New York Appears to Be 'Past the Plateau' of Virus Cases, Cuomo Says." *The New York Times,* 18 Apr. 2020. www.nytimes.com/2020/04/18/nyregion/ coronavirus-new-york-update.html.

Dargis, Manohla. "Review: 'The Wave' Is a Disaster Movie Making a Big Splash." *The New York Times,* 3 Mar. 2016. www.nytimes.com/2016/03/04/movies/the-wave-review.html.

"Deborah L. Birx, M.D." *United States Department of State,* 2017–2021.www.state.gov/ biographies/deborah-l-birx-md/index.html. Accessed 26 Jan. 2021.

Debruge, Peter. "Film Review: 'Pompeii.'" *Variety,* Variety Media, LLC., 19 Feb. 2014. www. variety.com/2014/film/reviews/film-review-pompeii-1201112224.

Deliso, Meredith. "Timeline: The Impact of George Floyd's Death in Minneapolis and Beyond." *ABC News,* ABC News Internet Ventures, 21 Apr. 2021. www.abcnews.go.com/ US/timeline-impact-george-floyds-death-minneapolis/story?id=70999322.

Editors, TheFamousPeople.Com. "Dwayne Johnson Biography." *TheFamousPeople.Com.* www.thefamouspeople.com/profiles/dwayne-douglas-johnson-1269.php. Accessed 30 Oct. 2021.

———. "Mark Fuhrman Biography." *TheFamousPeople.Com.* www.thefamouspeople.com/ profiles/mark-fuhrman-47579.php. Accessed 9 Oct. 2021.

Elsaesser, Thomas. "Tales of Sound and Fury: Observations on the Family Melodrama." *Film Genre Reader IV,* edited by Barry Keith Grant, Fourth Edition, Austin, TX, University of Texas Press, 2012, pp. 454–55.

Fear, David. "States of Emergency! Rating the Disaster Movie Canon." *Rolling Stone,* 8 Aug. 2014. www.rollingstone.com/movies/movie-lists/states-of-emergency-rating-the-disaster-movie-canon-26154.

Frishberg, Hannah. "Nick Cordero Had No Underlying Conditions before Dying of Coronavirus Complications." *New York Post,* NYP Holdings, Inc., 6 July 2020. www.nypost. com/2020/07/06/nick-cordero-had-no-underlying-conditions-before-coronavirus.

"Gene Hackman." *IMDb.* www.imdb.com/name/nm0000432/awards?ref_=nm_awd. Accessed 23 Nov. 2021.

"Governor Cuomo Signs the 'New York State on PAUSE' Executive Order." *New York State,* 20 Mar. 2020. www.governor.ny.gov/news/governor-cuomo-signs-new-york-state-pause-executive-order.

Grant, Barry Keith, editor. *Film Genre Reader IV.* Fourth Edition, University of Texas Press, 2012. *Google Books.*

Gunning, Tom. "An Aesthetic of Astonishment: Early Film and the (In)Credulous Spectator." *Film Theory & Criticism,* edited by Leo Braudy and Marshall Cohen, Seventh, Oxford University Press, 2009, pp. 736–37.

———. "The Cinema of Attractions: Early Film, Its Spectator and the Avant Garde." *Critical Visions in Film Theory: Classic and Contemporary Readings,* edited by Timothy Corrigan et al., Bedford/St. Martins, 2011, pp. 69–76.

Henderson, Cydney. "Broadway Actor Nick Cordero Went into 'septic Shock' after Lung

Infection Spread, Wife Says." *USA TODAY,* 28 Apr. 2020. www.eu.usatoday.com/story/entertainment/celebrities/2020/04/27/coronavirus-nick-cordero-on-ventilator-after-developing-fever/3037789001.

"Herstory." *Black Lives Matter.* www.blacklivesmatter.com/herstory. Accessed 22 Oct. 2021.

"The Hindenburg (1975)." *IMDb.* www.imdb.com/title/tt0073113/plotsummary?ref_=tt_stry_pl. Accessed 29 Oct. 2021.

"The Hindenburg (1975) - Overview." *IMDb.* www.imdb.com/title/tt0073113/?ref_=fn_al_tt_1. Accessed 24 Nov. 2021.

Hogan, Bernadette, Georgett Roberts, et al. "National Guard Deployed to NY Community With Nation's 'Largest Cluster' of Coronavirus." *New York Post,* NYP Holdings, Inc., 10 Mar. 2020. www.nypost.com/2020/03/10/national-guard-deployed-to-ny-community-with-nations-largest-cluster-of-coronavirus.

Hogan, Bernadette, Julia Marsh, et al. "Coronavirus in NY: 11 More People Test Positive in State, Bringing Total to 44." *New York Post,* NYP Holdings, Inc., 6 Mar. 2020. www.nypost.com/2020/03/06/coronavirus-in-ny-11-more-people-test-positive-in-state-bringing-total-to-33.

Impelli, Matthew. "Number of Coronavirus Cases in New York Surpasses Washington State to Become Most in Country." *Newsweek,* Newsweek Digital, LLC., 9 Mar. 2020. www.newsweek.com/number-coronavirus-cases-new-york-surpasses-washington-state-become-most-country-1491279.

"Inflation Calculator | Find US Dollar's Value from 1913–2021." *US Inflation Calculator |,* Coin News Media Group, LLC, 11 Aug. 2021. www.usinflationcalculator.com.

Keane, Stephen. *Disaster Movies: The Cinema of Catastrophe (Short Cuts).* 2nd ed., Wallflower Press, 2006.

Kelley, Sonaiya. "Broadway Actor Nick Cordero Dies at 41 after Long Battle with COVID-19." *Los Angeles Times,* 6 July 2020. www.latimes.com/obituaries/story/2020-07-05/broadway-actor-nick-cordero-obit-coronavirus.

Kenny, Glenn. "Pompeii Movie Review & Film Summary (2014) | Roger Ebert." *RogerEbert.Com,* Ebert Digital LLC., 21 Feb. 2014. www.rogerebert.com/reviews/pompeii-2014.

Kermode, Mark, host. "Top Ten Disaster Films." Kermode on Film, season 1, episode 23, *Apple Podcasts* app, 2 April 2019.

"Kevin Spacey." *IMDb.* www.imdb.com/name/nm0000228/awards?ref_=nm_awd. Accessed 23 Nov. 2021.

Kirshner, Jonathan. *Hollywood's Last Golden Age: Politics, Society, and the Seventies Film in America.* 1st ed., Cornell University Press, 2012.

Kloots, Amanda. "A Bronx Tale Cast in Prayer for Nick." *Instagram,* 16 Apr. 2020. www.instagram.com/p/B_DFURXgIXO.

_____. "New Home." *Instagram,* 28 Nov. 2019. www.instagram.com/p/B5aq8tpgHvr.

_____. "Nick Cordero." *Instagram,* 5 July 2020. www.instagram.com/p/CCSBM89Axt_.

_____. "Waitress - 'Live Your Life.'" *Instagram,* 26 Apr. 2020. www.instagram.com/p/B_dhXd5nOy9.

Levy, Emanuel. "Center Stage." *Variety,* Variety Media, LLC., 9 May 2000. www.variety.com/2000/film/reviews/center-stage-2-1200462348.

Lewis, Rebecca. "A Timeline of Cuomo's Handling of COVID-19 in Nursing Homes." *City & State NY,* Government Media Executive Group LLC., 5 Mar. 2021. www.cityandstateny.com/policy/2021/03/a-timeline-of-cuomos-handling-of-covid-19-in-nursing-homes/175185.

Lombardi, Joe. "Westchester Man Confirmed As Second Positive Case of Coronavirus in New York." *New Rochelle Daily Voice,* Cantata Media, 3 Mar. 2020. www.dailyvoice.com/new-york/newrochelle/news/westchester-man-confirmed-as-second-positive-case-of-coronavirus-in-new-york/784310.

Mason, Dancy. "Rebellious Facts About Natalie Wood, yhe Tragic Star." *Factinate.* www.factinate.com/people/facts-natalie-wood. Accessed 15 Feb. 2021.

MasterClass Staff. "How to Write Supporting Characters." *MasterClass,* 14 Nov. 2021. www.masterclass.com/articles/how-to-write-supporting-characters#what-are-supporting-characters.

Mayo Clinic Staff. "Extracorporeal Membrane Oxygenation (ECMO)." *Mayo Clinic, Mayo Foundation for Medical Education and Research* (MFMER), 30 July 2020. www. mayoclinic.org/tests-procedures/ecmo/about/pac-20484615.

Melas, Chloe. "Nick Cordero's Widow, Amanda Kloots, Thanks Fans for Making Her Husband a 'Rock Star.'" *CNN,* 7 July 2020. www.edition.cnn.com/2020/07/06/entertainment/ nick-cordero-amanda-kloots-final-instagram-live/index.html.

Mervosh, Sarah, et al. "See Which States and Cities Have Told Residents to Stay at Home." *The New York Times,* 20 Apr. 2020. www.nytimes.com/interactive/2020/us/coronavirus-stay-at-home-order.html.

Mouttet, Catherine. "Can You Feel It?" *Medium,* 24 Feb. 2021. catherinmouttet.medium. com/the-sensurround-effect-3bfcdf520577.

Mulvey, Laura. "Visual Pleasure and Narrative Cinema." *Critical Visions in Film Theory: Classic and Contemporary Readings,* edited by Timothy Corrigan et al., Bedford/St. Martin's, 2011, pp. 713–725.

Neale, Steve. *Genre and Hollywood (Sightlines).* 1st ed., Routledge, 2000.

———. "Masculinity as Spectacle." *Screen,* vol. 24, no. 6, 1983, p. 2. *Crossref* www.doi. org/10.1093/screen/24.6.2.

"The New York Times in Print for Tuesday, March 3, 2020." *The New York Times,* 3 Mar. 2020. www.nytimes.com/issue/todayspaper/2020/03/03/todays-new-york-times.

Nicas, Jack. "He Has 17,700 Bottles of Hand Sanitizer and Nowhere to Sell Them." *The New York Times,* The New York Times Company, 15 Mar. 2020. www.nytimes. com/2020/03/14/technology/coronavirus-purell-wipes-amazon-sellers.html.

"Nick Cordero—Obituary." *Playbill,* Playbill, Inc. www.playbill.com/person/viewmore?person=00000150-ac87-d16d-a550-ecbf5e8b0000. Accessed 6 Dec. 2020.

Nolan, Christian. "Lawrence Garbuz, New York's First Known COVID-19 Case, Reveals What He Learned About Attorney Well-Being From the Virus." *New York State Bar Association,* 11 Aug. 2020. www.nysba.org/lawrence-garbuz-new-yorks-first-known-covid-19-case-reveals-what-he-learned-about-attorney-well-being-from-the-virus.

Nugent, Annabel. "Nick Cordero's GoFundMe Page Raises Over $900k for Family After Actor Dies From Coronavirus." *The Independent,* Independent Digital News & Media Limited, 7 July 2020. www.independent.co.uk/arts-entertainment/theatre-dance/news/ nick-cordero-amanda-kloots-coronavirus-death-gofundme-donate-a9605226.html.

NY Book Editors. "Your Guide to Creating Secondary Characters." *NY Book Editors.* www. nybookeditors.com/2016/02/your-guide-to-creating-secondary-characters. Accessed 19 Oct. 2021.

"Parasite (2019)." *IMDb.* www.imdb.com/title/tt6751668/trivia/?ref_=tt_trv_trv. Accessed 6 Oct. 2021.

"Past CDC Directors/Administrators | About | CDC." *CDC: Centers for Disease Control and Prevention,* 20 Jan. 2021. www.cdc.gov/about/history/pastdirectors.htm.

Pesce, Nicole Lyn. "Who Is Deborah Birx—the Doctor That Both Trump and Pelosi Are Now Suddenly Criticizing?" *MarketWatch,* 3 Aug. 2020. www.marketwatch.com/story/ who-is-deborah-birx-the-doctor-whose-reaction-when-trump-suggested-people-inject-disinfectants-has-gone-viral-2020-04-24.

Podhoretz, John. "Anthony Fauci's Limitless Publicity Thirst Is Undermining the War on COVID." *New York Post,* NYP Holdings, Inc., 7 Apr. 2021. www.nypost.com/2021/04/07/ anthony-faucis-limitless-publicity-thirst-is-undermining-the-war-on-covid/?utm_ campaign=iphone_nyp&utm_source=mail_app.

"The Poseidon Adventure." *IMDb.* www.imdb.com/title/tt0069113/awards?ref_=tt_ql_sm. Accessed 15 Oct. 2021.

"Public Health Screening to Begin at 3 U.S. Airports for 2019 Novel Coronavirus ('2019-nCoV')." *Centers for Disease Control and Prevention,* 17 Jan. 2020. www.cdc.gov/ media/releases/2020/p0117-coronavirus-screening.html.

Ray, Rebecca. "Everyman Hero Definition | Everyman Examples." *Storyboard That,* Clever Prototypes, LLC. www.storyboardthat.com/articles/e/everyman-hero. Accessed 12 July 2021.

Reuters Staff. "Timeline: Key Events in the Month Since George Floyd's Death." *Reuters,*

25 June 2020. www.reuters.com/article/us-minneapolis-police-usa-onemonth-time1/timeline-key-events-in-the-month-since-george-floyds-death-idUSKBN23W1NR.

Rogers, Brooke. "You're Not My Dad, Gov. Cuomo—and Please Stop Pretending." *New York Post,* NYP Holdings, Inc., 19 Nov. 2020. www.nypost.com/2020/11/19/youre-not-my-dad-gov-cuomo-and-please-stop-pretending/?utm_campaign=iphone_nyp&utm_source=airDrop_app.

Salo, Jackie. "2020 Events: Yep, These Things All Happened in the Year from Hell." *New York Post,* NYP Holdings, Inc., 31 Dec. 2020. www.nypost.com/list/major-2020-events.

Sastry, Anjuli, and Karen Grigsby Bates. "When LA Erupted in Anger: A Look Back At the Rodney King Riots." *Npr,* 26 Apr. 2017. www.npr.org/2017/04/26/524744989/when-la-erupted-in-anger-a-look-back-at-the-rodney-king-riots

Schwirtz, Michael. "The 1,000-Bed Comfort Was Supposed to Aid New York. It Has 3 Patients." *The New York Times,* 6 Sept. 2021. www.nytimes.com/2020/04/02/nyregion/ny-coronavirus-usns-comfort.html.

Shaer, Brian. "Canonical Films of the 1970s Disaster Genre vs. the Genre Resurgence of the Late-1990s." Apocalypse, Dystopia, and Disaster 3: Dystopias and Disasters, Southwest Popular/American Culture Association 4th Annual Conference, February 21, 2020, Hyatt Regency, Albuquerque, New Mexico. Conference Presentation.

———. "*The Poseidon Protocol,* Or the Pedagogy of Survival According to Disaster Film Conventions in the Age of COVID-19." Film II, Midwest Popular Culture Association and Midwest American Culture Association Annual Conference, October 3, 2020, Virtual. Conference Presentation.

"Shelley Winters." *IMDb.* www.imdb.com/name/nm0001859/awards?ref_=nm_awd. Accessed 23 Nov. 2021.

Singer, Ben. "Female Power in the Serial-Queen Melodrama: The Etiology of an Anomaly." *Camera Obscura: Feminism, Culture, and Media Studies,* vol. 8, no. 1, 1990, p. 94.

"Snakes on a Plane." *Box Office Mojo,* IMDb.com, Inc. www.boxofficemojo.com/title/tt0417148/?ref_=bo_se_r_1. Accessed 22 Nov. 2021.

Sontag, Susan. "The Imagination of Disaster." *Against Interpretation, And Other Essays,* First eBook edition, Google Play ed., Picador/Farrar, Straus and Giroux, 2013, pp. 234–53.

Stlucas. "Grant Heslov." *Ethnicity of Celebs | What Nationality Ancestry Race,* 17 Dec. 2017. www.ethnicelebs.com/grant-heslov.

Stump, Scott. "Nick Cordero's Wife on His Coronavirus Leg Amputation: 'It Was Life or Leg.'" *TODAY.Com,* NBC Universal, 20 Apr. 2020. www.today.com/health/nick-cordero-s-wife-his-coronavirus-leg-amputation-it-was-t179215.

Taylor, Adam. "83 Not-Very-Flattering Things Foreign Officials Have Said About Trump." *The Washington Post,* 7 Dec. 2019. www.washingtonpost.com/world/2019/12/07/not-very-flattering-things-foreign-officials-have-said-about-trump.

Taylor, Andrew, and Tim Sullivan. "Trump Declares Emergency; World Steps Up Fight Against Virus." *AP NEWS,* The Associated Press, 13 Mar. 2020. www.apnews.com/article/north-america-donald-trump-ap-top-news-international-news-virus-outbreak-1b15b2f3f0b01eb66ea8116ff70bcb30.

Taylor, Derrick Bryson. "A Timeline of the Coronavirus Pandemic." https://www.nytimes.com/#publisher, 17 Mar. 2020. www.nytimes.com/article/coronavirus-timeline.html.

"The Towering Inferno (1974)." *IMDb,* www.imdb.com/title/tt0072308/trivia/?ref_=tt_ql_trv. Accessed 16 Nov. 2021.

"The Towering Inferno—Awards." *IMDb,* www.imdb.com/title/tt0072308/awards/?ref_=tt_awd. Accessed 8 Nov. 2021.

Truitt, Brian. "Broadway Star Nick Cordero Dies at 41 After Coronavirus Struggle Highlighted by Wife Amanda Kloots." *USA TODAY,* 6 July 2020. www.eu.usatoday.com/story/entertainment/movies/2020/07/05/broadway-star-nick-cordero-dies-after-coronavirus-battle/5232813002.

Tunzelmann, Alex von. "The Impossible Submerges the True Impact of the Tsunami." *The Guardian,* Guardian News & Media Limited, 3 Jan. 2013. www.theguardian.com/film/filmblog/2013/jan/03/reel-history-the-impossible.

"Turner Classic Movies—TCM.Com." *TCM: Turner Classic Movies,* Turner Classic Movies, Inc., www.tcm.com/unavailable#biography. Accessed 15 Feb. 2021.

———. *Box Office Mojo,* IMDb.com, Inc., www.boxofficemojo.com/title/tt0117998/?ref_=bo_se_r_1. Accessed 22 Nov. 2021.

———. *IMDb,* www.imdb.com/title/tt0117998/awards/?ref_=tt_awd. Accessed 23 Sept. 2021.

"2012." *Box Office Mojo,* IMDb.com, Inc. www.boxofficemojo.com/title/tt1190080/?ref_=bo_se_r_1. Accessed 24 Nov. 2021.

Villeneuve, Marina, and Jennifer Peltz. "NY Count: 6,300 Virus Patients Were Sent to Nursing Homes." *Washington Post,* 6 July 2020. www.washingtonpost.com/health/ny-count-6300-virus-patients-were-sent-to-nursing-homes/2020/07/06/e7e74946-bfef-11ea-8908-68a2b9eae9e0_story.html.

Warerkar, Tanay. "A Timeline of COVID-19's Impact on NYC's Restaurant Industry." *Eater NY,* Vox Media, LLC., 30 Dec. 2020. ny.eater.com/2020/12/30/22203053/nyc-coronavirus-timeline-restaurants-bars-2020.

Wee, Sui-Lee, and Vivian Wang. "China Grapples With Mystery Pneumonia-Like Illness." *https://www.nytimes.com/#publisher,* 21 Jan. 2020. www.nytimes.com/2020/01/06/world/asia/china-SARS-pneumonialike.html.

Woodward, A. "Anthony S. Fauci Biography—Family, Children, Name, Wife, Son, Born, Drugs, College, Time—Newsmakers Cumulation." *Encyclopedia of World Biography,* Advameg, Inc. www.notablebiographies.com/newsmakers2/2004-Di-Ko/Fauci-Anthony-S.html. Accessed 22 Jan. 2021.

Woodward, Aylin. "An Unsubstantiated Theory Suggests the Coronavirus Accidentally Leaked From a Chinese Lab—Here Are the Facts." *Business Insider,* Insider Inc., 15 Apr. 2020. www.businessinsider.nl/theory-coronavirus-accidentally-leaked-chinese-lab-2020-4?international=true&r=US.

Wu, Jiachuan, et al. "Coronavirus Lockdowns and Stay-at-Home Orders Across the U.S." *NBC News,* NBC Universal, 29 Apr. 2020. www.nbcnews.com/health/health-news/here-are-stay-home-orders-across-country-n1168736.

Wu, Katherine. "In Nick Cordero's Death, a Reminder of Covid-19's Unknowns." *The New York Times,* 6 July 2020. www.nytimes.com/2020/07/06/health/coronavirus-nick-cordero-underlying-conditions.html?auth=login-email&login=email.

Yacowar, Maurice. "The Bug in the Rug: Notes on the Disaster Genre." *Film Genre Reader IV,* edited by Barry Keith Grant, 4th ed., e-book, University of Texas Press, 2012, pp. 334–51.

Yamamitsu, Eimi, and Ben Dooley. "Trapped on a Cruise Ship by the Coronavirus: When Is Breakfast?" *The New York Times,* 5 Mar. 2020. www.nytimes.com/2020/02/05/world/asia/japan-coronavirus-cruise-ship.html.

Index